In No Ways Tired

The NAACP's Struggle to Integrate the Duval County Public School System

Abel A. Bartley

Clemson University

IN NO WAYS TIRED:
THE NAACP'S STRUGGLE TO INTEGRATE THE DUVAL COUNTY PUBLIC SCHOOL SYSTEM

Cover design by Jon White

ISBN: 978-1-886104-78-5

The Florida Historical Society Press
435 Brevard Avenue
Cocoa, FL 32922
http://myfloridahistory.org/fhspress

P•R•E•S•S

Dedication

I would like to thank God, Veronica, Brianna, Sarah and Aaliyah for your patience and support as I worked on this book. I also want to thank Irv Winsboro and Larry Zenke whose editing and help proved invaluable to me in completing this project. This is a reminder of what prayer, patience and perseverance can do.

Table of Contents

Introduction

In the book *Souls of Black Folk,* W. E. B. DuBois wrote, "The problem of the twentieth century is the problem of the color-line—the relation of the darker to the lighter races of men in Asia and Africa, in America and the islands of the sea." Race continues to be the defining issue in contemporary American life. No current issue has the same implications and controversial imperative as race. America is a nation of many faces, stories, and experiences. However, we often miss out on important aspects of the stories because we ask the wrong questions, which gives us the wrong answers. One of the most controversial questions facing the nation is the subject of public school education. There are very few places one can go in this country and find consensus on this issue. Since 1954 Americans have been struggling with the notion of what equal education is. As part of that question we have also been trying to figure out: What role does integrated education play in that notion?

In *In No Ways Tired: The NAACP's Struggle to Integrate the Duval County Public School System,* we have a case study of a large and important New South city that suggests lessons in desegregation and race relations relevant to a broader audience beyond both Jacksonville and Florida. This study, based on five years of research and writing, utilizes interviews, newspapers, books, and other primary sources, as well as the latest scholarly and secondary sources, to illuminate the historical lessons of school desegregation and community building in North Florida. In the process, the book presents important lessons for scholars and general readers alike about the turbulent history of race relations and public school desegregation in the nation, with special emphasis on the South. This book looks at the courage and strength of the black community, especially the leaders of the NAACP, who ignored threats and intimidation and refused to give up on the notion of integrated equal education for their children.

As noted, this work puts the Duval County story in context with a national story of school integration. It focuses on the NAACP's efforts to gain equal education for African American children in this New South city. Though school integration is a familiar story, each community brings a unique perspective to the struggle. Even though I focus on Jacksonville, Florida, I look at significant national issues such as busing, magnet schools, and achievement gaps, which have both local and national significance. By interviewing every living school superintendent, major local political figures, and several mayors, along with NAACP officials, school board members, school administrators, local and state activists, parents, and teachers, I present a unique perspective of the issues from a number of different viewpoints. Through interviews with both blacks and whites, we are better able to gauge their opinions, and also to find out why the integration process took so long and involved so many different people and political permutations. The manuscript ends with the aftermath of the Duval County Public School System being declared unitary and integrated by the courts. It concludes by asking some difficult questions about what the students, parents, politicians, and general citizenry of this important New South metropolitan area learned, and whether it was, in retrospect, worth the effort. These are issues much in the news today and in contemporary educational discussions and lessons across the nation.

This book will fit well in the evolving literature on educational equality and how that journey in America has resulted in yet unanswered questions and patterns of true school desegregation in this nation. It deals with civil rights, politics, education, and social changes, which never go out of style. Today, America is a much different place than it was in 1954, when the Supreme Court outlawed educational segregation. Dwight Eisenhower's consensus leadership has been replaced by the chaos of the Obama years, as Democrats and Republicans are locked in a life-and-death struggle over the future of this nation. Racial issues are literally no longer black and white, but have faded to brown and yellow. Hispanics are now the largest minority group and they are dealing with the same educational issues that African Americans are fighting. The more the nation has changed, the more it has remained the same. Those who fought against African American integration have regrouped and are now fighting new battles. There are growing calls to return the school systems to some idealized past era, when all the kids were taught in homogeneous neighborhoods with two-parent Protestant homes. The problem is, that America only exists in the imagination of certain people. Education is, for some, a "dirty word" because it has so many connotations. As Americans continue to fight this battle over education, I can hear the African American community, in the voice of associations like the NAACP, parent organizations, and others, saying, "We are in no ways tired. We will fight on as long as there is still a battle to be won."

Dr. Abel A. Bartley

Chapter Summaries

Chapter 1–Original Sin, Education in Black and White: A Brief History of Educational Efforts in Jacksonville, Florida

This chapter looks at the idea of educating African Americans and why it was such a controversial topic for whites. The chapter then focuses on how we gained public education and why it was such an important concept for the U.S. It also makes the point that we ensured an unequal society almost from the beginning by allowing educational segregation.

Chapter 2–Early Desegregation: Walk a Mile in My Shoes

This chapter covers the early efforts to integrate public schools in Florida and the U.S. It also looks at Jacksonville and the early pioneers who pushed for equal education. It provides some comparative analysis about what it was like to be black in a public school and what it was like being white.

Chapter 3–The Courts Have Spoken: And the Walls Came Tumbling Down

This chapter follows the path of the *Brown* decision and the reaction of white Floridians and other Southerners to the high court's decision. For African Americans it became immediately obvious that the South was not going to integrate its schools without a fight.

Chapter 4–Moving Toward a Unitary System: The University of Miami's Desegregation Center Writes a Plan

This chapter examines the first few integration plans submitted by the Duval County Public School System and why it can be argued that they did not take the integration effort seriously. The chapter also shows the determination of the NAACP and the black community to checkmate every effort to stall or delay integration.

Chapter 5–Disaccreditation, Delay, and Boycotts: Education in the Age of Chaos. Duval County Struggles to Fix Its Problems

This chapter explores the NAACP's efforts to integrate all areas of the city and how school integration was part of that effort. It also looks at the changing pattern of protest by the NAACP and how the efforts were becoming more pronounced.

Chapter 6–No Time for Delay: The 1970s and the Move Toward Full Integration

This chapter discusses the first serious efforts by the school system to integrate its schools. It focuses on how the long delays and other tactics hurt their credibility when they attempted to actually integrate the schools.

Chapter 7–Closing the Gap: Integrated But Not Unitary

This chapter investigates things like "white flight" and the growth of independent private schools which drained the school system of many white students and changed the meaning of "integration" and "unitary."

Chapter 8–The Battle is Over: What Have We Learned?

This chapter analyzes the end of the legal wrangling and what integration meant. It asks the question: Why did it take so long to integrate? It also looks at the statistics to see if integration actually produced what it originally promised.

Conclusion

The conclusion uses the celebrations associated with 2013 and the 150th, 100th, and 50th anniversaries of the Emancipation Proclamation to call upon President Obama to issue an executive order mandating equal education.

Duval County Public School Superintendents

Name	Start Date
R.C. Marshall	January 3, 1933
W. Daniel Boyd	January 7, 1941
J.W. Gilbert (Acting, Boyd was in the military)	1942-1945
Iva T. Sprinkle	January 6, 1953
Ish Brant	January 8, 1957
Dr. Cecil Hardesty	January 7, 1969
Dr. John T. Gunning	July 15, 1973
Dr. Herbert Sang	February 1, 1976
Dr. Charles H. Cline (Interim)	April 1, 1989
Dr. Larry L. Zenke	April 24, 1989
Dr. Donald S. Van Fleet (Interim)	February 4, 1997
John C. Fryer, Jr.	August 1, 1998
Dr. Nancy Snyder (Interim)	May 7, 2005
Dr. Joseph Wise	November 17, 2005
Dr. Ed Pratt-Dannals	October 17, 2007
Dr. Nikolai Vitti	November 12, 2012

* Information provided by the Duval County Public School System and personal files of Dr. Larry Zenke.

Chapter One

Original Sin, Education in Black and White:
A Brief History of Educational Efforts in Jacksonville, Florida

Education is the process of cultural, social, and intellectual procreation. It is an effective tool used by society to maintain and instill its values into future generations. In the United States, education has played a pivotal role as a unifying agent, defining cultural and racial identity nationally, regionally, and locally. Public education continues to hold promise as the great equalizer of the American mosaic, offering opportunities for improvement to those willing and able to take advantage of the public school system. Even so, public education remains a controversial and divisive issue, separating Americans along racial, social, political, and economic lines. Desegregation resonates as the most contentious issue facing education in the United States more than a half-century after the landmark 1954 *Brown v. Board of Education* decision outlawed segregation in public schools. The call for equal education has taken on more meaning in the increasingly politically, racially, and economically divided American society.

Jacksonville, Florida's, struggle to desegregate its schools and offer an equal education to its public schoolchildren provides a legitimate example for those interested in understanding the challenges of desegregating urban public school systems in the South. It also contradicts the continuing fiction that Florida was somehow different from other Southern states when it came to civil rights and race relations. Beginning on December 6, 1960, and not ending until November 18, 2001, the forty-one-year struggle underscores the multifaceted battle facing the integration of public schools. Like most controversial issues, educational desegregation is complicated and raises questions about the shortcomings of civil rights legislation and practices. It challenges white notions of privilege and highlights the lack of minority opportunity as a continuing problem in American education. If Americans can equalize educational opportunities, they can work on the other inequalities,

9

finally putting the legacy of slavery, racism, and segregation to rest.

Even though educational inequality involves more than the obvious struggle between blacks and whites, African Americans' historical struggle for equal education in Jacksonville underscores its significance and promise. Though opponents blame immigration, migration, budget policies, and social mores for contributing to contemporary educational disparities, no one can deny the legacy of prejudice in shaping American attitudes about race and school integration.

The African American struggle for educational equality is different from that of other minorities because Africans were historically excluded from the educational process in America. Colonial Americans told themselves that Africans were inferior and incapable of intellectual development above the elementary level. Slave owners realized the potential of education for destroying myths of white supremacy and rigidly limited educational opportunities open to slaves. Colonial Americans agreed that since Africans were brought here to be slaves, they would play a different role from whites in American society.[1]

By the time of the American Revolution, racial attitudes were so ingrained that color had become a rigid caste in itself. This color caste was grounded in the supposed supremacy of everything European over everything African. Africans were consigned to second-class status in environments controlled by whites. Africans locked in slavery were legally reduced to being chattel, or property, divorcing them from the human family and setting them apart from white society.[2]

By 1830 slavery had become a sectional entity, but racism was a national problem. Even though Southerners utilized slave labor, Northerners held racial beliefs that in many ways mirrored the worst of Southern attitudes. Across the country, blacks were recognized as de jure unequals. Legally, they were nonpersons, pariahs in a free land. For the few African Americans who were not subject to slavery, white Americans created a strange legal and social condition referred to as the "Free-Black." Those who were trapped in this status realized that they were neither legally free persons, nor were they slaves. Race scholar Winthrop Jordan described their position this way: "As for the Free-Negro's position in the community, the association of slavery with race had transformed a free black man into a walking contradiction in terms, a social anomaly, a third party in a system built for two. Not only did free Negroes provide an evil example to slaves, but, worse, their presence imposed a question mark on the rationale of slavery." In no region of the United States were African Americans recognized as equal to whites, and almost no whites believed they were capable of advanced intellectual development.[3]

This inferior status was confirmed and defended by nearly every institution in America. In 1857 the U.S. Supreme Court approved of this racial status in its *Dred Scott* decision. Dred Scott was a slave who sued for his freedom after his owner had taken him to free areas for several years. When Supreme Court Chief Justice Roger Taney delivered his opinion in the case, he simply stated what others already practiced. Taney said that African Americans had no citizenship rights that whites were obliged to respect. In essence, he confirmed African Americans' reduced status, arguing that they were never intended to be equal citizens under the law. According to Taney:

The question is simply this: Can a negro, whose ancestors were imported into this country, and sold as slaves, become a member of the political community formed and brought into existence by the Constitution of the United States, and as such become entitled to all the rights, and privileges, and immunities, guarantied (sic) by that instrument to the citizen?[4]

Taney's answer was an unequivocal No! He said blacks

. . . are not included, and were not intended to be included under the word "citizens" in the Constitution, and can therefore claim none of the rights and privileges which that instrument provides for and secures to citizens of the United States. On the contrary, they were at that time considered as a subordinate and inferior class of beings, who had been subjugated by the dominant race, and whether emancipated or not, yet remained subject to their authority, and had no rights or privileges but such as those who held the power and the Government might choose to grant them . . . they had no rights which the white man was bound to respect.[5]

For many whites, this decision settled the issue of African American inequality and lack of citizenship rights, but for African Americans it planted the seeds for their equality. Frederick Douglass said of the decision, "The Supreme Court was not the only power in this world. We, the abolitionists and colored people, should meet this decision, unlooked for and monstrous as it appears, in a cheerful spirit. This very attempt to blot out forever the hopes of an enslaved people may be one necessary link in the chain of events preparatory to the complete overthrow of the whole slave system." Douglass's words proved prophetic. The *Dred Scott* decision was preceded by the publication of Harriet Beecher Stowe's *Uncle Tom's Cabin* in 1853 and followed by John Brown's raid on Harper's Ferry in 1859, on the eve of the Civil War. With the catastrophic events of the Civil War, the debate over African American equality resurfaced.[6]

After President Abraham Lincoln issued his preliminary Emancipation Proclamation on September 18, 1862, promising freedom to slaves in areas still in rebellion, African American soldiers gave heroic service fighting to preserve the Union. As the war ground on, the issue of African American status and rights continued to befuddle the Lincoln administration. As the number of African American soldiers killed in action increased, there was a growing realization by Republican leaders that those who were paying such a terrible price were worthy of special consideration. As one Civil War commentator wrote, "From the day that bayonets were placed in the hands of the blacks . . . the Negro became a citizen of the United States. . . .This war has broken the chains of the slave, and it is written in the heavens that from this war shall grow the seeds of the political enfranchisement of the oppressed race." The war, and the major role blacks played in it, changed the attitude of the nation's leaders. By the war's end, Lincoln was giving cautious support for completely eradicating slavery and giving selected African American males voting rights. In his last public speech, he became the first American president to endorse African American suffrage when he stated, "I would myself prefer that (the vote) were now conferred on the very intelligent, and on those who serve our cause as soldiers." Lincoln's words presaged momentous changes.[7]

On Palm Sunday, April 9, 1865, General Robert E. Lee met with General Ulysses S. Grant in Wilmer McClean's front parlor in the hamlet of Appomattox Courthouse, Virginia, to surrender his Army of Northern Virginia. This surrender essentially ended America's bloodiest and most destructive war. The Civil War's destruction went beyond America's physical landscape, and included the nation's social, political, economic, and racial landscape as well. After four years of intense fighting, costing more than one million American lives, the sheer weight of Northern economic and military power overwhelmed the Southern resistance. As Southern opposition collapsed, Confederate leaders accepted military defeat, the overthrow of their institutions, and the possible reformation of their social system. The Civil War changed the nation and forced Americans to recognize their responsibility to the nearly four million African American freedmen.[8]

For slaves in Jacksonville, freedom did not come until May 14, 1865, when General Quincy Gilmore issued General Order 63, which formally ended slavery in Florida. Immediately there was strife between the former slaves and masters. Brigadier General Israel Vogdes reported that "as a body [former slave owners are] opposed to the freeing of the slaves, and many still have a lingering hope that some compensation will be awarded to them." The *New York Times* reported that whites viewed the former slaves from two radically opposite positions. Some wanted to elevate blacks at the expense of whites, while others wanted to annihilate blacks while accepting their own freedom. Much of the excitement was caused by the presence of black troops in the city.[9]

Once the fighting ended, the South faced the task of reestablishing a social order radically changed by emancipation and the overthrow of the slavocracy. Many Southerners refused to accept defeat and instead attempted to reestablish slavery under a different name, passing laws collectively referred to as "Black Codes." These Black Codes demonstrated that white Southerners had not changed their racist attitudes about African Americans and white privilege. Since the antebellum decades, Free Blacks had been second-class individuals who could legally be discriminated against by Southerners, who believed that it was permissible to treat the former slaves the same as they had treated the prewar Free Blacks. As a Florida politician stated, "Emancipation had not caused, '"any change in the social, legal, or political status' of those already free." They were expected to maintain the same racial etiquette they had followed before the war.[10]

When Florida's politicians wrote the state's Black Codes, they were simply giving the former slaves the prewar limited status of Free Blacks. Florida's Black Codes forbade African Americans from testifying against whites; enforced marriage restrictions; allowed civil authorities to whip blacks; outlawed interracial relationships; classified the rape of a white woman as a capital crime; segregated African Americans on public conveyances; forbade blacks from carrying weapons; set up special rules for vagrancy and labor contracts; and established apprenticeship laws. "In 1866 a capitation tax of $3 a year had been levied on all males between 21 and 55. Upon refusal to pay, the defaulter could be seized and hired out to anyone who would pay the tax and costs of proceedings." An additional one dollar tax was placed on black men to pay for schools. This ensured a cheap, stable labor supply for local employers. White supremacist ideas and the desire to keep African Americans in a condition as close to slavery as possible dictated the passage of these laws. Northern Republican politicians, such as Thaddeus Stevens and Charles Sumner, understood that radical changes needed to be made in Southern society as a necessary step to social harmony and reconstruction of the South.[11]

Northern reformers knew that changing Southern society required changing racial and social policies. As they debated the changes, the nation redefined the status of African Americans and identified their place within American society. This redefinition involved forcing the South to accept African American legal equality, a notion many Northerners had not fully accepted themselves. This shift required a social revolution and transformation of America's historical racial etiquette. Even in the North, racism remained a reality. An editorial in the *Cincinnati Enquirer* summarized whites' feelings on race: "Slavery is dead, the Negro is not, there is the misfortune."[12]

Though it salved the American conscience, ending slavery had not solved America's race problem. Reconstruction politicians made several moves which marked their determination to change the status and position of African Americans and bring them into the American family. On December 18, 1865, the Thirteenth Amendment was ratified, officially ending the nation's seventy-six-year odyssey with chattel slavery. This was followed three years later, on July 21, 1868, with the ratification of the Fourteenth Amendment, creating a national definition of citizenship that included the former slaves. The Fourteenth Amendment was a progressive piece of legislation, making all those born or naturalized in the United States, citizens. It was supposed to create a color blind society outlining the rights and privileges of citizens, with a legal definition of equality and citizenship that gave the former slaves equal rights, privileges, and legal status with whites. It provided for due process of the law to take away civil rights. It also assigned Congress the authority to reduce the political representation of states that violated equal rights. On March 30, 1870, Reconstruction politicians completed the transformation with the ratification of the Fifteenth Amendment. The Fifteenth Amendment protected the freedmen's franchise by punishing states that infringed on African American voting rights.[13]

By 1871, the United States had settled the legal issue of African American rights and citizenship. Between 1865 and 1870, the United States had radically transformed the nation: ending slavery, giving citizenship to African Americans, and providing measures for punishing states that denied the franchise. With the passage of the Thirteenth, Fourteenth, and Fifteenth Amendments, the United States government put itself on the side of African American rights. As historian David Kyvig stated, "The Fourteenth and Fifteenth Amendments . . . carried forward a social as well as a political and legal transformation hardly imaginable a few years earlier." With these political maneuvers, the radical Republicans had taken a major step toward creating an egalitarian society based on racial equality. By writing equality into the law, individual success would no longer be determined by race but rather by one's ability to navigate a hostile and confusing post-slavery world. In order to have enduring success and progress, African Americans would now have to eradicate the remnants of slavery and replace them with new initiatives.[14]

The linchpin of this revolution would become public education. For most parts of the South, little attention had been paid to educational issues before the Civil War, because only upper-class Southerners were educated while African Americans were generally confined to a lifetime of illiteracy. Once the war ended, the former freedmen were at a disadvantage to whites in educated settings. Education was the quickest way to improve life for African Americans. With a nearly ninety-five percent illiteracy rate in 1865, African Americans understood that they had a struggle before them to make up the intellectual ground lost during slavery. As Booker T. Washington wrote, "Few people who were not right in the midst of the scenes can form any exact idea of the intense desire which people of my race showed for education. It was a whole race trying to go to school. Few were too young, and none too old, to make the attempt to learn." W. E. B. DuBois said, "The uprising of the Black man, and the pouring of himself into organized effort for education, in those years between 1861-1871, was one of the marvelous occurrences of the modern world: almost without parallel in the history of civilization." With the introduction of free public education in the South, Southerners were beginning something new. According to DuBois, "Public Education for all at public expense was, in the South, a Negro idea." Even though Southerners demanded separate and unequal education, and protested paying for it, blacks were nevertheless able to make tremendous strides in education.[15]

Understanding why educational desegregation was so difficult requires familiarity with how segregated education started and a general understanding of Florida's educational structure. Jacksonville has been a part of Florida's history from the beginning. In 1562 French Huguenots, under the leadership of Jean Ribault, explored the banks of the St. Johns River. In 1564 René Laudonnière, with the help of French Huguenots, built the historic Fort Caroline. After Fort Caroline was destroyed by Spanish forces under the command of Pedro Menéndez de Avilés, the Spanish settled St. Augustine in 1565. Great Britain acquired Florida in 1763 and established one of Britain's first settlements in the area now known as Jacksonville. The British built indigo plantations and transportation routes, one of which was the famed "King's Highway."[16]

England ruled Florida from 1763 until 1783 before Spain regained control. In 1819 Spain ceded Florida to the United States. When Congress organized Florida as a territory in 1821, Jacksonville and Duval County were both chartered as areas of the Territory of Florida. Jacksonville was named after Florida's military governor, Andrew Jackson, and Duval County was named after Florida's first civilian governor, William P. Duval. The first governing document called for every sixteenth section of land in each township to be reserved for the aiding and the maintenance of primary schools. The care and administration of this land was given to the territorial government with provisions to spend the income from rentals on public education.[17]

This law was ignored for ten years. On January 22, 1831, the Florida Education Society, which had some of the most prominent people in Florida among its membership, was founded in Tallahassee. It would later develop branches in several townships in Florida. Its stated goal was "to collect and diffuse information on the subject of education, and to endeavor to procure the establishment of such a general system of instruction as is suited to the wants and condition of the Territory." This organization had limited success and soon failed. Florida's territorial legislatures passed a series of laws to care for and preserve the sixteenth-section lands between 1828 and 1835, even though no funds were used to support education. Florida's first constitution, written in 1838, made no mention of education with the exception of a relatively innocuous statement about land being reserved for schools. Each succeeding constitution made the same statement. Though the first constitution did not go into effect until 1845, it set the tone for educational policy in Florida. There was little centralized coordination of educational activities during Florida's early years.[18]

For the most part, Florida's officials left education to local entities. On March 2, 1839, state legislators passed their first school law, an act which appointed three trustees in each township "to care for and lease the sixteenth-section lands of their township and to apply the income to the support of common schools in that township, and in case there were no common schools in existence, to establish and maintain them." In 1840 the state passed another law, creating first a two, then ten, percent tax to educate poor children. On December 19, 1845, a new law was enacted which made the judges of county courts superintendents of common schools. It also required the trustees in the district to make a report to the judges on the first of each year.[19]

Jacksonville's role in public education was equally innocuous. Founded in 1821 by Isaiah D. Hart, Jacksonville grew slowly, but soon became an integral part of Florida's economic and social development. Its coastal location, good farming land, and deep river made it an ideal trading post and farming area. As the population expanded, so did the demand for education. Alexander Graham, an Episcopal minister, opened the first school in Jacksonville in 1835. Though the school was co-ed, it was reserved for white children. The records of this first school are scarce. One can only guess about the success or failure of Graham's educational efforts. Jacksonville remained a very small town with insignificant population numbers until the 1850s. According to the census in 1850, Florida had 47,208 whites and 40,242 African Americans. There were only 932 Free Blacks, all of whom resided in Key West.[20]

On July 26, 1845, judge of probate William F. Crabtree became the first county superintendent of education for Duval County. The same year, the Odd Fellows built a two-story wooden structure at the southeast corner of Adams and Market Streets. The building had steps leading to lodge rooms on the second floor. A school was run from the first floor where the Odd Fellows had their hall. Little is known about this school or the students who attended it.[21]

On January 10, 1849, the state passed legislation creating common schools for white children between the ages of five and eighteen. The legislation placed the director of land registry in charge of these schools. The judges of probate were also expected to serve as superintendents of schools, along with a board of trustees who were to be elected annually by taxpayers. Between 1849 and 1860, the state passed a series of laws to help communities support their schools. The most important of these laws was passed in 1851 when the state authorized the counties to levy taxes of up to four dollars per pupil on real and personal property to support schools. Next the state passed a law giving the proceeds from the sale of slaves, under the act of November 22, 1829, to be added to the school fund. The last attempt called for increasing the school fund to provide two dollars per child for every county that could not raise that much money. Neither of these laws solved Florida's public school financing problems. During the antebellum era, there were no African American schools in Florida. Indeed, during the 1830s and 1840s, the state passed laws making it illegal for African Americans to congregate for any purpose except work or attending divine services monitored by whites.[22]

In 1845 the state legislature in Florida, the country's newest state, passed a law stating that any "assemblies . . . by free negroes and mulattoes, slave or slaves, shall be punished . . . with a fine not exceeding twenty dollars, or stripes, not exceeding thirty-nine."

This measure, along with extensive and punitive slave codes, effectively eliminated opportunities to establish African American schools in the newest slaveholding state. Florida, like the rest of the white South, wanted to eliminate opportunities for slaves and free blacks to congregate and educate their children. Although based on the deep and pervasive racial norms of the antebellum South, the efforts by white Floridians to deprive African Americans of equal-opportunity education would last up to and even through the modern civil rights movement of the 1950s and 1960s. This study will explore the history of that educational inequality, and how the Sunshine State's reputed exceptionalism in the Deep South, as reported in the press, the media, and the literature, may not, in fact, match its record.[23]

Florida officials took steps to ensure that African Americans were not given access to public education early in the state's history. In 1846, just one year after Florida received statehood, officials passed a law which stated:

Be it further enacted that all assemblies and congregation of slaves, free Negroes and Mulattoes consisting of forty or more met together in a confined secret place is hereby declared to be an unlawful meeting, and the magistrates, sheriffs, militia officers of the patrol being commissioned, are hereby directed and required to enter into any such places and for that purpose to break open doors, windows, or gates if resisted, and disperse such slaves, free Negroes, or mulattoes as may be there unlawfully together; and magistrates, sheriffs, constables and militia officers of the patrol are hereby authorized to call to their assistance from the neighborhood such a force as he or they may judge necessary for the dispersing of such unlawful assembly of colored persons PROVIDED that nothing herein contained shall be construed to authorize any person to break into or disturb any church or place of public worship wherein they are assembled.[24]

Florida, like most Southern states, wanted to eliminate opportunities for slaves and free Blacks to congregate independently; thus denying them the ability to establish schools. Before the 1860s, most efforts to form a free public school system in Florida had failed. Few wealthy Floridians were interested in taxing themselves to pay for public schools. They believed that education was the responsibility of the family and not the state, and favored private school systems, which catered mainly to the upper class. "On plantations of those sufficiently wealthy or well-to-do, it was the practice to employ tutors for the sons and governesses for the daughters. These were generally college graduates from institutions in Northern and Middle States."

In antebellum Jacksonville, those who were educated were educated at their parents' expense even if the state offered assistance. Ironically, the first free public school opened in Jacksonville was an integrated school run by a Northern aid society. Esther Jane Hawks, a progressive reformer from New Hampshire, opened the state's first free public school in 1864. Hawks, a physician, was active in several movements, including the abolitionist movement, women's suffrage, and education. Hawks and her husband, Dr. John Milton Hawks, moved south soon after the start of hostilities. Hawks worked with the Freedman's Aid Society in South Carolina, opening a school at Port Royal Island. In 1864 she was authorized by the Freedman's Aid Society to open a school in Jacksonville, Florida. The school opened with twenty-nine white students and one African American. Northern soldiers occupied Jacksonville during this period, so most white families abandoned the area. Within three months, all but three of the white children had deserted the school, leaving it to the rapidly increasing African American population.[25]

After the war, whites returned to Jacksonville in large numbers. They once again attempted to reestablish a private school system exclusively for white upper-class children. There was discussion on the state level of establishing a state-controlled public school system. However, state leaders provided no money and gave no direction. Nevertheless, it was evident that African Americans wanted an education. Their wishes were combined with the philanthropic efforts of benevolent societies such as the American Missionary Association (AMA), AME Church, African Civilization Society, and the American Freedmen's Union Commission. With the help of these organizations, an educational foundation for freedmen was formed. African Americans placed pressure on local leaders to establish some sort of public school system in the city. The demand for education clearly outstripped the number of teachers. For Jacksonville and other Southern cities, the most immediate need was a place to train African American teachers.[26]

Even before the war ended, efforts were being made to increase the number of African American teachers. In 1864 E. B. Eveleth opened a school in Jacksonville for freedmen. By February 1865 there were more than 200 students attending this school. The students made so much progress that Eveleth was forced to offer morning and evening classes. Some students were so advanced that teachers had to divide the school into upper and beginning levels. Later that year, a school was organized to prepare female teachers between the ages of fifteen and twenty-five. During the Civil War and Reconstruction periods, Northern philanthropic organizations like the AMA came south to help African Americans establish educational institutions.

The AMA, which was founded on September 3, 1846, in response to the church's silence on slavery, became a major force for African American progress. The AMA believed that merely freeing African Americans from slavery was not enough. "They intended to free the bodies, souls, and minds of Black men. In their view the Civil War was a God sent punishment for the sin of slavery." The AMA argued that until the United States recognized African Americans as de jure equals, God's wrath would continue to visit the country. The organization's founders believed that the best path to equality was through education, where the spirit and lives of blacks could be refined, eventually destroying the caste system. The AMA selected Jacksonville as a center for establishing a normal school. Whites were leery of a general, free public educational system being established by the Reconstruction legislature because of their fear of race mixing. Thus, most whites chose to educate their children at home.[27]

In nearly every region of the South, the former slaves demonstrated a desire for education. With the help of Northern philanthropic societies, African Americans established a network of schools, attempting to ease the transition from slavery and prepare leaders for the future. By February 1865, the AMA was running a school in Jacksonville with both primary and advanced classes. The AMA believed that education should not only educate but also transform the former slaves into equal citizens. On January 16, 1866, the state passed legislation authorizing the first state-sanctioned education for African Americans. This legislation named Edward D. Duncan as the superintendent of common schools for freedmen. People both within and without the state widely praised and supported this appointment. As a result of this support, within a year there was a dramatic increase in the number of African American schools, from thirty to sixty-five. The number of teachers employed in African American schools increased from nineteen to forty-five, with an increase in overall enrollment from 1,900 to 2,726 students. "The teachers have been mostly colored, of good moral character, delighting in their work, maintaining good discipline, men of energy, and many well qualified. . . . I have never heard a single complaint of them," Duncan wrote in his first educational report. The first state superintendent of education, C. Thurston Chase, was recorded as stating that, "With the great mass of them [blacks], the avidity to learn was most intense with these first opportunities."[28] By all measures, blacks coveted an education and pursued all opportunities with vigor and commitment, a pattern that continued unabated for generations of African Americans in the Sunshine State.[29]

After passage of the 1868 State Constitution, Florida began offering free public education to its residents. Copying the Illinois public school plan, Florida's legislators outlined the state's version of public education. Article IX of the new constitution contained education provisions. These provisions were codified into law in January 1869, when the Florida legislature finally passed what became known as the "new school law." This law established standards for public schools and outlined a system for instruction, equipment, supplies, curriculum, and teacher qualifications. It also provided for a general and uniform system of tuition-free public instruction, "to all youth residing in the state between the ages of six and twenty-one years." Section 1 stated, "It is the paramount duty of the State to make ample provisions for the education of all the children residing within its borders, without distinction or preference." The supervisory oversight of this system was entrusted to the department of public instruction, a state board of education, a superintendent of schools, and a board of public instruction for each county, along with local school trustees, county treasurers and agents. Although the state allocated no immediate money to fund this new system, it had made public education available to African Americans and poor whites for the first time. Nevertheless, blacks continued to rely on the Freedman's Bureau for education.[30]

The school law permitted, but did not mandate, segregation. It called for, "separate schools for the different classes in such manner as will secure the largest attendance of pupils, promote harmony and advancement of the school, when required by the patrons." It also outlined the duties and responsibilities of each board of education. By 1870 Florida's educational problem had almost reached crisis proportion. Of the state's 178,748 residents, more than fifty percent were illiterate. Only one in four students had a school within commuting distance. The schools that were operating generally averaged just a few hours of instruction each day during an eighty-day school year. The school buildings were generally rented rooms in dilapidated one-room log cabins, typically lacking water or privies. The teachers and school officials faced constant harassment from local residents who resented educating their work force.[31]

As post-war Florida entered the 1870s, Ossian B. Hart, governor from January 1873 until March 1874, appointed Jonathan C. Gibbs, an African American graduate of Dartmouth College and the former Florida secretary of state, as state superintendent of public instruction. With this bold step, the governor sought to solidify Republican support, and to portray Florida as a progressive and compliant state, in an effort to avoid Washington's yoke of Reconstruction. Even as Gibbs feared the reactionary violence of the Ku Klux Klan in Florida, he rendered "all the assistance in my power" to create opportunities for "the education of the whole people of the South, without reference to race, color or previous condition."

The black community (almost one-half of the state's population) responded by committing large numbers of youth to the emerging educational system. Many of these schools, such as the subsequently famous Cookman School (Institute) in Jacksonville, opened under the auspices of local churches and households. There is evidence that educators looked at international models, such as the Bahamian schools, for curricula for African American children.

Often submerged in the historical literature is the fact that many black churches in Florida expanded their Sunday school programs into "Sabbath Schools." These offered African American children a once-a-week opportunity to learn grammar, arithmetic, and other academic disciplines that normally would not have been available to them because of the family and labor demands of the work week. During the Gibbs years, black students came to account for one-third of all the students in Florida facilities, even though they attended state-sponsored schools that were segregated and inferior. Moreover, African Americans at the local level created private educational endeavors and industrial schools in their own communities and churches to, as Booker T. Washington once termed it, uplift the race.[32]

Originally there was opposition to the school law, but that opposition began to subside after 1877 when white Democrats regained control of the state. Governor George Drew from New Hampshire surprised many by championing public education, arguing that it was cheaper than prisons and poorhouses. Drew had moved south before the war but claimed to be a Unionist, although he sold supplies to Confederates. African Americans were disheartened by Drew's election. One elderly African American who watched Drew's inauguration remarked, "Well, we niggers is done." Surprisingly, Drew said that, "Only through schools could the colored race become fit to exercise the privileges of voting intelligently to perform all the sacred rights of freedmen, to enjoy their liberty, to become wise and good citizens." Drew was more interested in building Florida's economy than he was in racial policy. In fact, he championed education as a means for expanding the economy.[33]

Inspired by Governor Drew's words the state superintendent of schools made a much-publicized tour of Florida's county schools. After his investigation, he came back with several recommendations. Among them were the consolidation of the schools into larger units; professional training for teachers; increasing the number of teachers; higher wages; development of a standard curriculum with textbooks; a guaranteed four-month term; and placing special emphasis on elementary education. Recognizing the tremendous opposition to African American education, he also suggested the establishment of a separate but equal system for blacks. The Florida press encouraged the expansion of public education and the number of children attending schools began to rise.[34]

In Jacksonville, Colonel Albert J. Russell and Louis Fleming served as the superintendent of public instruction and chairman of the board of public instruction, respectively. Russell was a former Confederate officer who had demonstrated his anti-black feelings. Seeing the potential of education for lifting African Americans from their degraded position and helping them gain political strength, he wanted to undermine this effort. Russell and Fleming built schools for white children all over the city, proving to be very efficient administrators who helped change white Floridians' attitudes about public education. Governor Francis Fleming chose Russell as Florida's superintendent of education in 1885. When

Russell left for Tallahassee, Jacksonville's school system was beginning to show progress. There were fifty-five public schools, with fifty of them continuously operating. These schools educated 2,665 students, who had a school term varying from five months, or 110 days, to eight months, or 176 days, depending on whether the school was a county or city school.[35]

This educational progress was made as the nation endured a period of retreat on racial issues. After Reconstruction and Democratic redemption of state and local politics, Florida's white Southerners rebuilt the social system, mandating segregation and African American subjugation. Using several unscrupulous measures, and supported by thousands of gruesome lynchings, the so-called Redeemers were able to relegate African Americans to second-class status within Southern society. Between 1877 and 1900, African Americans saw their citizenship rights robbed from them as white supremacy surged in the South. White politicians legally mandated racial separation in every area of Southern life. Moreover, from the beginning, school officials were careful to ensure that the educational systems did not challenge the existing social order nor upset the racial status quo. White supremacy had to be protected by every Southern institution, and African Americans could have no equal access to any entity which might lift them from their degraded position. To ensure the perpetuity of this system, every Southern legislature ordered segregation in its public schools to enforce this racial separation. There was little pressure to integrate schools during the early years of public education.[36]

Deep South Florida was part of this movement. Between June 9 and August 3, 1885, state lawmakers met in Tallahassee to write a new constitution, Florida's fifth, which codified educational segregation. The 1885 Constitution reflected the changing attitudes of white Southerners toward African American equality and citizenship rights. This constitution contained a new school law that ensured segregated public and private schools in Florida. Article XII, Section 12, stated, "White and colored children shall not be taught in the same school, but impartial provision shall be made for both." To protect themselves from Northern criticism and legal challenges from African Americans, legislators also mandated equal provisions for both races. As one commentator suggested, "This met the prejudices of the Southerners and disarmed the criticism of Northerners." In 1889 state lawmakers wrote a new school law which reinforced mandated segregation for all of Florida's public and private schools. Therefore, the notion of "separate but equal" was part of the state's racial behavior long before the 1896 *Plessy* decision mandated it. White parents demonstrated a reluctance to send their children to schools where African Americans were being educated. Even though the law mandated that schools be separate but equal, as in most Southern areas, local officials never enforced the *equal* provisions of the law. The result was generations of poorly educated African American children with few opportunities to improve their social condition. Although the new school law introduced in 1889 by Albert J. Russell made the school system less cumbersome and more efficient, it did nothing to improve African American education.[37]

Florida legislators made sure no one misunderstood their intentions when they wrote a statute that forbade white children from using the same books used by African American children. They went even further by mandating that books used in white schools be stored in separate facilities from those used in African American schools. The state constitution also required separate attendance zones for white and African American students to ensure there could be no mixing of the races through neighborhood schools. The 1885 Constitution made pariahs of African Americans and clearly degraded their social status in educational affairs. Duval County's white leaders eagerly enforced the state's Jim Crow laws and used them to reform the public school system. Generations of African American children were educated in segregated schools, where they received a daily dose of black degradation. Equally significant was that generations of white children were educated in separate schools where they were taught the superiority of the white race. By 1890 separate and unequal, though not the law of the land, was the practice of nearly every Southern institution.[38]

In Jacksonville educational policy clearly reinforced social attitudes as well. In 1866 the state legislature passed a law creating separate schools for African American and white children. By this time the state had become much more active in school issues. On March 1, 1869, the Board of Public Instruction was appointed. On November 24, 1869, the school board was organized, with Alonzo Huling as its first chair. The first school board was made up of five members chosen from recommendations by the state superintendent of public education.[39]

In 1889 the rules governing school boards changed in Florida. The state mandated that school boards must be elected by members of the local community. With a locally elected school board, the community gained control over school issues, and education became a local matter. Theoretically, this change ensured that African Americans would be included in all school decisions. However, because the state was actively involved in disenfranchising African Americans, their influence over school issues declined.[40]

With the aid of Northern philanthropic societies, Jacksonville's black community actually got involved in the educational process early. Jacksonville's African American community was fortunate to have former secretary of war Edwin M. Stanton headquartered in the city after the war. Stanton was serving as governor of the Fifth Military District, which was headquartered in Jacksonville. He was impressed with the level of knowledge African Americans possessed and he encouraged the Freedmen's Bureau to build a school in the city. With his support, educational activities increased dramatically. By 1866 there were already three schools and four teachers educating more than five hundred African American students in Jacksonville. Stanton Institute was the largest of these institutions, although the Cookman Institute, a normal and Biblical school built by the AME Church and the Freedmen's Aid Society in 1872, followed close behind with two teachers and fifty children by 1875.[41]

Stanton Institute also served as a model for what African Americans could accomplish if properly funded. On February 8, 1868, a group of African Americans created an organization called the Colored Educational Society of Jacksonville. Joining forces with the Freedmen's Bureau, the society raised $850 to purchase land between Beaver, Clay, Ashley, and Broad Streets from Ossian B. Hart. The Freedmen's Bureau then donated enough money to erect the "largest and finest school edifice in the state." The school opened on April 10, 1869, when $16,000 was dedicated, and was named after Secretary of War Stanton. It had six classrooms, a lecture hall, and a library. The school's function was to train African American teachers and to provide a solid grammar school education for Jacksonville's African American children. The school's principals were Celia E. and P. A. Williams, two sisters from Deerfield, Massachusetts. They supervised six teachers and 348 students.[42]

In 1869 Stanton offered coursework through eighth grade and graduates were allowed to teach in black schools. In 1870 Stanton had six classes with thirty-nine students in the normal class, eighty-eight in the first primary, sixty-four in the second primary, sixty-two in the first intermediate, sixty-two in the second intermediate, and fifty-seven in the third intermediate. The first graduation was held in 1880. The school was open to both races; however, only one white student attended. It was administered by the AMA, which paid one hundred dollars a month for rent; the county; and the Freedmen's Bureau. The school's administrators frequently changed its curriculum and upgraded its faculty during its first thirty years. State requirements and a fire helped administrators improve both Stanton's intellectual and physical landscape. Stanton had a board of trustees which helped run the school. Since people like Charles Anderson, Abraham Lincoln Lewis, and James S. McClane served on the school's board of trustees, Jacksonville's most prominent African American citizens were on the board. They were an influential part of the school's functioning and operational administration, and they had enough social and economic clout in the community to protect and advocate for the school.[43]

Stanton soon gained a reputation as the best African American school in the state. White tourists visiting Jacksonville flocked to the school to witness its operations. During the 1870s and 1880s,

African American teachers and administrators began to replace the Northern white teachers and administrators who ran the school. Jim Crow laws and African American independence led to a move to have African Americans lead their own institutions and exercise a greater say in their destiny. After Stanton joined the public school system in 1882, school officials named Dr. J. C. Waters to be Stanton's first African American principal.[44]

In 1894 James Weldon Johnson, a former student and graduate of Atlanta University, became Stanton's fourth African American principal. It was under his leadership that the school made its most dramatic changes. During the next decade, Johnson improved the curriculum and added courses, upgrading the school to high school status. Stanton was the only high school or secondary educational facility in the city, and, for a while, one of the few serving the state. The May 1, 1901, fire which devastated Jacksonville destroyed Stanton along with several other downtown buildings. The school's insurance policy paid to have the school rebuilt. The new building was a wooden structure inadequate for the children's needs. By 1912 everyone agreed the building housing Stanton's students was a firetrap.[45]

Stanton's board of trustees recommended renovating and expanding the school. The school board rejected that idea and instead recommended replacing Stanton with three smaller buildings, located in different areas of the city, in order to create neighborhood schools. Almost immediately, African Americans organized to save Stanton. The board of trustees filed a lawsuit challenging the school board's decision. Their lawyers argued that the school board was trying to dilute African American education and destroy a functioning black high school. This was the first civil rights suit filed in Jacksonville. In 1915, after it became obvious that the lawsuit might succeed, the school board reversed itself and agreed to renovate Stanton. In 1917 the school board funded the construction of a modern three-story brick structure on the spot where the original building had been located.[46]

The Stanton High School story is one of the few successes involving African American education in Jacksonville. For most African

Americans, Jacksonville offered only a rudimentary education, totally inadequate for the changing society. To concentrate only on the success of Stanton does a disservice to the other African American schools in Jacksonville.

As historian Barbara Richardson noted, most researchers tend to concentrate on Stanton and ignore the other aspects of African American education in Jacksonville. Even though the educational experience was generally positive, African Americans suffered from all the consequences of a separate and vastly unequal educational system. Although no Florida school district dedicated itself to equal education, that was no excuse for the appalling conditions black children in Jacksonville faced. Florida's educational policy was wedded to its racial policies; thus, even before the state mandated segregated education, schools were already de facto segregated and vastly unequal. For the most part, white parents refused to send their children to integrated schools and African American parents were reluctant to trust the education of their children to white teachers. This racial polarization had a devastating effect on African American education in Jacksonville.

Most white politicians and leaders refused to advocate school integration when they established the public school system. There are a number of reasons that can be given, but ultimately racism was the cause. Most whites understood the significance of equal education and the impact of educational competition. If African Americans could be educated on an equal basis with whites, the notions of white supremacy and African American inferiority, the linchpins of Southern racial policy, would be destroyed. Also, with the close daily contact of a school environment, it would be virtually impossible to enforce the prohibitions against interracial mixing, long a taboo in Southern society. Therefore, no Southern state made a legitimate effort to integrate schools because of the potential adverse effect on the social order. South Carolina and Louisiana were the only Southern school systems that experimented with integrated education, but both were forced to abandon the experiment when whites resisted.[47]

In 1877 there were 2,158 students enrolled in the forty-nine schools in Duval County. Of those forty-nine schools, twenty-eight educated the 889 white children and twenty-one schools educated the 1,269 African Americans. The school board appropriated $2,969.18 for the white schools and only $65.12 for the African American schools. Although there were more African American children than whites, the county spent seventy-three percent more on white education than African American education. Even Stanton was not nearly as impeccable as the best white schools. Stanton, with eight teachers and 469 students, was worth $20,000 in 1880, while East Jacksonville, the best white school, had four teachers and eighty students but was valued at $25,000. Stanton's student-teacher ratio was 58 to 1, while East Jacksonville's student-teacher ratio was only 20 to 1.[48]

During the 1880s and 1890s, little changed in the condition of African American education in Jacksonville. In 1890 there were 4,296 students enrolled in Duval County schools. The 2,476 African American students were educated in thirty-two schools where the county spent only $14,418, while the 1,820 white students were educated in forty-nine schools where the county spent $20,619. Even when the successful Stanton Normal School was compared with the East Jacksonville White Graded School, the best white school was considerably better than the best African American school.[49]

The examples of inequality in education were numerous. On all levels of the system, white children were provided more and better educational support than African Americans. For example, in 1880 the La Villa Colored Graded School, with 134 pupils, was valued at $500. The La Villa White Graded School, with just forty-nine students, was also valued at $500. The white Jacksonville High School, with an enrollment of just eighty-three students, was valued at $5,000, while the Oakland Colored School, with 226 students, was valued at only $3,000.[50]

When the school system built new schools, they were generally for whites. Usually African Americans were forced to accept the old school buildings and supplies left over when whites moved to better surroundings. In 1893 the county completed construction on a new school at the cost of $4,450 for white children. They gave the school that the white children had left to the African American students, who had been meeting in a church. This was a pattern that would become all too familiar as time went on and would expand from buildings to include books, jerseys, desks, and supplies. Whatever was used or discarded by whites was given to African Americans. This meant that African American supplies, books, and other learning materials were chronically outdated.[51]

In every Southern city, local officials practiced discrimination in the allotment of educational funds. State officials consistently denied that educational discrimination existed, all the while continuing the discrepancies. William Sheats, the state superintendent of public instruction, denied that Florida discriminated in providing education. Sheats argued that the funding inequities could be explained by the fact that it was cheaper to educate large numbers of students in large buildings than to educate smaller numbers in small buildings. Sheats ignored the fact that there were more African American students enrolled in a smaller number of schools than white students. S. Paul Brown said of black facilities in Jacksonville, "The facilities for the education of the colored race in Jacksonville are superior to those of most places. In fact I doubt that any town of its size has so many institutions devoted to this end. Aside from their equal share in the system of public schools and funds, there are three colleges here: The Cookman Institute, where all higher branches are taught, Edward Waters College, an industrial institution, and Florida Baptist Academy, a colored theological school."[52]

Educational inequities extended even to teacher pay. In Jacksonville the highest pay a white male teacher could earn was $187 per month. The highest pay an African American male could earn was $100 per month. The most that a white female teacher could earn was $80 per month while the most an African American female could earn was $50 per month. Joel D. Mead, the Duval County superintendent of public instruction, issued a report for the school term ending June 30, 1894. It reported ninety public schools in

34

Duval County, forty-seven for whites and forty-three for African Americans. Of the 5,048 students, 2,637 were African Americans. There were eighty-nine teachers for the white children and only sixty-three for the African American children. In 1893 kindergarten classes were started. They educated more than 200 students annually.[53]

Florida slowly began to make improvements and offer new benefits to those using its public schools. In 1916 state officials began providing free transportation for pupils attending public schools. In Jacksonville, school officials originally used eight horse-drawn vehicles to transport 150 students to schools. This system allowed the district to close isolated small schools by shipping the students to better schools in the city. Busing also helped increase the number of students who went to middle and high school. By 1939 there were forty-five modern buses transporting more than 5,000 students. The state passed a series of laws designed to regulate these buses and also to ensure their safe travel on highways and streets. These laws called for regular inspections of the buses and certification of the bus drivers. There was no opposition to busing children then.[54]

During the post-Reconstruction period, the racial climate of the South declined rapidly, causing a shift from a policy of separation to a policy of subjugation of African Americans. The post-Reconstruction period has garnered a great deal of attention from historians, and explanations for the racial decline follow a number of directions. The reasons for the decline are almost irrelevant. The reality is that what had started out as a promising period of racial cooperation quickly disintegrated into a racial catastrophe, which ended in African Americans being locked in a cruel cauldron of racial segregation and systematic discrimination.

After an initial period of racial progress, the South slowly descended into a racial abyss where African Americans were relegated to second-class citizens. As Reconstruction ended, white Southerners erected a brutal system of racial segregation, designed to separate African Americans from whites and reduce them to a second-class status. This movement toward segregation was a slow, deliberate process, which involved legal and extra-legal efforts. Most researchers agree that African Americans were the collateral damage of a struggle among the executive, legislative, and judicial branches for control of the nation's future from the 1870s through 1900.[55]

After the failed attempt to impeach President Andrew Jackson in 1865, there was a clear imbalance between the legislative and executive branches of the government. This came on the heels of the reduced role of the judicial branch during the Civil War and the liberties taken by the Lincoln administration. The result was that the legislative branch seemed to be gaining the upper hand in ruling the government. The balance of power, an important aspect of our system, was lost. After the tremendous growth in legislative power and the expansion of federal authority there was a backlash from the judicial branch.[56]

African American civil rights suffered from the struggle between the legislature and the judiciary. These newly gained rights given to African Americans were only as legitimate as the legislation that assured them and the courts that enforced them. Many people became concerned with the level of federal intervention in the personal lives of citizens. They were also concerned with the size of the federal government and the newfound power concentrated within the hands of federal officials. Many of the functions generally associated with state government had been taken over by federal officials.[57]

A series of cases signaled a reduced role by the federal government in protecting African American rights. After the country ratified the Thirteenth, Fourteenth, and Fifteenth Amendments, which ended slavery; outlined citizenship rights along with the notion of equality; and ensured the franchise, respectively, the federal courts were responsible for defining those rights. The federal courts, especially the Supreme Court, were supposed to protect citizens from encroachments by an overbearing government and define the parameters of citizenship rights. Clearly, these amendments were designed to define equality, protect African American citizenship, and outline the boundaries of a multiracial democracy.

However, the framers of these laws wrote them with such vague language that they opened the door to varying interpretations.[58]

By the time these amendments were ratified, the U.S. Supreme Court was in the midst of a power struggle with the legislative branch for control over the direction of the nation. After a period of executive domination during the war years, followed by legislative supremacy in the period immediately after the war, the judicial branch of the government began to exert itself. The courts began to narrow the powers of what they viewed as an overbearing federal government.[59]

The federal activism of the judicial branch was a reaction to its perceived loss of power with the expansion of the legislative and executive branches. To adequately enforce the provisions of the Thirteenth, Fourteenth, and Fifteenth Amendments would clearly expand the powers of the federal government. Tracing the entire case law leading to segregation would be beyond the scope of this book; however, it is important that one understand the steps and background leading to racial segregation.

In 1870 Congressman Charles Sumner, a representative from Massachusetts and a prominent Republican politician, introduced a law to Congress guaranteeing equal rights to African Americans. The bill prohibited discrimination in railroads, steamboats, public conveyances, hotels, restaurants, theaters, public schools, church organizations, and cemeteries. The law was designed to define freedom and give federal officials the authority to enforce its meaning. The bill had a two-fold nature, involving the right to political participation and the right to equality before the law. Sumner's original bill went further than any other definition of freedom and included the right to escape racial insult and be free from racial violence.[60]

Opposition to the bill was strong and unrelenting. Opponents did not want to broaden the definition of freedom as far as Sumner envisioned. They argued that Sumner's bill expanded the federal role too far and regulated noncriminal behavior of citizens by outlining whom they could serve in private establishments. They also argued that the constitutional basis of the law was suspect. Sumner modified the bill, keeping the basic assumption that freedom meant more than political equality and protection from violence; it included the destruction of the stigma of caste. He reintroduced the bill each year from 1870 until 1874. By March 1874, Sumner was near death. As he lay on his deathbed, he gathered his closest friends and colleagues around his bed and whispered, "Take care of the civil rights bill. My civil rights bill, don't let it fail."[61]

In 1875 two of Sumner's Republican colleagues, Ben Butler and Levi Morton, took up the bill and pushed it through Congress. The Republicans were on the decline, suffering major reversals in the midterm elections. Progressives knew that passing this type of legislation was getting difficult. However, these two men were adamant. They removed the portion calling for integrated education, opting instead for equal education. This compromise allowed them to put together a coalition which passed the legislation. The bill prohibited discrimination on racial grounds in the operation of inns, public conveyances on land or water, theaters, and other places of public amusement. An aggrieved party could seek redress in federal court in the form of monetary damages. The guilty party could also be charged with a misdemeanor accompanied by a fine and jail time. The 1875 Civil Rights Act put the force of the law behind African American rights. With this law we knew what equality meant and had guidelines for punishing those who violated its principles. It also laid the foundation for separate but equal educational settings.[62]

Almost immediately there were challenges to the new law. Ordinary citizens in all regions of the country questioned the expanded activities of the federal government. Many whites viewed the Civil Rights Act as an unfair infringement on their citizenship rights. It touched their day-to-day behavior as it related to African Americans, forcing African Americans on whites in all of their social settings. African Americans could purchase tickets and sit next to whites in theaters, taverns, and on public conveyances. With the changing racial attitudes, it was only a matter of time before the legislation would be challenged in the courts.[63]

On October 15, 1883, the U.S. Supreme Court handed down its decision in a series of cases filed by African Americans challenging racial discrimination in public accommodations. In each of the cases the defendants had clearly violated provisions of the Civil Rights Act. The decision settled five cases of discrimination against blacks regarding access to public accommodations and violations of Sections 1 and 2 of the Civil Rights Act of 1875. The cases involved cities from New York to California. They also involved a variety of entities: an opera house, a dining room, hotel lodging, a theater, and seating in the ladies' section of a train. The issues involved in the case were national, not regional, because they originated in different parts of the country.[64]

The federal government, in the person of Samuel Field Phillips, argued that the Fourteenth Amendment prohibited states from denying equal protection of the laws. Because private businesses required state licenses, they must be constrained to follow state law. He then argued that the Fourteenth Amendment had already set the precedent for the state's forcing individuals to adhere to state laws even in the regulation of private property. The court rendered its decision on October 15, 1883. In an 8 to 1 decision, the court said the Fourteenth Amendment protected African Americans from state-sanctioned discrimination but not from private individual discrimination. In essence, the court ruled that states could not discriminate but that individuals could.[65]

After the court rendered its decision, a wall of segregation was erected, separating African Americans in all areas of public life, mainly in the South. Between 1883 and 1895, the tenor of segregation changed from general separation to a policy of subjugation. "At the state level private and public agents quickly seized on the two-tiered system of justice. . . . African Americans were excluded from jury service . . . paving the way for nullification of criminal prosecutions of Whites for violence against Blacks." The facilities provided to African Americans were clearly inferior to those offered to whites, but when African Americans complained, they faced a hostile justice system. By 1895 Southern state governments had created a series of laws that supported a ruthless system of segregation, separating African Americans from the society at large and relegating them to an inferior social status. To African Americans and their friends, this was a violation of the Equal Protection Clause of the Fourteenth Amendment.[66]

African Americans refused to accept their reduced status and organized a legal challenge. On June 7, 1892, Homer Plessy purchased a first-class ticket for a trip from New Orleans to Covington, Louisiana. Plessy sat in the white section of the train and proceeded on his trip. Plessy, a light-skinned African American, was arrested when he refused to move to the African American section after it was learned that he was passing for white. He was charged with violating the state law mandating segregation. During his first trial in the Louisiana State Court, Judge John H. Ferguson found him guilty. The Louisiana State Supreme Court upheld this decision. Plessy then appealed the decision to the U.S. Supreme Court.[67]

Albion Tourgee, a North Carolina judge and Republican leader who advocated African American civil rights, argued Plessy's case before the Supreme Court. Alexander Porter Morse, a Washington, D.C. lawyer, argued the case for the State of Louisiana. Morse contended that the separate accommodations for African Americans did not violate the Thirteenth Amendment's prohibition against racial distinctions, nor did they violate the Equal Protection Clause of the Fourteenth Amendment because the accommodations were equal even though they were separate. Tourgee countered that the mere act of separating people for no reason except their color represented discrimination, which placed a badge of inferiority on blacks.[68]

On May 18, 1896, the Supreme Court rendered its decision. In a stunning 8 to 1 decision, the court ruled in favor of the State of Louisiana, establishing a new doctrine often referred to as "separate but equal." This decision gave state agencies license to separate African Americans from whites in all social and educational settings, with the caveat that the accommodations had to be equal. This separation inevitably led to suppression wherein *equal* was ignored and *separate* became the law of the land.[69]

Even before the court rendered its decision, Florida had mandated school segregation. The 1885 Florida Constitution specified, "White and colored children shall not be taught in the same school, but impartial provision shall be made for both." Separate but equal was law in Florida even before the Supreme Court legitimated it. Along with constitutional restraints there were state laws that forbade the teaching of white and African American children in the same building. They also mandated separate attendance zones for African American and white children. Even children living in the same neighborhood were required to attend separate schools. By state law, there was no such thing as a neighborhood school. The laws were so far-reaching that state superintendents were even required to keep books used in African American and white schools separate. These three laws, along with the state constitution, regulated the way Duval County public schools were operated.[70]

The underpaid, overworked African American teachers in Jacksonville performed miracles with their limited resources. They were able to raise the African American students to a level of literacy which outdistanced cities of similar size. After the African American schools were integrated into the public school system, they dedicated themselves to a path of liberal arts education. African American teachers emphasized reading, writing, and arithmetic and produced one of the most literate groups of African Americans in the state.

Between 1914 and 1924, the gap between African American and white education expanded. There were several bond issues that increased revenue for improving existing school structures. African American schools did not receive their fair share of these funds. In 1915 a $1 million bond issue allowed the city to replace most of the wooden structures utilized by white students. A subsequent bond issue was passed on August 1, 1919, producing another $325,000; on April 19, 1922, a third bond issue was passed, providing an additional $1 million to fund the replacement of the other schools. By 1924 all twenty-four schools serving white students were fireproof brick structures, equipped in a modern fashion. In comparison, there were only five brick African American schools.[71]

It is difficult to explain just how unequal conditions were between African American and white schools. The disparities increased as each decade passed. The Great Depression and the associated economic constrictions harmed African American schools disproportionately. Educational surveys conducted during this time showed that African American and white children had a different educational experience.

The Duval County Public School System had several levels of organization. These included a county superintendent; a supervisor of primary grades; a supervisor of elementary grades; a supervisor of rural schools; and supervisors of various subjects such as physical education and health; music; art; vocational education and manual arts; household arts; ancient languages; romance languages; classification; and vocational guidance; as well as the principal of each local school. In high schools, they established one additional level of administration called a department head. With so many levels of administration, the superintendent had very little actual day-to-day control over the schools. Some of the tiers of administration overlapped, which caused friction. The rural schools in the county had almost no day-to-day supervision.[72]

During the 1920s, the Institute of Educational Research, Division of Field Studies, released a telling report of a study conducted by the Teachers College of Columbia University. It was one of the first in-depth studies of education in Jacksonville. The study concluded that the city was doing a poor job on education. Researchers especially pointed out problems with funding education. The low tax assessments, coupled with little concern for public education, had created a system with high debt and low standards. The survey estimated Jacksonville's population at 135,024. There were 18,183 students attending public schools in Jacksonville. Of that number, 71.64 percent were white, with 17.68 percent in junior high school and 10.68 percent in senior high school.[73]

The study found that Jacksonville lagged behind the rest of the nation in teacher pay. The average starting salary for an elementary teacher was $900, while the national average for U.S. cities was $1,067. The maximum salary for an elementary teacher in Jacksonville was $1,440, compared to $1,841 in comparable cities. The median salary for elementary teachers in Jacksonville was $1,290, compared to $1,565 for similar cities.[74]

The salaries for junior high teachers were also low. While the minimum salary for a junior high teacher in Jacksonville was $1,300, and the U.S. average was $1,263, the maximum salary for a Jacksonville junior high teacher was $1,700, while the national high was $2,229. The median junior high school teacher's salary in Jacksonville was $1,590, while comparable cities had a median salary of $1,804.[75]

High school teachers faced similar reduced pay scales. Jacksonville's high school teacher salaries ranged from $1,500 to $2,150, compared with $1,438 to $2,462 for comparable locations. In Jacksonville the median high school salary for teachers was $1,776, while that of similar cities was $2,060. It must be stated that the maximum salary was a median of the highest salaries and did not accurately show the highest salary for the city. Several of the cities used in the comparison were, in actuality, much smaller than Jacksonville.[76]

The low salaries created a number of problems for the Duval County Public School System. To begin with, there was an unusually high turnover rate for teachers. Second, there were a large percentage of teachers who had attained less than the minimum standard of training for their group. Third, the average level of teacher experience in Jacksonville was low. Researchers predicted, "Well-trained teachers cannot be expected to remain in the system for many years if better salaries can be obtained in other cities. Jacksonville, on the other hand, will find it difficult to secure the most competent teachers available because of the low salaries paid." This observation, made in 1927, is still appropriate for Jacksonville's contemporary situation.[77]

School teachers who worked outside of the city were actually paid less than teachers who worked in Jacksonville. County teachers were paid on a different scale from city teachers. The rationale behind this pay difference was that living costs in outlying areas were less than in the city. However, this did not make up the difference in the pay scales. Living cost was defined as the cost for room rent, summer school, laundry, board, and other incidentals. The problem with salary versus living cost was not unique to Duval County teachers. In 1927 the median annual living cost in Jacksonville was $783 for elementary teachers. Therefore, living cost ate up 87 percent of the minimum salary, 60.5 percent of the median salary, and 54.3 percent of the maximum salary paid to Jacksonville's teachers.[78]

For junior high teachers the cost was $879. That meant that living cost consumed 67.6 percent of the minimum salary, 55.3 percent of the median salary, and 51.7 percent of the maximum salary. The living cost for senior high teachers was $1,033, meaning that living cost absorbed 68.8 percent of the minimum salary, 58.1 percent of the median salary, and 48 percent of the maximum salary. For county teachers, living costs of $527 used up 82.3 percent of the minimum salary, 55.2 percent of the median salary, and 42.5 percent of the maximum salary.[79]

Raises were small and incremental. Between 1920 and 1926, the median salary for elementary teachers increased just 3.4 percent, from $1,250 to $1,293. High school teachers' salaries increased by 15.8 percent, from $1,534 to $1776. Teachers in Duval County saw their salaries change from $747 to $953, an increase of 27.5 percent. The larger increases for high school teachers and county residents were designed to keep up with the rest of the profession.[80]

Also related to salary was the notion that salary schedules valued experience, education, recruitment, and cost of living. There should be no difference in pay for similar work in different school divisions. An elementary teacher with four years of schooling beyond high school could make $1,440, but a teacher with identical qualifications and training could earn $1,700 in junior high and $2,150 in high school. The report found that, "the educational demands made upon the teachers in various departments do not vary sufficiently to warrant such a difference in salary." The report went on to argue that teaching in elementary schools is no less difficult than teaching in high schools. The result of the unequal pay was that better-trained elementary teachers were leaving the profession.[81]

The 1927 report recommended abolishing the existing salary schedules and creating what was known as a single salary schedule. With a single salary schedule, each teacher would be paid the same salary, with the only differences being based upon training. A teacher with two years of post-high school training would receive a minimum salary of $1,080 and a maximum of $1,647. A teacher with three years of education would receive $1,260, minimum, and $1,854, maximum. Teachers with four years of training would receive $1,440, minimum, and $2,304, maximum. A teacher with five years of training would receive a minimum of $1,620 and a maximum of $2,484. This type of system would establish automatic salary increases, encourage teachers to seek further training, and reduce the turnover rate.[82]

A 1927 study surveyed 117 teachers in Jacksonville. The typical white junior high school teacher in Jacksonville had four years of training beyond high school. There were forty-one, or approximately thirty-five percent, who had less than four years. There was a need for specialized training for teachers who had an education degree but taught courses outside of their specialties. The average high school teacher had four-and-a-half years of training. Of the teachers interviewed only eight reported having less than four years of training. There were fifteen who had five or more years. It was recommended that high school teachers have at least some post-graduate work. Local leaders ignored most of the recommendations made by the study group.[83]

As expected, the report did not mention segregation or its impact on African Americans. It did, however, recognize that poor facilities hampered educational activities among African Americans. Researchers also expressed concerns about the danger of fires and other hazards prevalent in black schools.

The educational problems African Americans faced were many. During the 1925-1926 school year, 9,045 of the 12,576 African American children were enrolled in ten Duval County schools.

Nearly twenty-eight percent of the black school-aged children were not enrolled. Even at the newly rebuilt Stanton High School, there were serious problems. In 1925 Stanton, the only African American school that offered courses above the eighth grade, was not accredited because the school board refused to build a science laboratory.[84]

The educational inequities continued through the 1940s. Overcrowding became such a problem in African American schools that most were forced to operate dual sessions. There were twenty-two schools for the more than 11,000 African American students in Duval County. Most of the African American schools operated on a nine-month basis as dictated by the state's compulsory education law. However, there were almost no attendance officials to ensure compliance.[85]

For the 25,000 white students attending public schools in Duval County, the school system provided 1,100 classrooms. For the more than 11,000 African American children, there were only 272 classrooms. The classroom ratio for white students was 1 to 22. The ratio for African Americans was 1 to 40. Schools that offered two shifts generally had the first session from 7:00 a.m. to 12:00 p.m. The other students arrived at 12:00 p.m. and were dismissed at 4:00 p.m.[86]

The educational needs of black students were usually ignored by the community since they had few advocates. Rufus E. Payne, who served as the first supervisor of Negro education, was the exception. Payne had a difficult job getting even the basics for black children. Rufus Payne was born in Greenland, Florida on April 13, 1892. He attended Florida Baptist Academy and Atlanta University and served two years in the Army during World War I. He lived briefly in New York City before returning to Jacksonville to teach in the school system. Payne served as assistant principal of Stanton High School, where he also taught math. When Franklin Street Elementary School opened, Payne was promoted to become its first principal. After two years he was tapped as the first supervisor of Negro education in Duval County.[87]

Payne was much adored by his students and the community. He coached football, often funding the teams from his own pocket, since the state provided no extracurricular funds. He pushed forcefully to get Matthew Gilbert Middle School opened. Payne died unexpectedly on June 24, 1929, at the age of thirty-seven, from a bleeding hemorrhoid and his position was not filled. In honor of his work, School No. 163 was renamed Rufus Payne Elementary School in 1964.[88]

Segregated education harmed African American children in many ways. The unequal educational facilities, coupled with the prevalence of segregation within society, worked a double evil on African Americans, providing them with a poor education and instilling in them a disregard for their race. By the 1940s, the educational policies of the past were no longer a viable practice for the rapidly changing post-war society. Things were going to have to change. How much things actually changed can be debated.

Despite the many polemics about education and race, Jacksonville's problem is that it has only recently made a legitimate effort to create a unitary educational system. The blame for this is not entirely on the school board, but must also be shared by society at large. Despite the racial progress of the last thirty to forty years, most whites still display an unwillingness to sacrifice for racial progress. This can be easily seen in the widespread opposition to busing and the continued slow progress in neighborhood integration and educational equity plans.

The roots of this problem stem from the failures of the civil rights era. As the civil rights movement progressed, African Americans broke free of the confines of their traditional neighborhoods. Whites then fled the urban areas, surrendering their once segregated neighborhoods to newly arriving African Americans. This movement compounded a race problem by expanding it into a class problem as well. African Americans who could afford to move left their previously all-black neighborhoods and escaped into suburbs. With the open housing laws of the late 1960s and early 1970s, most minority neighborhoods experienced a brain drain as better-educated, socially mobile African Americans moved into the sub-

47

urbs or into exclusive areas away from the urban core. The result was a two-tiered educational structure which catered to the wealthier areas.

The article, *Reading, Writing and Racism: The Fight to Desegregate the Duval County Public School System,* by the author, looks at this process and its impact on educational integration. Public school integration remains a crucial factor in establishing social and economic equality for African Americans. School integration has served as the foundation for societal integration in the past and will probably serve the same purpose in the future. We assume that each generation makes racial progress, gradually becoming more tolerant as, through education, they learn more about others. Though tremendous strides have been made, it is obvious that, as the poet Robert Frost wrote, "We have miles to go before we (can) sleep."

Notes

1 Winthrop Jordan, *White Over Black: American Attitudes Toward the Negro, 1550-1812* (Chapel Hill: University of North Carolina Press, 1968), 134.

2 Ibid., 20.

3 Ibid., 134.

4 Paul Finkleman, *Dred Scott v. Sandford: A Brief History With Documents* (New York: Bedford/St. Martins Press, 1997), 34.

5 Ibid., 35-36.

6 John Hope Franklin and Alfred A. Moss, *From Slavery to Freedom: A History of African Americans,* 8th ed. (New York: Alfred K. Knopf, 2000), 216; Finkelman, *Dred Scott v. Sandford,* 1-4.

7 James McPherson, *The Negro's Civil War: How American Blacks Felt and Acted During the War for the Union* (New York: Ballantine Books, 1991), 285-286; Eric Foner, *Reconstruction: America's Unfinished Revolution, 1863-1877* (New York: Harper & Row Publishers, 1988), 74.

8 Franklin and Moss, *From Slavery to Freedom*, 244-249.

9 Richard Martin, *The City Makers* (Jacksonville: Convention Press, 1972), 80-81.

10 Joe Richardson, *The Negro in the Reconstruction of Florida, 1865-1877* (Tallahassee: Florida State University Press, 1965), 135.

11 Richardson, *The Negro in the Reconstruction of Florida*, 43, 135-136; Lerone Bennet, Jr., *Before the Mayflower: A History of Black America* (Chicago: Johnson Publishing, 2003), 206.

12 Foner, *Reconstruction*, 31.

13 David Kyvig, *Explicit and Authentic Acts: Amending the US Constitution 1776-1995* (Lawrence: University of Kansas Press, 1996), 166-169; James McPherson, *Ordeal By Fire: The Civil War and Reconstruction*, 2nd ed. (New York: McGraw-Hill Press, 1992), 540-541.

14 Kyvig, *Explicit and Authentic Acts*, 155.

15 Frankin and Moss, *From Slavery to Freedom*, 293; James Anderson, "Ex-Slaves and the Rise of Universal Education in the New South, 1860-1888" in *Education and the Rise of the New South*, eds. Robert Goodenow and Arthur White (Boston: G. K. Hall and Co., 1981), 2; W. E. B. DuBois, *Black Reconstruction in America 1860-1880* (New York: Touchstone Books, 1935), 123, 638. Goodenow and White, *Education and the Rise*, 3.

16 *Duval County Public Schools A Survey Report: Division of Surveys and Field Services* (George Peabody College for Teachers, Nashville, Tennessee, 1965), 3.

17 Ibid, 3; Lee Bigelow, *Public Schools of Duval County*, Prepared for the State Library Project, Works Progress Administration, Jacksonville, Florida, 1939, 3.

18 Thomas Cochran, "History of Public Education in Florida," Thesis, University of Pennsylvania (Lancaster: The New Era Printing Company, 1921), 1; Bigelow, *Public Schools of Duval County*, 3.

19 Pleasant Gold, *History of Duval County Including Early History of East Florida* (St. Augustine: The Record Company, 1929), 118; Cochran, *History of Public Education in Florida*, 1-2.

20 Bigelow, *Public Schools of Duval County*, 5.

21 Gold, *History of Duval County*, 121; T. Frederick Davis, *History of Jacksonville, Florida and Vicinity 1513 to 1924* (Jacksonville: Florida Historical Society, 1925), 415.

22 Cochran, "History of Public Education in Florida," 1-2, 18-19; Bigelow, *Public Schools of Duval County,* 8.

23 "Title Fourth: Of Offenses Committed by Slaves, Free Negroes, and Mulattoes, and of Certain Civil Remedies Against Free Negroes and Mulattoes," ch. 1, sect. 2, in Leslie A. Thompson, *A Manual or Digest of the Statute Law of the State of Florida, of a General and Public Character, in Force at the End of the Second Session of the General Assembly of the State, on the Sixth Day of January, 1847. Digested and Arranged under and in Pursuance of an Act of the General Assembly, Approved December 10, 1845* (Boston: Charles C. Little and James Brown, 1847), 539, see 531-46 for the extensive and punitive slave codes; Donald G. Nieman, "Introduction," in Donald G. Nieman, ed., *African Americans and Education in the South, 1865-1900* (New York: Garland, 1994), vii.

24 J. Irving Scott, *The Education of Black People in Florida* (Philadelphia: Dorrance Press, 1974), 6.

25 Bigelow, *Public Schools of Duval County,* 12; Davis, *History of Jacksonville, Florida,* 416-417; Richardson, *The Negro in the Reconstruction of Florida,* 98.

26 Scott, *The Education of Black People in Florida,* 7.

27 Joe Richardson, "Christian Abolitionism: The American Missionary Association and the Florida Negro," *Journal of Negro History,* vol. 40, issue 1, Winter 1971, 35, 37, 41; Bigelow, *Public Schools of Duval County,* 14.

28 Quoted in Sheats, "Administration of Superintendent Chase," 12.

29 Richardson, "Christian Abolitionism," 38; Scott, *The Education of Black People in Florida,* 7.

30 Richardson, "Christian Abolitionism," 41; Cochran, "History of Public Education in Florida," 34; Bigelow, *Public Schools of Duval County,* 17; Richardson, *Reconstruction,* 114.

31 Arthur White, "State Leadership and Public Education in Florida: The Evolution of a System," Goodenow and White, eds., *Education and the Rise,* 238.

32 Hon. J. C. Gibbs, *Report of the Superintendent of Public Instruction of the State of Florida, For the Year Ending September 30, 1873* (Tallahassee: Hamilton Jay, State Printer, 1874), 49; Jonathan C. Gibbs, "Education in the South," in Scott, *The Education of Black People in Florida,* 141; "The Florida Conference," *Southwestern Christian Advocate* (New Orleans), February 26, 1874; "Letters from Florida," *Southwestern Christian Advocate* (New Orleans), December 31, 1874; "Florida Letter," *Southwestern*

Christian Advocate (New Orleans), March 1, 1877; "Letter from Florida," *Southwestern Christian Advocate (*New Orleans), August 16, 1877; Florida Notes-Sabbath School Convention," *The Star of Zion* (Salisbury, N.C.), September 26, 1889; see Maxine D. Jones and Kevin M. McCarthy, *African Americans in Florida* (Sarasota: Pineapple Press, 1993), 44-45; Joe M. Richardson, "Jonathan C. Gibbs: Florida's Only Negro Cabinet Member," *Florida Historical Quarterly 41* (April 1964), 363-68; James D. Anderson, *The Education of Blacks in the South, 1860-1935* (Chapel Hill: University of North Carolina Press, 1988), 135.

33 Richardson, *Reconstruction,* 235-240; White, *Education and the Rise,* 238.

34 White, *Education and the Rise,* 239.

35 Ibid., 237; Richardson, *Reconstruction,* 113-114; Bigelow, *Public Schools of Duval County,* 19-20.

36 Bennett, Jr., *Before the Mayflower,* 233-245; Rayford Logan, *The Betrayal of the Negro: From Rutherford B. Hayes to Woodrow Wilson* (New York: Collier Books, 1968), 286-287.

37 1885 Florida State Constitution; Bigelow, *Public Schools of Duval County,* 19, 21; Gerald Schwartz, ed., *A Woman Doctor's Civil War: Esther Hill Hawks' Diary* (Columbia: University of South Carolina Press, 1989), 1, 5-7.

38 Mims v. Duval County School Board, filed June 23, 1973, US District Court 4; C. Vann Woodward, *The Strange Career of Jim Crow,* rev. 3rd ed. (New York: Oxford University Press, 1974), 102.

39 *School Board History,* document received from the School Board containing information gleaned from County Archives of Florida, no. 16, Duval County, book no. F352, H673, I #16, 123.

40 Ibid.

41 Richardson, *Reconstruction,* 121; Richardson, "Christian Abolitionism," 41; Barbara Jackson, unpublished paper, March 17, 1981, UNF Library.

42 Richardson, *Reconstruction,* 109; Barbara Jackson, unpublished paper, March 17, 1981, UNF Library. Richard Martin, *The City Makers* (Jacksonville: Convention Press, Inc., 1972), 91.

43 Program for the Benefit of the Piano Fund, Stanton High School, and Brief History, December 3 and 4, 1917.

44 Ibid.

45 Ibid.

46 Ibid.

47 Foner, *Reconstruction,* 322.

48 *Daily Florida Union,* August 4, 1877; Richardson, *A History of Blacks in Jacksonville, Florida,* 158-160.

49 Florida, Superintendent Reports 1890, 31-35; Richardson, *A History of Blacks in Jacksonville, Florida,* 159.

50 Richardson, *A History of Blacks in Jacksonville, Florida,* 160.

51 Ibid.

52 Bigelow, *Public Schools of Duval County,* 25.

53 Ibid., 22, 25.

54 Ibid., 59.

55 Joel Williamson, *After Slavery: The Negro in South Carolina During Reconstruction, 1861-1877* (New York: WW Norton & Company, 1965), 280-294; Allen Trelease, *Reconstruction: The Great Experiment* (New York: Harper & Rowe Publishers, 1971), 196-204; Eric Foner, *The Story of American Freedom* (New York: WW Norton & Company, 1998), 131; Rayford Logan, *The Betrayal of the Negro: From Rutherford B. Hayes to Woodrow Wilson* (New York: Collier Books, 1965), 48.

56 James McPherson, *Ordeal by Fire: The Civil War and Reconstruction,* 2nd ed. (New York: McGraw-Hill, 1992), 528-531, 585-586.

57 Kyvig, *Explicit and Authentic Acts,* 182-187.

58 Ibid.

59 Ibid.

60 Foner, *Reconstruction,* 504.

61 Ibid., 533.

62 Ibid., 553-554.

63 McPherson, *Ordeal by Fire,* 569-570; Kyvig, *Explicit and Authentic Acts,* 184-185; Trelease, *Reconstruction: The Great Experiment,* 179-180; Logan, *The Betrayal of the Negro,* 114-115.

64 John Howard, *The Shifting Wind: The Supreme Court and Civil Rights From Reconstruction to Brown* (Albany: State University of New York, 1999), 125.

65 Ibid, 61-62.

66 C. Ogletree, *All Deliberate Speed* (New York: WW Norton, 2004), 98-99.

67 Richard Kluger, *Simple Justice: The History of Brown v. Board of Education and Black America's Struggle for Equality* (NewYork: Alfred K. Knopf, 2004), 72.

68 Howard, *The Shifting Wind,* 144-148.

69 Logan, *Betrayal of the Negro,* 211.

70 Howard, *The Shifting Wind,* 148-151.

71 *Report of the Surveys of the Schools of Duval County, Florida, including City of Jacksonville.* The Institute of Educational Research Division of Field Studies Teachers College. Columbia University George D. Strayer, Director Bureau of Publications Teachers College, Columbia University, New York City, 1927, 51.

72 Ibid., 51.

73 Ibid.

74 Ibid., 79.

75 Ibid.

76 Ibid., 79-80.

77 Ibid., 80.

78 Ibid., 81.

79 Ibid.

80 Ibid., 82.

81 Ibid., 83.

82 Ibid., 85.

83 Ibid., 66-67.

84 *The National Negro Bluebook North Florida Edition* (Jacksonville: Florida Blue Book Publishing Company, 1926), no pagination, but on pages 11-12.

85 *Jacksonville Looks At Its Negro Community: A Survey of Conditions Affecting the Negro Population in Jacksonville and Duval County, Florida,* Conducted by a Survey Committee of the Council of Social Agencies (Jacksonville: Council of Social Agencies, 1946), 41-49.

86 Ibid.

87 Interview with Grace Payne Webb; Biographical information about Rufus Elvin Payne, cdm16025.contentdm.oclc.org

88 Ibid.

Chapter Two

Early Desegregation: Walk a Mile in My Shoes

Casual observers may not see the connection between World War II and the African American civil rights movement. However, perceptive thinkers can discern how the war set the stage for the societal changes that followed it. World War II profoundly changed the United States and its relationship with the rest of the world. The massive effort expended to end the madness of Nazi Germany and Imperial Japan awakened within American leaders the need to end racial prejudice and legalized discrimination in America. The war confirmed America's role as the new superpower, challenged its commitment to equality, and initiated the nearly forty-five-year struggle between the Soviet Union and the United States over the ideological domination of the Third World. A debate between communism and totalitarianism on one side and democracy and capitalism on the other side was played out on the world stage. As part of that internecine struggle, each side highlighted contradictions and hypocrisies in the other's system. The Soviet Union drew considerable attention to America's treatment of African Americans and other minorities as proof that American pronouncements of liberty and justice were insincere utterances designed to fool a gullible world audience. Soviet leaders mocked the so-called Four Freedoms advocated by Americans, questioning the nation's position as the world's moral leader. These criticisms focused a negative light on the United States and embarrassed its leaders in their efforts to win the hearts and minds of people living in Third World countries.

In areas like Asia and Africa, where the United States and the Soviet Union fought a number of proxy wars, Jim Crow segregation and racial discrimination disadvantaged the United States in its efforts to attract friends and convince skeptics. As a result, civil rights became a foreign policy issue and a matter of national security. As the Cold War expanded, many American leaders found themselves in the uncomfortable position of defending segregation, an embarrassment that threatened the nation's status as the leader of the free world. As historian Donald Nieman has written, segregation gave Soviet propagandists ammunition "to prove our democracy an empty fraud, and our nation a consistent oppressor of underprivileged people."[1]

Accordingly, the federal government switched sides and gave cautious support to the burgeoning African American civil rights movement. Nearly every branch of government took cognizance of the need to protect America's international image. The federal courts began enforcing the *equal* part of the separate but equal policy permitted by the 1896 *Plessy* decision. This new emphasis on equality led to the federal courts' outlawing the infamous White Primary in 1944, opening the Democratic Party to African Americans. This action gave African Americans a chance to challenge the ruling powers of the South and demand changes in the Jim Crow system, foreshadowing the shift in the federal government's commitment to civil rights. After African Americans engaged in sustained legal action and grassroots protest, the courts began limiting the states' right to discriminate against citizens, gradually eroding the walls of segregation.[2]

Once World War II ended, despite intense opposition from white Southerners, the federal government placed greater emphasis on minority rights, mainly because of concerns about America's image on the international stage. According to historian John Hope Franklin, "The courts . . . took cognizance of racial questions and rather frequently ruled in favor of equality. The executive branch, moreover, sensitive to both domestic and foreign pressures, exerted considerable influence in eradicating the gap between creed and practice in American democracy." The shift in federal opinion encouraged African Americans to press a new historical struggle for civil rights.[3]

Because of its carefully cultivated image, most people believed that Florida was not part of this struggle. In 1949 V. O. Key Jr., in his classic *Southern Politics in State and Nation,* declared Florida an exception within Dixie, "scarcely part of the South," in fact, a "world of its own," whose history emitted only "a faint tropical rebel yell." Even though Key's work proved flawed in many respects, as Pearl Ford Dowd and others have underscored in *Unlocking V. O. Key Jr.: Southern Politics for the Twenty-First Century,* the message of Key's classic, of Florida's exceptionalism, has endured and provided a baseline for many interpretations of race relations in the proverbial Sunshine State. This structural narrative of Florida as a state apart from its Dixie neighbors has long endured in the scholarship of Southern apologists such as Ulrich B. Phillips and later Hugh Douglas Price; Donald Matthews and James Prothro; and Manning J. Dauer. It has also permeated many popular accounts of the Sunshine State. More recently, scholars such as those writing in *Old South, New South, or Down South?: Florida in the Modern Civil Rights Movement* have begun to revise previous interpretations of Florida as deviating from the racial norms of the Deep South, especially with regard to educational inequalities. Continuing in that vein, this study focuses also on the pioneering actions of grassroots African Americans in the struggle to combat school segregation, and the sociocultural boundaries that are so ingrained in the daily and political life of Florida.[4]

The NAACP, America's oldest surviving civil rights organization, took advantage of the federal government's changing position and pushed an aggressive strategy to end the disparities in American society, focusing initially on education. Their lawyers knew that Florida was no different from any other part of the South. Working from a blueprint principally drawn up by Charles Hamilton Houston, the NAACP lead counsel, NAACP lawyers challenged obvious areas of inequality in an attempt to force America to live out its creed that, "All men are created equal." Houston, the NAACP's leading legal strategist, was born on September 3, 1895, in Washington, D.C., where he received his early education in the segregated public schools. His father, William Houston, was a successful lawyer who wanted to ensure that his son succeeded academically. He sent young Charles to the renowned M Street School (later called the Paul Lawrence Dunbar High School), acclaimed as one of the best African American high schools in the country.[5]

On June 11, 1911, at age 15, Houston graduated from M Street School and went on to Amherst College where, in June 1915, he graduated Phi Beta Kappa. Upon graduation, Houston taught English at Howard University before joining the Army and serving as a lieutenant in Europe during World War I. After the war, Houston returned to the U.S. where he studied law at Harvard, graduating cum laude and receiving a prestigious Langdell Scholarship to work on his doctorate of law. Supreme Court justices Roscoe Pound and Felix Frankfurter, two of the best legal minds in the country, tutored Houston during his legal training. They gave him invaluable insight into how the Supreme Court made its decisions and how the law worked. After leaving Harvard, Houston won the prestigious Frederick Sheldon Traveling Fellowship. This was an annual award given to Harvard graduate students who wanted to study abroad. Houston used this fellowship to study civil law at the University of Madrid, graduating in 1924 with his juris doctorate.[6]

When Houston returned to the U.S., he joined his father's law firm in Washington, D.C. Later that year, Houston joined the Howard University Law School faculty, where, in 1929, he was appointed vice dean of the Law School. There he helped overhaul the Law School's program, revising its curriculum and improving the facilities while strengthening the student selection process. Under Houston's guidance, Howard's Law School became the chief training ground for future African American civil rights lawyers. Concentrating on constitutional law, with special emphasis on civil rights, Howard trained some of the best African American legal minds. Houston believed that every African American lawyer had to be better than his white opponent and also had to be a social engineer. He explained his philosophy this way: "A social engineer was a highly skilled, perceptive, sensitive lawyer" who understood the Constitution of the United States and knew how to explore its uses in solving problems of . . . local communities and in "bettering conditions of underprivileged citizens." Houston taught students at Howard Law School that, "discrimination, injustice, and the denial of full citizenship rights and opportunities on the basis of race and background of slavery could be challenged within the context of the Constitution if it were creatively, innovatively interpreted and used." He argued that African American lawyers had a better opportunity to force societal reforms than politicians.[7]

In 1929 the NAACP's legal team suffered a loss when Moorfield Storey, the organization's brilliant eighty-four-year-old legal strategist, died. Storey had argued all five of the cases the NAACP brought before the Supreme Court. Arthur Springarn, a competent Manhattan attorney who had been a part of the NAACP for years, took his place. Springarn was successful at recruiting a cadre of very good civil libertarians to serve on the national legal committee. He admittedly was no great legal thinker, nor was he known for his skills as an advocate. Sensing the possibility of receiving financial assistance to fight segregation, he took the opportunity to become much more aggressive in challenging discrimination. The legal office needed more attention. Also, many argued that it might be advantageous to bring in some African American lawyers to argue some of the cases, so he invited Charles Houston to join the legal team.[8]

In June 1935 Houston joined the staff of the NAACP's national office in New York to advise on NAACP activities and guide the work of those spending the Garland Fund. The Garland Fund was a $100,000 donation given to the NAACP by Charles Garland, a Harvard undergraduate and champion of progressive causes. He was the son of a wealthy Boston merchant who chose to use his $1,000,000 inheritance to aid liberal reform. His funds went to organizations like the American Civil Liberties Union (ACLU), the NAACP, progressive periodicals, and labor organizations. Nathan Margold, a Romanian-born Jew serving as chief counsel for the NAACP, was commissioned to develop a national strategy for defeating segregation. Margold, a Felix Frankfurter prodigy, wrote the *Margold Report* to serve as a blueprint for ending segregation. He advised a full-frontal attack on segregation, using the 1886 Supreme Court precedent in *Yick Wo v. Hopkins*. This case dealt with discrimination against Chinese laundry workers. The

Supreme Court ruled that cities could not discriminate when enforcing city ordinances. He called for a massive national suit challenging segregation and discrimination. He wrote:

> . . . If we boldly challenge the constitutional validity of segregation if and when accompanied irremediably by discrimination, we can strike directly at the most prolific source of discrimination. We can transform into authoritative adjudication the principle of law now only theoretically inferable from *Yick Wo v. Hopkins*, that segregation coupled with discrimination resulting from administrative action permitted but not required by state statutes, is just as much a denial of equal protection of the laws as is segregation coupled with discrimination required by express statutory enactment.[9]

Margold resigned from the NAACP in 1933 to accept a position as solicitor of the Department of Interior, leaving his blueprint behind for others to follow. The NAACP chose Columbia University law professor Karl Llewellyn, an expert on constitutional law, to replace Margold. Llewellyn, believing he did not have enough court experience, declined. With the encouragement of Walter White, the NAACP next turned to Charles Houston. Houston accepted the challenge of carrying out the organization's efforts to end discrimination, particularly in education and transportation. Houston was especially galled by educational discrimination. He wrote, "Since education is a preparation for the competition of life, poor education handicapped Black children who with all elements of American people are in economic competition." In 1935 Houston initiated a special appeal for support of the NAACP's educational work with a quote from Frederick Douglass. "To make a contented slave you must make a thoughtless one, . . . darken his moral and mental vision, and annihilate his power of reason. He must be able to detect no inconsistencies in slavery, . . . It must not depend upon mere force; the slave must know no higher law than his master's will."[10]

Houston believed that educational discrimination was the linch-pin of America's racial segregation. He thought that whites hid behind alleged beliefs in African American inferiority to entitle themselves to superior educational life opportunities over African Americans. He argued, "Discrimination in education is symbolic of all the more drastic discriminations which Negroes suffer in American life. And these apparent senseless discriminations in education against Negroes have a very definite objective on the part of the ruling Whites to curb the young (Blacks) and prepare them to accept an inferior position in American life without protest or struggle. In the United States the Negro is economically exploited, politically ignored and socially ostracized. His education reflects his condition; the discriminations practiced against him are no accident." Hence, Houston committed himself to attacking educational inequality. He announced that he wanted, "to use every legitimate means at (the NAACP's) disposal to accomplish actual equality of educational opportunity for Negroes." He proposed equalizing education by leveling the various areas where inequities existed: the school term; pay for teachers with similar qualifications; transportation opportunities; buildings and equipment; per capita expenditure for education of black and white children; and graduate and professional training for African American and white students.[11]

The effort gained momentum when, in the early 1930s, African American teachers filed lawsuits challenging pay disparities between black and white teachers. Employing Houston's plan, the NAACP attempted to use these equalization cases as part of a national strategy to challenge obvious inequities throughout America society. The strategy called for a gradual program of attacking clear violations of the separate but equal doctrine as a prelude to a general assault on segregation and discrimination. The disparities between teachers' pay were an unequivocal violation of the court's mandate for separate but equal. Where school districts had teachers with equal credentials making different salaries, the usual explanation for the pay differences was race. "School districts' salary schedules clearly showed that Black (sic) teachers received substantially lower pay than Whites (sic) with comparable training and experience." Proving discrimination in these cases would have been fairly easy and inexpensive.[12]

Teachers in Florida took the initiative and pushed the NAACP to move on the equalization suits. In 1937 people representing Florida's African American teachers contacted Walter White and asked him to file a suit. Charles Houston was leery of moving too fast and wanted to make sure that they had answers for the many defenses the school districts would offer. Houston knew that district officials would argue that black teachers had a lower cost of living and needed less money. They were also afraid that the NAACP would not be able to find plaintiffs willing to file suit. Attorney Simuel Decatur McGill of Jacksonville handled most NAACP cases in Florida. He was nearly sixty and had been practicing law for over thirty years, successfully handling accident cases, when the teacher equalization suits came to him. He had been litigating civil rights cases for years but was unfamiliar with Houston's approach.[13]

In the midst of such racial inequities, virtually every school district in Florida practiced systematic discrimination, not only in school assignment but also in disbursement of funding, term of academic year, student per capita funding, and, most glaringly, in pay for teachers. By the eve of World War I, Florida allocated $12.50 per capita for white schools versus $2.87 per capita for black schools for construction and maintenance, and $8.35 per capita versus $4.92 per capita between the races for educational programs. Although blacks comprised roughly forty-one percent of Florida's population in 1910, the state invested $2,067,356 in white schools, while black schools received only $184,255, or roughly 8.2 percent of total school spending. Moreover, not one accredited high school for blacks existed in the state's major urban areas of Jacksonville, Tampa, and Pensacola.[14]

Into the 1920s, the average annual pay for black teachers shadowed that of white teachers. For example, in Gainesville the annual salary was $562 for blacks and $970 for whites. Across the state, white female teachers averaged $115.20 per month and white male teachers averaged $169.20 per month. Black female teachers earned just over $60 per month and black male teachers earned roughly $80 per month, with some Florida counties paying blacks a paltry $30 monthly. In the practice of pay disparity, Florida did not prove exceptional, but rather conformist, compared to other former Confederate states. Black teachers in Mississippi in 1890 earned $23 per month while white teachers earned about $33 per month, and in Alabama in 1900, blacks tended to earn $17.66 a month and whites about $25 per month. From 1911 until 1913, the average yearly salary in Virginia was $322.69 for a white teacher, and $172.63 for a black teacher. Similarly, in Georgia during the same years, a white teacher earned $318.63 a year, while a black teacher earned $119.35 per year. White teachers in South Carolina earned $333.28 a year during the same time, and black teachers earned $110.54 per year.[15]

In addition, Florida provided black schools (generally one-room schoolhouses) with dramatically less funding than that given to the white schools. For instance, between 1897 and 1898, white schools statewide were budgeted $565,465; that same year, black schools were budgeted only $171,486. The amount of money spent per student also differed significantly in other states of the Deep South as well as in conformist Florida. In Beaufort County, South Carolina, in 1910 the average expense for each white student was $40.68, while only $5.95 was spent for each black student. The same was true in Alabama. In 1910 Macon County, Alabama, spent approximately $39.99 per white student. Each black student, conversely, received only $3.89. In North Carolina in 1914-15, $7.40 was spent for each white student, while $2.30 was spent on each black child. In Amelia County, Virginia, in 1915, $11.63 was spent for each white child, and $0.94 was spent for each black child for teachers' salaries. By the time of the crash leading to the Great Depression, little had changed in Florida; Tallahassee budgeted $703,454 for the state's thirty-seven percent black population and $11,364,476 for the state's white population. Thus, Florida paralleled its Jim Crow counterparts in miserly support for black education. The *Pittsburgh Courier* decried the situation to its widespread black audience in the following headline: "Says Negro Education in Florida Needs Help: Amazing Situation Revealed."[16]

Presumably, proving discrimination in Florida would be easy. For example, in 1938 Florida's school budget allocated $800 annually per teacher for salaries, yet African Americans received an average of only $510 a year. In some Florida counties, African American teachers were paid as little as $30 per month. Originally, lawyers representing the African American teachers asked only that their clients earn the full $800 a year the state allocated. When confronted with the disparities, county officials refused to discuss the issue. NAACP lawyers developed a strategy to combat this by pressuring large urban counties to equalize pay, hoping that this would induce smaller, rural counties to follow suit. But NAACP lawyers had difficulty finding a teacher willing to put their name on a lawsuit. Harry T. Moore, a state NAACP leader, convinced John E. Gilbert, an eleven-year teaching veteran and principal of the Cocoa Junior High School, to sign on. The Florida State Teachers' Association agreed to pay Gilbert's salary once he was fired. On May 24, 1938, Attorney S. D. McGill accompanied Gilbert in filing a suit to equalize teachers' pay in Florida. The school district fired Gilbert after he lost the case, and the Florida Supreme Court refused to overturn the lower court's ruling. Gilbert never taught again in a Florida school. The Florida court's ruling shifted the equalization fight to local courts, forcing a county-by-county struggle centered on the large urban counties.[17]

Gilbert appealed the state court's decision to the Supreme Court. While his appeal was pending, Vernon McDaniel, another African American teacher, successfully challenged the unequal pay schedules used in Escambia County, Florida. In November 1941, Mary White Blocker, a sixty-nine-year-old school teacher in Duval County, sued the Duval County Public School System challenging the unequal pay scales for African American and white teachers used in Jacksonville. The 285 African American teachers in Jacksonville watched the case closely, because their pay would be affected by the court's decision.[18]

Because Jacksonville was Florida's largest city, the NAACP focused on this lawsuit. Several events occurred just before the case was to be argued before the court. The school district retired Blocker in an attempt to evade the case. However, the 285 African American teachers voted to pay Blocker's salary, a benefit they provided for her until her death twenty-three years later, to keep the suit going. The school district's plan failed and McGill continued to pursue the case with the assistance of Thurgood Marshall a special NAACP counsel. Marshall would later gain fame for arguing other school desegregation cases and for being the first African American to join the Supreme Court.

Thurgood Marshall was born on July 2, 1908, in Baltimore, Maryland. He graduated from Lincoln University and Howard Law School, where he had been a part of Charles Houston's first class. In 1934 he joined his teacher and mentor Houston on the NAACP's legal counsel staff. Marshall combined the Duval County suit with cases from Tampa, Miami, Palm Beach, and four other counties. Judge Louie W. Strum chose the Duval County case as the representative case as he deliberated the arguments.[19]

Teacher equalization suits posed a potential economic catastrophe for Southern school districts. A 1941 report cited in the *Baltimore Afro-American* found that Florida's African American teachers earned just forty-eight percent of what white teachers earned. In Florida, a typical white teacher earned $1,030 a year, while the typical African American teacher earned just $493 a year. The NAACP had already waged a five-year struggle to correct these inequities in other states, producing more than $25 million in salary adjustments for African American teachers. In Maryland and Virginia alone, the NAACP forced officials to spend $629,000 equalizing teachers' pay. The Office of Education estimated the cost of equalizing educational facilities in the South at more than $35 million. Just equalizing teachers' pay in Florida would cost taxpayers $1,588,104 annually.[20]

Marshall and McGill of Florida made a compelling argument in favor of the African American teachers' position. The state's public school systems were clearly violating the law with a dual pay scale, which paid white teachers double the base salary of black teachers. Also, white teachers received one-third more money for years of college completed, and white principals earned a larger stipend than black principals. This situation had not changed since 1917, when white teachers earned an average of $383 while African American teachers earned $181. In 1939-1940, white teachers earned, on average, $1,104, compared to $574 for black teachers. Once it became obvious that they were going to lose the case, school board officials offered a nonracial salary equity plan. The plan called for a rate based on countywide teacher examinations and level of training. Teachers who liked their pay could have their salaries frozen at their current rate or take the exam and receive an adjustment based upon the results. Thurgood Marshall complained that the plan unfairly advantaged white teachers, who could have their salaries frozen at the higher rate, while African American teachers had to take exams that might or might not be administered fairly. After some initial balking, on June 20, 1942, NAACP lawyers reluctantly accepted the school district's plan. Though not a panacea, this equalization suit put the state on notice that long-standing areas of discrimination were going to be challenged by African Americans. It also reestablished in the state the issue of equality in all areas of educational affairs.[21]

The teacher equalization suits were a symbolic gesture; however, they in no way made up for the inequities existing in education. They provided African American teachers with some tangible benefits, improving black teachers' pay from fifty percent of what white teachers earned in 1930 to sixty-five percent of what white teachers earned in 1945. Nevertheless, these victories came with a price and were generally dependent on state courts enforcing the settlements. Also, though they improved their salaries, they did not necessarily equalize them. State officials often found ways around the agreements by using objective merit rating systems that fostered discrimination. Also, teacher equalization suits generally only benefited teachers in large urban settings. The suits often did not affect teachers in smaller rural areas, where judges were less inclined to support such measures and where teachers were afraid to challenge the system. Another consideration was that the school districts found that teachers' exams were an effective tool in maintaining a racially biased pay scale. They also found that they could divide black teachers by separately negotiating with specific teachers.[22]

There were numerous other areas in which African Americans experienced inequality in education. In 1937 over half of Florida's sixty-seven counties had no public high school for African Americans. Less than ten percent of the state's 95,000 high-school-aged African American students were enrolled in junior or secondary schools. There were other obvious discrepancies, including outdated textbooks; no school buses; leaky roofs; poorly ventilated and heated buildings; and a lack of indoor restrooms. Many students had to run out into the rain or use unsanitary privies for restroom facilities.[23]

By 1952, the NAACP had sprung into action. The Legal Fund mounted a national assault on educational inequities. The organization sued school districts in South Carolina, Virginia, Kansas, Delaware, and the District of Columbia, challenging inequities in education. Though the lawsuits originally challenged obvious disparities, they eventually evolved into a collective challenge of de jure racial segregation in the public schools. NAACP lawyers questioned the separate but equal principle used by Southern and some Northern states to guarantee racial segregation in their public school systems. The U.S. Supreme Court combined the cases and chose the Topeka, Kansas, case of *Brown v. Board of Education* as the representative case to hear. Veteran civil rights attorney Thurgood Marshall, lead counsel for the NAACP, argued the case before the high court. His arguments were buttressed by hundreds of friends-of-the-court briefs written by sympathetic parties. One of the most powerful was written by attorney general Herbert Brownell, who encouraged the courts to dismantle segregation because, "racial discrimination furnished grist for the Communist propaganda mills, and it raises doubt even among friendly nations as to the intensity of our devotion to the democratic faith." The segregated school boards were represented by one of the country's most respected jurists, John William Davis.[24]

John W. Davis was a lawyer of almost mythical reputation. A man with impeccable legal skills, Davis was one of the most respected legal litigators in the country. Famed Supreme Court justice Oliver Wendell Holmes once said that no lawyer who had argued before him was, "more elegant, more clear, more concise, or more logical." Davis, a native of Clarksburg, West Virginia, and trained at Washington and Lee University, was a legal genius who had a distinguished legal career in both the corporate and political worlds. He had served as President Woodrow Wilson's solicitor general, and in 1924 was the Democratic Party's vice presidential candidate. Davis had argued sixty-seven cases before the Supreme Court, winning forty-eight of them. By the time he was tapped by South Carolina's governor and former Supreme Court justice James Byrnes to defend the South's segregation policies, Davis was an eighty-one-year-old legal strategist. Thurgood Marshall, then forty-three years old, had followed Davis's career and, while a law student at Howard, had often skipped classes to watch him argue before the high court. Marshall viewed Davis as a legal mastermind.[25]

Marshall compiled a talented team of lawyers, historians, sociologists, and psychologists to argue that segregation had detrimental mental and social effect on African American children. He centered his arguments on the Equal Protection Clause of the Fourteenth Amendment, arguing that segregation in and of itself was a denial of equal protection because, by segregating African American children, the state had reduced them to second-class status and denied them their equal protection rights. He also argued that segregation represented a Jurassic approach to racial control in a technologically advancing, progressive, and contemporary era. Marshall contended that segregating African American children placed a stigma of inferiority on them and separated them from the rest of the human family. This segregation, he argued, violated the American principle of equality and insulted America's claims of democracy and equal treatment. He played upon fears that the

Western world, still reeling from the effects of the Second World War, would watch to see how Americans handled racial issues.[26]

Davis argued that the South had improved African American education and, given more time, black schools would be brought up to equality with white schools. He also stated that African American schools had proven effective at educating black children, even pointing to Marshall's success. He argued that educational segregation was an original intent of the framers of the Fourteenth Amendment, because they recognized the inherent differences between African American and white children. Davis pointed to the fact that when the Fourteenth Amendment was ratified, segregated education was a fact throughout the South, including Washington, D.C., where the amendment was written, debated, and passed. He also cautioned the high court about the social consequences of ending segregation in the South, saying, "This Court may judicially notice the fact, that there is a large body of respectable expert opinion to the effect that separate schools, particularly in the South, are in the best interest of children of both races as well as of the community at large."[27] The high court then gave careful consideration to the two arguments.

At 12:52 p.m. on May 17, 1954, the Supreme Court issued its ruling in *Brown*. A unanimous Supreme Court ruled that segregation was a violation of the Equal Protection Clause of the Fourteenth Amendment. Chief Justice Earl Warren, writing for a unanimous court, said, "To separate them, (African American children) from others of similar age and qualifications solely because of their race generates a feeling of inferiority as to their status in the community that may affect their hearts and minds in a way unlikely ever to be undone. . . . Segregation with the sanction of law, therefore has a tendency to retard the educational and mental development of Negro Children." With this decision, school segregation was outlawed in America.[28]

However, the victory was not total or complete. The high court allowed for a fifty-four-week cooling-off period while the justices decided the technical difficulties of desegregating the school systems. After listening to oral arguments about differing plans and ideas on how best to implement their decision, the court, in 1955, made its second ruling in the school desegregation issue in what has been called *Brown II*. Chief Justice Earl Warren, speaking for a unanimous court, reaffirmed its first decision and said that segregation must go with all deliberate speed. On May 31, 1955, the court ordered the ruling implemented.[29]

In the landmark *Brown II* decision, the court remanded the cases back to the lower courts where the judges were more familiar with them and with local sentiment. Subsequently, each school district was required to develop its own schedule and plan for implementing desegregation. Because the U.S. is such a vast area, with differing numbers of African Americans and whites in each region, the Supreme Court made local school districts responsible for implementing desegregation plans. They agreed to allow local officials to negotiate the parameters of desegregation in each area.[30]

Initially, the *Brown* decision had little impact on Florida's schools. No school district made any effort to change its operational structure or integrate African Americans into white schools. As in other areas of the South, Florida's leaders chose to go slowly with their desegregation plans or make no movement at all. The Continuing Education Council, a group composed of white businessmen and professionals established to advise the state on integration issues, met immediately after the *Brown* decision and advised using every legal means to delay integration. They saw no reason to move ahead of the country with desegregation. A group of concerned citizens met with the attorney general, state superintendent of schools, and leaders of the House of Representatives and agreed that they would maintain a strong public school system, "for every child regardless of race or locality, and that any attempt to do away with the public school system to circumvent the Supreme Court decision was unthinkable." In June 1954, the state allocated $10,000 for a survey conducted by the University of Florida and the University of Miami to gauge public opinion on *Brown*. The attorney general used the results of the survey to submit a brief to the Supreme Court.[31]

Florida officials had already demonstrated opposition to educational integration during the *Virgil Hawkins* case. While other states had reluctantly opened their graduate programs to African Americans, Florida's officials continued to defend segregation. In 1948, five blacks applied for entrance into the University of Florida. Virgil Hawkins and William T. Lewis applied for admission to the University of Florida's Law School, while Oliver Moxey, Rose Boyd, and Benjamin Finley all applied for entrance into graduate programs at the University of Florida. All of their applications were rejected by the university, citing Florida's state constitutional codes against integration. Hawkins cited the new court rulings in *Gaines v. Maryland* to argue that the university's decision violated his equal protection rights. When he appealed to the Supreme Court they referred the case back to the State Supreme Court. The State Supreme Court refused to admit him. In St. Petersburg, two African Americans applied for admission to the St. Petersburg Junior College for Whites. There were no educational institutions offering courses past the twelfth grade for blacks in that part of the state. To block them from suing, a group of whites raised money and sent the boys out of state for schooling. State officials used every tactic to block African American admission into public schools, demonstrating a recalcitrance that would forebode bad times ahead for all those seeking school integration in the state. This action contradicted Florida's unearned moderate image.[32]

The *Virgil Hawkins* case demonstrated the lengths that state officials were willing to go in order to fight school integration. Virgil Darnell Hawkins will go down in Florida history as the man who opened up Florida's public colleges and universities. His case made heroes out of villains and villains out of heroes. Those who argue that Florida was a moderate state on civil rights would do well to study his story. Hawkins paid a terrible price for challenging Florida's segregationist customs. The Supreme Court showed a remarkable lack of commitment to integration. Virgil Hawkins's story helps those who want to know how difficult school integration was in Florida.[33]

Florida state officials were content to wait and see what would happen. Florida's officials joined with six others states in supporting the Southern position in the *Brown* case. Florida's attorney general Richard Ervin filed an *amicus curiae* brief in the Supreme Court which counseled delaying implementation of the ruling. Florida's legal strategist used what was called the "community attitudes" argument to fight integration. Ervin argued that the court should consider the psychological and sociological effects of integration on whites. He wrote "Give the people a chance through the democratic process to change the attitudes . . . of the community." State officials further argued that the only way to integrate without destroying the entire system was to give time for public opinion to soften so that they could integrate peacefully. Florida officials spent $10,000 conducting a poll to measure public sentiment. The poll found that three-quarters of white leaders disagreed with the *Brown* decision in principle. Another thirty percent disagreed violently and thirteen percent stated that they would not enforce integration law. Florida officials put together a suggested plan for integrating which was a clarion call to delay and obstruct the process. Among the things the plan called for was that the black petitioner's application had to be made in good faith and not for capricious reasons, nor for the general uplift of the race.[34]

Despite the state leaders' opposition, public school integration was clearly coming; the only questions remaining were W*hen?* and *How?* An editorial in the *St. Petersburg Times* summarized the situation: "For a little while the Red Shirts and the Crackers may be able to keep up a front for their white supremacy movement but it is dead. Like the traditional snake that wiggles and continues to wiggle until sundown even with its head cut off, white supremacism and segregationism may continue for a little while yet. But its proponents are a loud mouthed and largely discredited minority. Not for long can their will prevail over the decent and thoughtful majority of Southerners. And Florida will do itself honor and increase its stature in the eyes of the nation if it is first to adopt a plan for a rational, workable and reasonably speedy end to segregation." Several religious figures joined in arguing that segregation was wrong and should be abandoned as quickly as possible. African American leaders opposed a gradualist approach, instead preferring immediate action.[35]

There were others who tried to maintain segregation. Bryant Bowles attempted to organize a chapter of the National Association of White People in Tavares, Lake City, Jacksonville, and Apopka. He met with little success as less than one thousand people attended his meetings. Most Floridians were content to just delay the inevitable as long as possible. Ervin's brief had outlined the framework from which those who wanted to delay implementation of the *Brown* decision could work. In his brief he wrote:

There is a need for reasonable time and planning by state and local authorities in any revision of the existing legal structure of the state of Florida (which now provides an administrative framework for the operation of a dual system of public schools) in order to provide a legal and administrative structure in which compliance with the Brown decision can be accomplished in an orderly manner.

The basic change which must be made if Florida is to comply with the non-segregation decision is either a repeal or revision of the Florida constitution which provides White (sic) and colored schools. White and colored children shall not be taught in the same school, but impartial provision shall be made for both.[36]

Florida's political leaders decided to follow a two-track strategy on public school integration. They publicly argued that integration was inevitable while they continued to support segregated schools. Florida, like other Southern states, had seen the handwriting on the wall and had been trying to equalize public school education since the end of the Second World War. Their answer to separate but equal was the formation of the Minimum Foundation Act of 1947. They also elevated Florida A&M College to university status in September 1953.[37]

Despite all of their talk about progressive education, Florida's officials were united in their belief in segregated education. Much of their supposed progressive steps were only designed to forestall the inevitable. They wrongly believed that by just equalizing their schools they could keep them segregated. The Minimum Foundation Program (MFP) established state-mandated standards and provided state aid on a needs basis. By improving education statewide, supporters realized that African American education would be improved. "Before the passage of the law in 1946-1947, capital outlay per pupil enrolled was $2.35 for Negroes and $7.24 for whites. In 1952 it became $68.78 for Negroes and $59.84 for whites."[38] However, responsible white leaders understood the MFP's improvements could not make up for years of African American educational neglect.

In the 1950s and the early part of the 1960s, Florida had one of the nation's most progressive and well-run public school systems. Thomas D. Bailey, state superintendent of education, had put together a coalition of politicians, educational experts, civic leaders, and state officials who protected schools and ensured that they were adequately funded. Born on October 31, 1897, in Lugoff, South Carolina, Thomas David Bailey received an A.B. degree from Wofford College in Spartanburg, South Carolina in 1919, and a master's degree in education from the University of Florida in 1939. Bailey served as principal of various high schools and served on several educational committees in Florida during the twenty-year period prior to his election as state superintendent of public instruction in 1948. He served as superintendent from January 1949 to September 1965. Bailey worked closely with Ed B. Henderson, the executive secretary of the Florida Educational Association (FEA), an organization Bailey had served as president of, to protect Florida's schools. Nearly ninety percent of the state's teachers and administrators were members of this organization, making it a powerful educational advocacy organization.[39]

Henderson was an important part of Florida's educational establishment. He held executive positions in the state's School Board Association, Continuing Education Council, the Council of 100, and the Florida PTA. The Bailey-Henderson team proved to be very effective at placing educational issues at the forefront of Florida's legislative agenda. Bailey concentrated on creating and maintaining good schools while Henderson worked to improve conditions for Florida's teachers. Henderson worked through his FEA and popular teachers to pressure state leaders to support school bills. Bailey worked with legislative leaders and legislative committees to convince state leaders to improve schools. Together with their organizations, they created what became known as the Florida School Lobby.[40]

Originally, the Florida School Lobby wanted to strengthen the MFP, which was begun in 1947 and served as a model for forty-four other states. In Florida the MFP distributed state funds according to each county's taxpaying ability, the number of instructional units, and the type of instructional activity. The MFP distributed funds based upon their goal of one teacher for every twenty-seven students. The Florida School Lobby flexed their muscle in 1949 when they pushed the state legislature to fund this program. In 1949 the state legislature appropriated $89 million for education, more than $52 million more than the previous year. The additional funds went to pay for increased per-pupil spending from $170 to $294 and providing large salary increases for Florida's teachers. It also guaranteed a 180-day school year. The passage of this legislation solidified Bailey's and Henderson's position as Florida's most powerful educational leaders.[41]

The School Lobby reached its zenith in 1957, when the legislature voted record increases for education. The Florida School Lobby took advantage of census data, which showed the state's population was increasing rapidly. An alliance was formed between the Department of Education and the Florida Educational Association to increase educational opportunities for Florida's children. The legislature appropriated money for building more classrooms, increasing teachers' pay, and building community colleges. Governor Leroy Collins, who believed that a good educational system attracted businesses and investment, helped the Florida School Lobby by pushing its agenda through the legislature.

Collins came to power in 1954 after defeating Charlie Johns in a special election held after Florida's forty-one-year-old governor Daniel McCarty died of pneumonia. In 1956 Collins defeated three rabid segregationists to win election, projecting himself as a racial moderate during an increasingly reactionary period. His principal Democratic primary opponent, Sumpter Lowry of Tampa, staked out such an extreme racial position that Collins was able to easily capture the moderate ground, even though he also supported segregation. Lowry once told an audience, "I've got one plank: Segregation, it's a four by four, it's a mile long, and there's room for every cracker in the state of Florida to get on it right now."[42] Circumstances forced Collins to deal with educational issues as one of his priorities. In 1957 Collins asked the legislature to increase taxes to fund six new segregated community colleges, build new classrooms, and increase teacher salaries.[43]

The legislature responded by endorsing a plan to use the first $36 million from the state's three percent sales tax to be designated for education. This increase raised the education budget to $115 million, meaning that the state's contribution to local education would increase to 57.7 percent. Bailey referred to this bill as the "Magna Carta for teachers and children in Florida." The Department of Education spent $23 million of the new money on classroom construction, while $36 million went to relieve rural classroom shortages and create programs for driver's education, exceptional child education, vocational education, and adult education. Florida's teachers also received between $300 and $1,500 in salary increases. Florida's progressivism attracted national attention. The *New York Times* education editor praised Florida for "the greatest improvement in the nation at every level from grammar schools through the graduate courses at state universities." Florida continued to maintain segregation.[44]

However, despite the early success, Florida's educational fortunes turned quickly when the nation's economy began to falter in 1959. As the economy slowed, so did the economic boom which had fueled Florida's growth, drying up precious state funds. In 1959, sixty cents of every state dollar was going to education. With the economic slowdown there were calls to reduce spending and tighten up the budget. Also, the Supreme Court's ruling in the *Brown* case forced state officials to begin to deal with the very controversial issue of school desegregation. There were several conservatives who wanted to take political advantage of the issue and push through a conservative agenda.[45]

Bailey, Collins, and Henderson worked with the state's attorney general Richard Ervin to develop a delaying policy for school desegregation. Their plan was to delay desegregation as long as possible, while making the court think that Florida was developing a plan. Collins worked with other moderates to write what was called the Pupil Assignment Law. This law was designed to delay school integration while placating federal officials. The law did not mention race but allowed pupils to transfer between schools only if they matched the moral, psychological, and socioeconomic background of the pupils in the school of admission. Most people believed that this would stop African American children from transferring to white schools.[46]

A battle erupted between the advocates of delay and the reactionary "Pork Chop Gang," a group of ultraconservatives representing twenty-two rural North Florida counties. Because of Florida's nonrepresentative legislative apportionment system, legislators from rural counties made up the majority of both of Florida's state houses. This Pork Chop Gang, which had a reputation for voting for self-interested legislation–often called pork–had fought Collins's attempt to make the legislature more representative in 1955. Their constituents were mostly racists and agriculturalists, vehemently opposed to changing the dual educational system in Florida. In 1956 they tried to introduce legislation calling for an interposition resolution, which would have authorized the state to use its power to nullify federal authority. Collins terminated the legislative session to block the move.[47]

In 1957 there was an attempt to pass a strict segregation bill. The Pork Chop Gang took advantage of the furor over the possible lack of qualifications of a few African American children to attend white schools under the Florida pupil assignment law. With the help of the Senate president and speaker of the Florida House, the ultra-conservatives passed an interposition resolution. Collins denounced the legislation, referring to it as "a hoax." The legislature struck back by passing a "last resort bill," enabling a vote of twenty-five percent of the property holders in a district threatened with desegregation to abolish their public schools.[48]

Bailey and Collins blasted the bill. Bailey argued that it was more important to keep the schools open even if it meant integrating them. Collins vetoed the legislation, referring to its supporters as agitators. The veto was upheld and the school crisis seemed averted until September of 1957, when President Dwight D. Eisenhower sent federal troops into Little Rock, Arkansas, to enforce a federal court-ordered school desegregation plan at Central High School. The plan called for nine African American children to be integrated into the Little Rock, Arkansas, Central High School.[49]

In October the conservatives regrouped and passed a second last resort bill. Collins put together a coalition which included a more moderate speaker of the House and thirty-one legislators to block this second bill. The constant infighting between those who supported harsh measures to block desegregation and those who saw integration as inevitable severely weakened the School Lobby. Fortunately, Collins proved to be an effective chief executive. In 1959 he opened the state legislative session with a powerful protest to any school abolishment law. He said, "Never, never, never set up any plan or device by which, our public schools can be closed." With this support the School Lobby was able to block thirty-seven radical segregation bills and halt moves to call a special session to revise the state constitution to include a school closing provision.[50]

Even though the reactionaries admitted defeat, the much-publicized battle convinced Floridians that the public schools were a potentially dangerous bastion of racial liberalism. This change in attitude, coupled with an economic downturn, pushed many Floridians to support reductions in educational spending as a way to reduce the power of the School Lobby. In 1959 a special committee investigating the 1957 school bill referred to many of the programs as frills. In response the legislature reduced the MFP by $5 million below estimated need. This was the first revenue reduction since the MFP had been enacted. Following this reduction, teacher salaries were frozen and the School Lobby was defeated on a number of additional proposals.[51]

Meanwhile some Southerners organized violent demonstrations to warn state officials not to interfere with the existing school structure. Throughout the South there was a series of bombings all aimed at "bastions of integration" to show the South's defiance. Between January and May of 1958, there were forty-five racially motivated bombings in the South. The last two were in Jacksonville, where the all-black James Weldon Johnson Middle School was bombed along with a Jewish Community Center. Senator Clifford Chase of New Jersey called for a federal investigation into the bombings, and what he termed, "a campaign of terror which extends through a number of southern states."[52]

As the educational situation deteriorated, some areas refused to wait for state action and began the process of integrating their school districts on their own. In 1959 the Dade County Public School System was the first Florida public school system to put forward an integration plan. Local officials in Miami voluntarily integrated their public schools ahead of a federal court mandate and even before the state changed its constitution outlawing school integration. Even though most of the residents in the neighborhoods where integration was coming moved, the plan represented a first, albeit failed, step for Florida. This action returned educational integration to the top of the state's agenda and fired up the anti-integrationist forces.[53]

In 1961 Farris Bryant came to power as Florida's new governor. Unlike his predecessor, Bryant did not make education the capstone of his administration. Bryant's major constituents were industrialists who wanted him to reduce spending and keep the state's budget under control. In order to please them, he cut expensive state-supported programs. Since the costliest program the state ran was public education, Bryant attacked the school budget. The legislature was equally austere in its allocations. Legislators reduced increases in textbook purchases and teacher salaries. By the 1960s educational issues were increasingly being relegated to the back burner of the state's agenda, at precisely the time when, nationally, the integration process was gaining momentum.[54]

State officials knew that they could not stop integration, but they hoped to delay it until the political tides turned in a more favorable direction. Public school integration was coming to Florida, but state officials determined to do nothing that would hasten the process or make it easy. The 1960s would prove to be a pivotal period for integration of the public school system.

Notes

1 Harvard Sitkoff, *The Struggle for Black Equality: 1954-1980* (New York: Hill & Wang, 1981), 19-21; Donald Nieman, *Promises to Keep: African Americans and the Constitutional Order 1776 to the Present* (New York: Oxford University Press, 1991), 143.

2 Steven Lawson, *Running for Freedom: Civil Rights and Black Politics in America Since 1941* (Philadelphia: Temple University Press, 1991), 14-18; Nieman, *Promises to Keep,* 145.

3 John Hope Franklin and Alfred Moss, *From Slavery to Freedom: A History of African Americans,* 7th ed. (New York: McGraw-Hill, 1994), 461.

4 Pearl Ford Dowe, "V. O. Key Jr.'s Missing Link: Black Southern Political Culture and Development," in *Unlocking V. O. Key Jr.: Southern Politics for the Twenty-First Century,* Angie Maxwell and Todd G. Shields, eds. (Fayetteville: University of Arkansas Press, 2011), 23-38. On the issue of Florida gaining a reputation for moderation and exceptionalism as a Deep South state, see V.O. Key Jr., *Southern Politics in State and Nation* (New York: Alfred A. Knopf, 1949 [1950]), 83-84; Ulrich B. Phillips, "The Central Theme of Southern History," *American Historical Review 34* (1928), 30; Hugh Douglas Price, *The Negro and Southern Politics: A Chapter of Florida History* (New York: New York University Press, 1957), 26-113; Donald Matthews and James Prothro, *Negroes and the New*

Southern Politics (New York: Harcourt, Brace and World, 1966) 136-170; Manning J. Dauer, "Florida: The Different State," in *The Changing Politics of the South,* William C. Harvard, ed. (Baton Rouge: Louisiana State University Press, 1972), 92-164; Irvin D. S. Winsboro, "Image, Illusion, and Reality: Florida and the Modern Civil Rights Movement in Historical Perspective," in *Old South, New South, or Down South: Florida and the Modern Civil Rights Movement,* Irvin D. S. Winsboro, ed. (Morgantown: West Virginia University Press, 2009), 1-21; Marvin Dunn, "The Illusion of Moderation: A Recounting and Reassessing of Florida's Racial Past," in Winsboro, ed., *Old South, New South, or Down South,* 22-46; Paul Ortiz, "Old South, New South, or Down South? Florida and the Modern Civil Rights Movement: Towards a New Civil Rights History in Florida," in Winsboro, ed., *Old South, New South, or Down South?,* 220-44.

5 Genna Rae McNeil, *Groundwork: Charles Hamilton Houston and the Struggle for Civil Rights* (Philadelphia: University of Pennsylvania Press, 1983), 26.

6 Ibid., 24-26, 30-6, 51-55.

7 Ibid., 59-61, 68-85.

8 Richard Kluger, *Simple Justice: The History of Brown v. Board of Education and Black America's Struggle for Equality* (New York: Alfred A. Knopf, 2004), 131-139.

9 McNeil, *Groundwork: Charles Hamilton Houston,* 115.

10 Ibid., 114-117; Kluger, *Simple Justice,* 131-139.
  * The Garland Fund was started in 1922 by Charles Garland who used his $1 million inheritance for philanthropic endeavors. He wanted the money to benefit the poor as well as the rich, and blacks as well as whites. Its official name was The American Fund for Public Service. In 1930 they selected the NAACP for a $100,000 gift.

11 Ibid., 134; Howard Ball, *A Defiant Life: Thurgood Marshall and the Persistence of Racism in America* (New York: Crown Publishers Inc., 1998), 51.

12 Donald Neiman, *Promises to Keep: African Americans and the Constitutional Order to the Present* (New York: Oxford University Press, 1991), 136-137.

13 Mark Tushnet, *The NAACP Legal Strategy Against Segregated Education, 1925-1950* (Chapel Hill: UNC Press, 1987), 94.

14 See Thomas A. Bailey, *Narrative Reports of County Superintendents, 1892-94 to 1898-1900, Research Report-21, Division of Research*

(Tallahassee, 1962), 35-181; Thomas A. Bailey, *Narrative Reports of County Superintendents, 1900-1902 to 1904-1906, Research Report-27, Division of Research* (Tallahassee, 1963), 3-189; Thomas A. Bailey, *Narrative Reports of County Superintendents, 1906-1908 to 1910-1912, Research Report-37, Division of Research* (Tallahassee, 1965), 3-204; William M. Holloway, *Bi-Ennial Report of the Superintendent of Public Instruction of the State of Florida, For the Two Years Ending June 30, 1912* (Tallahassee: T. J. Appleyard State Printer, 1912), 448, 454; W. S. Cawthon, *Biennial Report of the Superintendent of Public Instruction* (Tallahassee: Florida Department of Public Instruction, 1926), 218-19; "Whites Must Not Teach Negroes: Not One Public High School in All Florida for Colored Boys and Girls," *Baltimore Afro-American,* January 24, 1914; James D. Anderson, *The Education of Blacks in the South, 1860-1935* (Chapel Hill: University of North Carolina Press, 1988), Table 6.3, 194.

15 W. S. Cawthon, *Biennial Report of the Superintendent of Public Instruction* (Tallahassee: Florida Department of Public Instruction, 1930), 176; Charlton W. Tebeau, *A History of Florida* (Coral Gables, FL: University of Miami Press, 1971), 305; Maxine D. Jones, "The African-American Experience in Twentieth-Century Florida," in Michael Gannon, ed., *The New History of Florida* (Gainesville: University Press of Florida, 1996), 384; Scott, *The Education of Black People in Florida,* 64; Adam Fairclough, *A Class of Their Own: Black Teachers in the Segregated South* (Cambridge: Belknap Press, 2007), 126; Louis R. Harlan, *Separate and Unequal* (New York: Atheneum, 1968), 257.

16 W.S. Cawthon, *Biennial Report of the Superintendent of Public Instruction of the State of Florida for the Two Years Ending June 30, 1928* (Tallahassee: T.J. Appleyard, 1928), 255; Cochran, *History of the Public-School Education in Florida,* 199; William H. Chafe et al., *Remembering Jim Crow: African Americans Tell About Life in the Segregated South* (New York: The New Press, 2001), 153; Harlan, *Separate and Unequal,* 131-32, 167; "Says Negro Education in Florida Needs Help: Amazing Situation Revealed," *Pittsburgh Courier,* December 28, 1929.

17 J. Irving E. Scott, *The Education of Black People in Florida* (Philadelphia: Dorrance Press, 1974), 64; Ben Green, *Before His Time: The Untold Story of Harry T. Moore, America's First Civil Rights Martyr* (Gainesville: University of Florida Press, 2005), 40-41.

18 Barbara Walch, *New Black Voices: The Growth and Contributions of Sallye Mathis and Mary Singleton in Florida Government* (Jacksonville:

Barbara Walch, 1990), 58; Scott, *The Education of Black People,* 74; *Atlanta World,* February 3, 1942.

19 Ball, *A Defiant Life,* 45-49; Juan Williams, *Thurgood Marshall: An American Revolutionary* (New York: Random House Press, 2000), 22; Walch, *New Black Voices,* 58; Scott, *The Education of Black People,* 64, 74.

20 *Baltimore Afro-American,* December 14 and 27, 1941.

21 Ben Green, *Before His Time,* 36; *Pittsburg Courier,* June 20, 1942.

22 Charles Ogletree, *With All Deliberate Speed: Reflections on the First Half Century of Brown v. Board of Education* (New York: WW Norton & Company, 2004), 120; Tushnet, *The NAACP Legal Strategy,* 96-97.

23 Green, *Before His Time,* 36.

24 Franklin and Moss, *From Slavery to Freedom,* 453; Kluger, *Simple Justice,* 527-529.

25 Kluger, *Simple Justice,* 527-533.

26 Ball, *A Defiant Life,* 119-121; Kluger, *Simple Justice,* 564-584.

27 Kluger, *Simple Justice,* 547, 564-584.

28 Ibid., 705.

29 Ibid., 747-749.

30 Ibid., 747.

31 R. W. Puryear, "Desegregation of Public Education in Florida-One Year Afterward," *Journal of Negro Education,* vol. 24, no. 3 (Summer 1955), 221.

32 Algia Cooper, "Brown v. BOE and Virgil Darnell Hawkins 28 Years and Six Petitions to Justice," *Journal of Negro History* (vol. 64, no. 1, Winter, 1979), 1-6; Ibid., 222.

33 *St. Petersburg Times,* May 16, 2004.

34 Kluger, *Simple Justice,* 726-728, 734.

35 Puryear, "Desegregation of Public Education in Florida," 223.

36 Ibid., 219.

37 Ibid., 220.

38 Ibid.

39 Arthur White, *Florida's Crisis in Public Education: Changing Patterns of Leadership* (Gainesville: University of Florida Press, 1975), 2-3.

40 Ibid.

41 Ibid., 3-4.

42 Martin A. Dyckman, *Floridian of His Century: The Courage of Governor Leroy Collins* (Gainesville: University of Florida Press, 2006), 120-121.

43 White, *Florida's Crisis in Public Education,* 4-5; Dyckman, *Floridian of His Century,* 60-71.

44 White, *Florida's Crisis in Public Education,* 6-7.

45 Ibid.

46 Ibid., 8-9.

47 Ibid.

48 Ibid.

49 Ibid.

50 Ibid.

51 Ibid., 10.

52 *New York Times,* May 11, 1958.

53 *New York Times,* February 19, 1959; August 16, 1959.

54 White, *Florida's Crisis in Public Education,* 10-11.

Chapter Three

The Courts Have Spoken:
And the Walls Came Tumbling Down

While Florida may have been praised for its progressive educational policies in the 1950s, Jacksonville's local schools continued to face daunting challenges. The 1950s set the stage for public school integration nationally, but in Jacksonville schools struggled just to keep pace with the rapidly growing city. As the city's population expanded, public school officials found themselves in a constant struggle to improve the school system. The schools were chronically overcrowded and woefully underfunded. While African Americans in other areas like Baton Rouge and Montgomery were making slow progress toward integration, Jacksonville's African American community faced stiff opposition to even the smallest efforts to integrate.

In 1950 Duval County had seventy-five public schools. These schools educated 43,000 students. To alleviate the classroom shortage, the school district introduced its so-called Jacksonville Plan. This plan called for the school system to spend $14.5 million building 600 new classrooms. Local officials touted the proposal as a major step forward, particularly when people considered that the value of the existing structures was only $13 million. However, what the residents did not know was that county schools were so overcrowded that the new proposal was inadequate for the county's needs. Those who pushed the Jacksonville Plan and bond funding ignored a developing trend. Between 1940 and 1950 Jacksonville's population was growing so rapidly that school officials would need much more money to keep up. In 1940 Jacksonville had 173,065 residents. By 1950 the population was at 204,517. The areas outside of the city were growing even faster. Those areas grew from 37,078 to 99,512, a 168.4 percent increase.[1]

School issues dominated the city's agenda during the late 1950s and early 1960s. The 1960s were a period of racial, social, and economic turmoil for Jacksonville, Florida. After years of segregation and discrimination, cracks finally appeared in the Jim Crow system. In 1959 a frustrated police officer name Frank Hampton challenged racial segregation on the city's golf courses. Hampton was a Jacksonville native who grew up caddying for white golfers at the San Jose Country Club. From this experience Hampton developed a love for golf which followed him into adulthood. Hampton was insulted by the limitations placed on African American golfers. Jacksonville's parks system allowed African American golfers to use public courses at Brentwood and Hyde Park on Mondays and Fridays, respectively, but at all other times the parks were off limits.[2]

On April 7, 1959, city officials, responding to a lawsuit filed by Hampton and other black golfers, closed the public parks as an alternative to integrating them. This action reflected the feelings of many whites who preferred no services to integrated services. Hampton's lawyer, a local attorney named Ernest Jackson, filed a federal lawsuit challenging the legality of the golf course closings. Dallas Thomas, parks and recreation commissioner for Jacksonville, responded by threatening to sell the city golf courses before the courts could force their integration. Despite a petition from a biracial golfing group and the support of several organizations, local officials refused to negotiate with African American golfers and continued to keep the parks closed.[3]

This recalcitrance forced Hampton and his lawyers to seek desegregation of all city facilities. If city leaders would not negotiate on golf courses, there was little hope of bargaining on larger issues like education. Jacksonville's mayor, Haydon Burns, joined forces with other commissioners in defending Jacksonville's segregationist stance. Much of the community supported the commission's actions as local leaders defied the federal courts and continued to segregate. However, the resistance faced trying to integrate golf courses paled in comparison to the fight against school integration. City leaders were united in their opposition to integration and vowed to use every weapon at their disposal to block, delay, and obstruct it. There was no shortage of individuals who were ready to man the breach to stop African Americans from integrating their facilities.[4]

After seeing the federal court's resolve in enforcing the *Brown* decision, most Southerners knew that school desegregation was inevitable. The best they could hope for was to delay the process and interfere with its implementation. Jacksonville, like most southern cities, was split between those who supported integration and those who opposed it. There were few people who were indifferent. With the full force of the law as support, the NAACP was determined to see Jacksonville's schools desegregated.

Even in the most conservative areas of the South, most people could see integration was coming, but there was no shortage of people willing to do whatever it took to delay its arrival. As the new school year began, Jacksonville's school board wanted local residents to know that it opposed school integration. In the middle of this struggle were a number of well-intentioned whites who wanted to avoid violence and accept the inevitable integration. There were many others who wanted people to know that they opposed integration and disagreed with the Supreme Court.[5]

In 1959 a new unnamed high school was opened in Jacksonville. School Board Superintendent Ishmael (Ish) W. Brant, whom many described as a "good ole boy," chose someone who, he thought, shared his views on race and integration as the principal of this new school. In 1957 Brant was elected as superintendent of schools in Duval County. He served in this position until 1969.[6]

Brant, a former football coach, surrounded himself with men who shared his ideas on education and who also had football experience. One of them was Billy Parker, a former University of Florida quarterback and high school teacher and coach. Brant chose him as principal of the new high school that was to open in the new school year. Parker naively wanted the students to name the school so he allowed them to make recommendations. Valhalla High School, Wesconnett High School, and Nathan Bedford Forrest High School were the three names eventually offered for consideration.[7]

Parker put the names in big letters over different parts of the school's façade and asked the students to stand in line under the name they wanted. The students overwhelmingly chose Valhalla High School as the name and Wesconnett as the alternative. There was little support within the student body for naming the school after Nathan Bedford Forrest, of KKK fame. Few students knew who Forrest was and they had not proposed his name. Following the students' wishes, Parker chose to use Valhalla High School as the name, with Wesconnett as the alternative. He submitted the name and alternative to the school board for approval and then went about preparing for the school year, expecting the name Valhalla High School to be approved with little fanfare.[8]

He went as far as to choose colors and purchase jerseys and other products with the new school emblem and the name Valhalla on them. He had no problem with the name Valhalla High School, even though he preferred the name Wesconnett because it identified the school with the neighborhood. Parker was unaware of any controversy around the name and felt that the election process had been fair and legitimate. The students had chosen the name they wanted, and as their principal, he was comfortable with their choice. He was unaware of the political atmosphere surrounding the city and school at the time. He did not know that parents were concerned about the students' choice and wanted to deliver a strong message to those pushing integration.[9]

Religious leaders were also disturbed about the students' choice of names. They joined forces with concerned parents to object to the name Valhalla. The parents had investigated and discovered that Valhalla referred to a Scandinavian myth about the palace or hall of immortality in which the souls of Norse, or Norwegian, heroes slain in battle dwell. This upset the delicate sensibilities of the parents and religious leaders, who demanded that the students choose another name more befitting an educational facility. Parker, who at first objected to the parents' involvement, relented and called for a new election to choose a different name. He kept the two remaining names, Wesconnett and Nathan Bedford Forrest. The students then held a second election in which they over-whelmingly chose Wesconnett as the school's name.[10]

However, in the interim, women connected with the Daughters of the Confederacy lobbied the school board to select Nathan Bedford Forrest as the name of the high school to honor Jacksonville's Confederate past and to show pride in its Southern traditions. They also wanted to deliver an unmistakable message about where they stood on educational integration. Parker went before the school board and argued in favor of the name Valhalla because that had been the students' first choice. He expressed outrage that the parents were meddling in an issue that was not their business. However, the school board, wanting to make a statement to those who supported integration and show where they stood on the issue, chose Nathan Bedford Forrest as the school's name. They also chose the Rebel as the school's mascot. This was a deliberate slap in the face to the NAACP, the African American community, and the spirit of the *Brown* decision. Most people were familiar with Forrest's background as a founder and member of the Ku Klux Klan and also his involvement in the controversial Fort Pillow incident where more than 270, mostly black, Union soldiers were murdered. The school board downplayed these criticisms and overwhelmingly voted for the name of Nathan Bedford Forrest. They arguably wanted to send a message to Jacksonville's integrationist forces.[11]

Several civil rights organizations criticized the school board's decision as insensitive and untimely. The decision represented the feelings of the vast majority of white residents who vehemently opposed changing the segregated school system. They were not in favor of desegregating the schools and had given the superintendent and the school board their support in doing whatever it took to fight integration. It is no secret that Ish Brant, the school superintendent, and most of the school board publicly opposed school integration and openly worked to block its implementation. Brant described his opposition this way, "I grew up in the South and all I knew was segregation. It worked for both races at that time."[12]

This opposition was countered by an aggressive push for civil rights by a determined African American community. Throughout the city and the nation, civil rights demonstrators were pressuring local officials to integrate public facilities. African Americans were standing up and demanding their full citizenship rights, using non-violent protest as their weapon. In 1960 Haydon Burns, Jacksonville's mayor since 1949, entered Florida's gubernatorial race. In order to attract support from conservatives in western agricultural regions of Florida, Burns advocated a conservative social agenda which included opposition to integration, angering civil rights leaders and many blacks who had been a part of his political coalition. Rutledge Pearson, a Jacksonville school teacher and local leader of the NAACP, challenged Burns's conservative positions and used civil rights demonstrations to pressure local leaders to improve conditions for African Americans.[13]

Pearson organized a youth division of the NAACP which engaged in demonstrations to force local officials to end segregation. These young people, most of whom were high school students, challenged local leaders by joining the rapidly growing sit-in movement. This movement began in Greensboro, North Carolina, in February 1960 and rapidly spread to other parts of the country. Sit-ins were instrumental in desegregating lunch counters and diners all over the South. They were part of the economic warfare used by NAACP leaders to force integration.[14]

Student leaders like Rodney Hurst, a high school student studying in Rutledge Pearson's class, were enraged by the injustices they saw in Jacksonville. Hurst worked with Pearson in organizing students to help fight for improvements in the city. The students concentrated on prominent stores in downtown Jacksonville that practiced segregation. Their first goal was to desegregate the lunch counters in the Woolworth's store.[15]

The protests eventually led to a violent outbreak that embarrassed the city leaders. In an August 27, 1960, incident, which has now come to be known as "Ax Handle Saturday," Klansmen from North Florida and southern Georgia attacked peaceful civil rights protesters in Jacksonville's downtown streets. Local African American street gangs counterattacked the Klansmen, creating a disgraceful racial scene which garnered international attention. In the midst of this social chaos and the state's marginalizing of educational issues, African American parents pressed school officials to begin the process of integrating the public schools. School integration was an essential part of the African American struggle for equality. 1960 proved to be an important year on Jacksonville's civil rights timeline. As the nation geared up to remember the centennial of the Civil War, the South prepared to fight a second round over the issue of African American civil rights.[16]

On December 6, 1960, NAACP attorney Earl Johnson filed a lawsuit challenging school segregation in the Duval County Public School System on behalf of a group of African American students. Johnson served as the attorney of record for the Jacksonville branch of the NAACP. Earl Johnson was born on August 11, 1928, in Huntington, West Virginia, the eldest of fifteen children. His father worked for the railroads while his mother did day labor. Johnson grew up poor in a housing project in Huntington, but excelled at both sports and academics. He graduated as the salutatorian of his high school class and was remembered for a speech he gave in which he talked about growing up to become a lawyer who would help integrate society. In 1946 he joined the Army hoping to use the GI Bill to underwrite his college education. In 1948 Johnson left the military and entered Howard University, where he joined the ROTC program, graduating in 1952. After graduation, he reentered the military to fight in the Korean Conflict. In 1953 he returned from the Korean War and in 1954 reentered Howard University as part of their Law School.[17]

After graduating from law school in 1957, Johnson moved to Jacksonville to accept an offer from his father-in-law to work in the legal department of the Afro-American Life Insurance Company. His father-in-law was working at the company during that time and encouraged his bosses to hire the young lawyer. Johnson passed the Florida Bar in 1958 and, after spending several years working in the legal office at the Afro-American, on July 1, 1960, resigned to go into private practice with Leander Shaw, an old friend from the Army. Shaw, whose father was the dean of the Florida A&M University Graduate School, was a fellow Virginian, even though Johnson was from West Virginia. Shaw and Johnson made a formidable legal team. They agreed to allow Johnson to work on community issues while Shaw handled many of the important private legal cases. In 1983 Shaw was appointed to the Florida Supreme Court. In 1990 he was appointed chief justice, a position he held until 1992. He was the first African American to hold that distinction.[18]

The plaintiffs in the December 1960 case were Daly N. Braxton, a thirteen-year-old eighth grader at James Weldon Johnson Junior High School and Sharon Braxton, a fifteen-year-old tenth grader at New Stanton High School. They were named under their mother, Sadie Braxton, the spouse of a naval seaman who was away at sea. In addition to the Braxton children, there were six other children listed as plaintiffs: Hattie Bell Neal, 15; Gladene Neal, 11; Bruce Jones Goodson, 8; James Bodie, 9; and his sister Annette Bodie, age unknown. Because of the high-profile nature of the case, the NAACP's national offices sent Thurgood Marshall and Constance Motley Baker to help argue the case. The plaintiffs' legal team consisted of Earl Johnson, Constance Motley Baker, and Thurgood Marshall, who was later to serve on the Supreme Court. The plaintiffs paid a heavy cost for their involvement in the case. Braxton was forced out of the city after receiving numerous threatening phone calls. The family eventually relocated to Miami but several of the children returned to Jacksonville as adults. Two of the original families involved in the suit were forced to drop out of the case for fear of reprisals from employers and others in the community. Earl Johnson also endured death threats and the loss of several friends because of his involvement in the case.[19]

The NAACP's case was simple. NAACP lawyers charged the Duval County Public School System with operating segregated, dual schools, a clear violation of the Supreme Court's 1954 mandate in *Brown*. The Duval County case was just one of a series of cases involving school districts in Florida. Volusia, Hillsborough, and Escambia Counties were also being sued during this period.

Even after the federal courts had reaffirmed their demand that public schools must "effectuate a transition to a racially nondiscriminatory school system . . . with all deliberate speed" in May 1955, Jacksonville, along with the other cities included in the suits, had taken no steps toward desegregation. Johnson argued that the school system operated a dual system with eighty-nine schools attended and staffed exclusively by whites and twenty-nine schools operated and attended only by African Americans. This educational duality resulted in an unequal educational experience for African American children.[20]

He also accused the superintendent's office of being racially structured, with white and African American educational issues being decided separately. He pointed to the fact that there was a director of Negro education whose sole job was the overseeing of African American schools. Before the *Brown* decision most Southern school districts assigned the administration of African American schools to a separate all-African American educational office. This office was staffed and run solely by African Americans. It was common practice to have a director of Negro education who would report directly to the superintendent and exercise broad administrative authority over the total program of African American education. After the 1954 *Brown* decision, most school districts, especially ones as large as Jacksonville's, had eliminated this position. As a reflection of how bad race relations were in Jacksonville, in 1965 the Duval County Public School System still had a director of Negro education, although most Southern states had abolished this office years earlier.[21]

Dr. John Irving Elias Scott served as the director of Negro education in Duval County. Scott was a man ahead of his time. He distinguished himself as a brilliant educator, an excellent administrator, and a successful businessman. He was also a noted civic and social leader and a first-class researcher and author. Scott had a chemistry degree from Lincoln University, a master's degree from Wittenburg University, and a PhD in educational administration from the University of Pittsburgh, making him one of the best-educated men on the Duval County School Board's payroll.[22]

93

Scott served in a number of positions within the Duval County Public School System. He was a principal on the elementary, junior, and high school levels. Dr. Scott became the first person with a PhD hired by the Duval County Public School System. Between 1944 and 1953 Scott served in a number of administrative positions at various colleges. In 1953 the Duval County Public School Board hired Scott to serve as director of Negro education. Over his term the name of this position constantly changed, first to assistant director of education and then to director of special education studies. Scott was deeply interested in African American history and culture and fought to have schools named after African American figures. He was responsible for at least ten schools in Jacksonville being named after African Americans.[23]

Over his long career, Dr. Scott wrote eight books and edited an educational journal, the *Negro Educational Review*. This journal was started by Scott and Dr. Gran Lloyd in January 1950 and continues to be published today. Lloyd, like Scott, was highly educated. He had a master's degree from Columbia and a PhD from New York University. Lloyd was an expert on economic issues. Like Scott, he was concerned with educational issues in Jacksonville.

Scott summarized his experiences in Jacksonville when he wrote of an incident that occurred while he was serving as a principal. The superintendent came by Scott's school and told an audience that he was the best-prepared African American principal in the county. The next day Scott asked the superintendent how many people working for the school board had PhDs. The superintendent replied, "None." Then he explained that if he had called Scott the best-prepared principal in the county, some of the whites sitting in the audience would have been offended. This summarized the experience of African Americans in Jacksonville's schools. They could never be seen as better than whites. Everything had to be separate and unequal to be accepted by many whites. It was this notion of inequity that had to be discarded. That was the motivating factor for the parents filing the lawsuits.[24]

The rest of the school system was run by Ish Brant. Ishmael Winford Brant was born on October 3, 1906, in Ocala, Florida. He graduated from high school in 1933, and then went to the University of Florida where he played football, baseball, and basketball, and ran track. He lettered in both football and track. He eventually earned a master's degree from the University of Florida. Brant received his teaching certificate and was hired in Cocoa, Florida, where he distinguished himself as a high school football coach and athletic director. He was also elected to the Rockledge City Council.

In 1942 Brant moved to Neptune, Florida, where he served as assistant principal, athletic director, and head football coach at Fletcher High School. During Brant's successful coaching career, Fletcher High won 176 games while losing only fifty-six. The Florida Athletic Coaches' Association praised Brant for his success, making him a popular figure in the community. A few years later, Brant ran for mayor of Neptune and completed three terms. He then served one term as city manager of Jacksonville Beach.[25]

By 1957 Brant was disillusioned with the school situation in Jacksonville. He believed the elected school superintendents were to blame for the poor condition of schools in the city. He thought the current superintendents were politicians more than educators. Brant told many people that he could do a much better job supervising the school system than anyone else in the running. He entered the race for school board superintendent, won the election, and served until 1969.[26]

Brant's election coincided with the school integration crisis in the state. He knew that integration was inevitable, nevertheless, he wanted to fight it because that was what the white community wanted. His strategy was to delay the process as long as possible in hopes that the composition of the court might change and the ruling be reversed. He joined with the other community leaders in developing a series of schemes designed to forestall school integration. Although Brant was a man of his time who opposed integrated schools, he did support equal education for blacks and whites. Brant argued that even black children needed a good education—they just needed to receive it in their own schools. His dedication to equal education in Jacksonville meant that he sometimes took positions that were unpopular in the white community.[27]

Brant believed that the *Braxton* lawsuit covered two issues. The first was unequal spending on African American students compared to white students. The other issue was segregation. Brant mistakenly believed that by guaranteeing equal spending on African American and white schools, he could satisfy the African American parents while blocking the integration process. He completely misread the will of the African American community and did not understand the events surrounding him. Brant's initial reaction to the lawsuit was to promise equal educational spending. He had no idea that blacks were way beyond that point.[28]

The case was argued before federal judge Bryan Simpson on December 21, 1961. Simpson, a native of Kissimmee, Florida, was nicknamed "Cowboy" by his friends and people in his court. Local attorney Sam Jacobson said of Simpson, "Bryan Simpson was a giant of the federal legal system in Jacksonville in the 20th century. He personified the federal courts in this area from the period of the 50s into the 80s. . . . He was a person of huge courage as far as racial matters were concerned and had just an exquisite sense of fairness."[29] The NAACP's case was simple. Jacksonville maintained a dual system and had made no effort to modify or change it since the *Brown* decision. There were clear and obvious disparities between African American and white schools. The school board lawyers admitted that they had a dual system, but argued that they were operating under state law and could not change their operation until the state changed its constitution. Their argument was an old one which had been rejected by earlier courts in Miami and Tampa. The lawyers argued state law trumped federal law and, since the state constitution continued to outlaw integrated education, they could not integrate local schools. This argument did not impress Judge Simpson.[30]

On August 21, 1962, district judge Bryan Simpson found that the school board and superintendent "have pursued and are presently pursuing a policy of operating the public school system of Duval County on a racially segregated basis. In the eight years since the first *Brown* decision they have not operated any plan whatever for eliminating racial discrimination in the public school system committed to them for administration." The judge went on to say, "No schools may be constructed, designed, maintained, and operated for white pupils only, nor may any school be constructed, designed, maintained, and operated for Negro pupils only." With this ruling Judge Simpson had outlawed generations of segregation in the Duval County public schools.[31]

Simpson ordered the school board to end its dual system and to draw up a plan for integrating public schools in Jacksonville. The court found several issues related to the Duval County School System. The judge's order mandated that the school board write, "a complete plan for the removal of dual attendance zones for the system-wide opening of all schools on a nonracial basis." Judge Simpson's orders were clear and unmistakable: Duval County's schools had to be integrated.[32]

No one was surprised by the judge's decision. It was clear that Jacksonville had a segregated school system which had policies designed to maintain that segregation. Everything about the Duval County Public School System was segregated, from the numbering of the schools to the way attendance zones were written. Teacher and administrative assignments were made on a racially segregated basis, with 3,940 teachers and administrators being given their school assignments based on their race. The 1,014 African American teachers and administrators were all assigned to schools with numbers from 101 and up. These were the school number designations for black schools. African American parents who wished to have their children transferred under the Florida Pupil Assignment Law were always rebuffed by county officials.[33]

State Representative George B. Stallings, who represented Jacksonville from 1959 until 1968, introduced another plan on October 4, 1962, designed to block integration. He called his plan controlled choice. This plan called for allowing parents free choice of which type of school they wanted their children to attend. According to Stallings, "Instead of pupils being assigned to a particular school because of race or school districts or any other usual reasons, the sole criterion for assignment would be exclusively the choice of the child's parent or guardian." Stallings argued that the plan was fair because everyone, white and black, had a choice. Stallings begged the board to use his plan for their October 30th deadline for an integration plan. The court and school board rejected this plan.[34]

The school board filed its plan on October 30, 1962. It called for a deliberate process of integrating one grade per year. The plan would have created geographical attendance zones, which opened all schools on a nonracial basis. Under this plan, grades one and two would be integrated in 1964 and one additional grade would be integrated every year, with full integration occurring by 1974. The school board's plan also proposed a so-called Freedom of Choice clause that allowed any student to transfer to a school where he or she was in the majority. In essence, it allowed parents the opportunity to choose if they wanted their children to attend integrated schools.[35]

The school board challenged the provision of the desegregation order prohibiting the assignment of teachers and staff on a racial basis. In addition, the board ignored the judge's rulings on the following issues: approving budgets, making available funds, approving employment contracts, and approving construction programs that would maintain or support a racially segregated school.[36]

Meanwhile, the school board's plan was appealed by the *Braxton* plaintiffs because they viewed it as too slow. NAACP lawyers asked the court to amend the school board's plan and have grades one through six integrated in 1964 and the rest of the grades integrated one-year-at-a-time thereafter, with full integration coming in 1970. On August 13, 1964, the federal court denied the appeal and ordered the school board's plan implemented as written on May 8, 1963.[37]

Under the school board's plan, the first African American students were integrated in September 1963. Thirteen African American children, all from the first grade, took part in this initial process. These young people endured protest and abuse but paved the way for later generations. Opposition to this limited integration was fierce. Jacksonville was replete with anti-African American and anti-integration organizations, one of which was the KKK. The Klan promised determined resistance to integration and protested areas and organizations that refused to tow the line.

The initial integration started off smoothly even though there were daily protests by parents and local toughs. The calm came to a sudden and violent end on February 16, 1964, at about 3:00 a.m., when a bomb exploded under the home of Iona Godfrey, a former NAACP member. Her six-year-old son Donald, a student at the formerly all-white Lackawanna Elementary School, was one of the original thirteen children who had integrated the public school system. The explosion ripped an eighteen-inch-deep hole in the floor of the family's house, located in the Murray Hill section of Jacksonville at Gilmore and Owens Streets. The blast splintered boards in the kitchen and dining room floors, dropping most of the family's appliances through the hole. The bombing followed a bomb threat given to the family just days earlier and signaled the first organized violence against school integration. On March 5, the FBI arrested a thirty-year-old Klansman from Indiana named William Rosecrans. Ten days later six Klansmen collaborators were also arrested. This bombing came in the midst of very tense NAACP-sponsored civil rights demonstrations in Jacksonville. The bombing followed days of verbal harassment directed toward both Donald and his mother. Even though his mother was not active in the civil rights movement, the boy was targeted by the protesting parents.[38]

By 1965 the failure of the Duval County Public School System's integration plan was apparent. On March 19, 1965, the NAACP lawyers went back to court challenging the school board's plan as being too slow and ineffective. They pointed out that only sixty-two of the more than 30,000 African American children in the Duval County Public School System were integrated under the school board's plan. African American high school students at the

Beaches and in Baldwin continued to travel to the urban core for their education. In Baldwin, the students traveled more than twenty miles one way to school, often passing operating whites-only schools.[39]

The lawyers also argued that under the school board's plan, the school attendance zones were drawn in such a way that they perpetuated segregation instead of alleviating it. The NAACP lawyers also criticized the freedom of choice rule as an obvious tool to preserve segregation. Students were being transferred in such a way as to maintain separate schools instead of integrating schools. By July 9, 1965, the school board agreed to accelerate its desegregation plan so that the first four grades of each elementary school would be integrated in the 1965-1966 school year, with all six grades integrated by 1966-1967. NAACP lawyers rejected this offer. A hearing was held on November 3 and 4, 1965, to discuss the school board's plan. Both sides argued their case on February 5, 1966.[40]

On January 24, 1967, Judge Simpson once again ruled on the school board's plan. The judge recognized that this plan had not integrated the school system. The attendance zones were defined so they actually prevented school integration or allowed for only token integration. He found that the school board did not make cross-racial school assignments. However, the school board freely permitted transfers of white students to all-white schools or African American students to all-African American schools even if a school of another race was near. African American children trying to transfer to all-white schools were routinely denied transfers even though they were freely allowed to transfer to predominantly African American schools.[41]

Judge Simpson also found that African American elementary schools continued to feed into African American junior high schools, which, in turn, continued to feed into African American high schools. African American high school students in Baldwin and the Beaches continued to attend the African American high school in downtown Jacksonville, a distance of twenty miles away. Black students at the Beaches were still traveling past white schools on their way to African American schools. In September 1965, of the 118,000 students enrolled in Duval County schools, there were 137 African American students attending twelve previously all-white schools and no white students attending previously all-African American schools. That meant that nearly five years after the original case had been filed, only .0045 percent of the 30,000 African American students had been integrated. The school board kept routinely assigning African American teachers, administrators, and staff to African American schools and white teachers, administrators, and staff to white schools.[42]

The school board's primary vehicle for integrating the schools continued to be the freedom of choice rule, even though it was clearly ineffective. The federal courts customarily maligned the freedom of choice rule as a useless tool for integration. In the 1966 *Singleton v. Jackson Municipal Separate School District* case, the court described the freedom of choice rule as a "haphazard basis for administering public schools." Another court wrote, "If this court must pick a method of assigning students to schools within a particular school district, barring every unusual circumstance, we could imagine no method more inappropriate, more unreasonable, more needlessly wasteful in every respect, than the so-called 'freedom of choice' system." The court said freedom of choice did not allow school boards to plan transportation, curricula, schedules, or lunch allotments because they did not know which students wanted a transfer or how many would receive transfers. Also, because of freedom of choice, certain schools were constantly dealing with overcrowding, resulting in even more transfers once the school year began.[43]

The resulting widespread transfers violated the very notion of freedom of choice. Students were forced to leave the school that they had chosen to attend, disrupting both their education and the school they transferred to. Even though the courts rejected freedom of choice, the school board continued to support it. Judge Simpson found that the school board made no initial assignments of white or African American students to schools attended only or primarily by students of the opposite race. White students living in black districts were not required to attend the schools in their district. They were allowed to transfer to schools where their race was in the majority. Similarly, African American students living in white attendance zones were not required to attend the schools in their district. They were freely allowed to transfer to schools where their race was in the majority. In some instances, they were assigned to African American schools outside of their neighborhoods. Finally, the court found that the school district continued to maintain unequal or inadequate and inferior facilities for African Americans.[44]

The federal courts ordered the following: First, starting with the 1967-1968 school year, a single system of nonracial attendance zones must be established for all grades. The school board had to withdraw all zone boundaries and feeder patterns used to perpetuate or promote segregation. All zone boundaries or feeder patterns used to maintain the current system were dismantled. Second, the courts ordered that students had to attend the schools in their zone of attendance no matter where they had attended school previously. A student could not be transferred unless he or she required a special course of study not offered at the school serving his or her zone. Students with physical handicaps could transfer to schools designed to fit their special needs, if they provided written application. Students whose race was in the majority could transfer to a school where their race was in the minority.[45]

On February 3, 1967, the school board challenged the minority transfer policy, arguing that the policy was, "contrary to the law [as] it affirmatively imposes a discrimination by race as a criterion for transfer." Around the same time, the plaintiffs filed a new motion charging the school board with failure to comply with the January 24 order. School board lawyers argued that the school board had not redrawn their district lines.[46]

The federal court conducted hearings on August 10 and 11, 1967, on both motions. In an order entered on August 22, 1967, the court ordered that the school board abide by its minority transfer order. On the other motion, the court found that the school board had ignored its order to redraw attendance zones. The court found that

the school board was either unwilling or unable to make meaningful changes to comply with the court's order. Judge Simpson said,
"It is convincing on the record before me that the defendant Board,
the individual members thereof, the defendant Brant, and the subordinate employee personnel of said defendants, are either incapable or unwilling to undertake full and meaningful compliance with
either the strict tenor or broad objectives of the provisions of the
January 24, 1967 Order."[47]

The courts could no longer trust the school board to govern itself.
In response, the federal court ordered the school board to immediately request the assistance of school administrators and the
Department of Health, Education, and Welfare, located at the University of Miami under the South Florida Desegregation Center.
The University of Miami Desegregation Center would then help the
school board write a new plan for integrating Jacksonville's
schools. The school board was ordered to submit its plan of student assignment to the University of Miami Desegregation Center
for the center's review. The center would serve as an impartial
mediator to look at the school system to see where changes could
be made.[48]

The new study was to include revisions of zone boundaries and
feeder patterns; staff assignments; faculty assignments; new
school construction; and general board practices, with respect to
desegregation of schools, and with a view to complete elimination
of segregation and racially discriminatory practices in Duval
County schools. The courts were especially angry because, after
four years of court-ordered desegregation, only 137 of the more
than 30,000 African American students attended predominantly
white schools in Jacksonville. That represented just .0045 percent
of the African American students. No whites attended predominantly African American schools. The school board made no initial
assignments of white students to African American schools. White
and African American students who lived in the same attendance
zone attended different schools. Clearly, the school board had
failed to integrate the Duval County Public School System. There
was little hope that more time would improve their efforts.[49]

The courts found that the school board had an obligation to create a unitary school district where there were no clearly defined African American or white schools. The local government had to convert the school system to one that provided educational opportunities on equal terms to all its citizens. The courts went on to say, "The criterion for determining the validity of a provision in a school desegregation plan is whether the provision is reasonably related to accomplishing this objective. If the plan is ineffective, longer on promises than performance, the school officials charged with initiating and administering a unitary system have not met the constitutional requirements of the Fourteenth Amendment; they should try other tools."[50]

During the fall semester of 1966, African American civil rights leaders handpicked ten young people to integrate the formerly all-white Ribault High School. Jean Downing, Pat Pearson, Chris Johnson, Maxine Engram, Linda Sutton Denkins, Longinea Parsons, Martha Mitchell Hemphill, Alton Idowa, Kenneth Hart, and Thomas Crompton pioneered Jacksonville's school integration. They were the sons and daughters of civil rights activists specially chosen because of their academic records, behavior, and resilience. Ribault High was picked because it offered courses in foreign languages whereas the school the students were transferring from did not. Their move did not violate the school board's transfer policy. The students were ferried to the school in two black Cadillacs volunteered by Holmes Funeral Home.[51]

The initial response of the white students was predictable. "I remember . . . people sort of looking and gawking at us and people calling us niggers," said Martha Mitchell Hemphill, one of the students. The students were hurried into the cafeteria, amid chants and monkey noises, to sign in and get their class schedules. Maxine was hit with a raw egg as she sat in the lunchroom. Jean Downing recalled being pushed and punched by several people. Longinea remembered being stuck with a dissecting needle used in science lab to pin back frog and cat skins. Chris Johnson, who rode his motorcycle to school, remembers his book falling off the motorcycle and some kid driving over it and spinning his tires. Later that week someone cut the tires on his motorcycle.[52]

In class Pat Pearson was subjected to other humiliations. Students threw spitballs at her while the teacher taught. Most students just ignored the African American students. The girls, for the most part, did not participate in sports. However the boys starred in track, football, and basketball. There they were able to break down some of the racial barriers. All of the students were subjected to insults and racism. When Chris Johnson and Thomas Crompton were invited to a pool party, it was with the stipulation that they not enter the pool.[53]

Each student was traumatized by the experience. Many have refused to return to Ribault while others have put the whole affair behind them. Longinea Parsons regrets his decision to return to Ribault as a substitute teacher. In describing the events, he said, "It was like a rape victim revisiting the scene of the crime, . . . that's what I feel like now when I pass by there . . . it's not as intense an experience as, say, a rape, but after being drawn out over time I would say the trauma, the effect on a life, is that kind of effect." All of the students attended college after graduation, with eight of them attending Historically Black Colleges and Universities (HBCUS).[54]

Jacksonville's integration process was a painful one for those who experienced it. However, it was a necessary step on the way to integration. The courage and resilience of those students made them unsung heroes of the civil rights struggle. While the leaders of the struggle are often highlighted in books and newspapers, the foot soldiers who actually carry out the battle are often forgotten. The role these children played is immeasurable because they sacrificed their high school experience for the good of their race. The abuse they faced blazed a path for those who followed.

Because of the school board's half-hearted efforts, the Duval County Public School System remained a segregated entity with little real progress being made toward integration. The Supreme Court made a major contribution toward defining integration with its decision in a case in 1968. In *Green v. County Schools of New Kent County*, the federal courts outlined the factors used to determine integration. In this case the courts said that the test of compliance with *Brown* was the practical consequences of any given school district's desegregation program, and that freedom of choice plans had proven predictably ineffective. The court shifted the burden of proof to the school boards to create a plan that was realistic and would completely remove, "root and branch," the vestiges of state-imposed segregation. With this decision, the federal courts put the onus on the school board to prove that they were doing everything within their power to integrate the schools.[55]

The *Green* case established six areas that needed to be desegregated in order for a school system to be declared integrated. These were: student assignment, faculty, staff, transportation, extracurricular activities, and facilities. These so-called *Green* factors, or categories, were the official areas of evaluation when considering a school system's degree of segregation. They set the foundation upon which a school system and the African American community could debate the perimeters of integration.[56]

In August 1969 Judge McRae met with NAACP lawyers and school board officials about the progress of school integration. As expected, the judge heard two different opinions about what was happening. NAACP lawyer Earl Johnson asked the judge to force the school district to do more to desegregate its schools. Johnson argued that there were still twenty-two all-black schools in Duval County. He also pointed out that only 1.8 percent of the total school body was integrated. Johnson argued that the desegregation process should be furthered immediately, using all necessary measures short of disrupting the system. He encouraged the judge to order that teachers and students be transferred even if it meant busing them.[57]

School Board Superintendent Cecil Hardesty criticized that recommendation. He said that such a move would lead to chaos. He asked the judge to make no "drastic changes," with little more than three days left before school opened. William Durden, the school board's lead counsel, disagreed with Johnson's numbers, arguing that the percentage of students integrated was higher. He claimed that almost ten percent were integrated and, in some schools, the numbers had reached twenty percent. He outlined the school board's efforts since the judge had given his order. The school system had closed Matthew Gilbert and Stanton Schools and moved the students to integrated schools. The lawyers could not agree on the important issues of how to integrate students, faculty, and administrative personnel. There was also no agreement on how to integrate the remaining twenty-two all-black schools in Duval County.[58]

The school board was under court order to hold an assembly in all twenty-two all-black schools to inform the students of their right to attend any school to which they could obtain transportation. The board was required to phase out Matthew Gilbert and Stanton Vocational Schools. The school board had to put racial balance issues at the forefront when hiring new teachers and administrators, and to submit to the court a written report of its progress in complying with this ruling. One of the most important requirements was that the board had to file a comprehensive desegregation plan by December 1, 1969, ending segregation of students, faculty, and administrative personnel above the classroom level in school activities, including sports. The school officials assured the judge that they were working toward that end.[59]

In response, Judge McRae granted the school board a one-year reprieve to complete the process of integration. Therefore, in 1969, more than fifteen years after the Supreme Court had issued its initial ruling in the *Brown v. Board of Education* case, Jacksonville's school system had made only limited progress toward integration and ending the dual system. Once again, African Americans were hearing the familiar refrain, often associated with Martin Luther King Jr.: "Wait."

Notes

1 Richard Martin, *Consolidation: Jacksonville-Duval County, The Dynamics of Urban Political Reform* (Jacksonville: Crawford Publishing Company, 1968), 30.

2 *Florida Times-Union,* April 7, 1959.

3 *Florida Times-Union,* September 23, 1959.

4 Ibid.

5 Interview in person with Billy Parker, former principal of Forrest High School, September 20, 2001.

6 *Florida Times-Union,* October 17, 2001; Ibid.

7 Ibid.

8 Ibid.

9 Ibid.

10 Ibid.

11 Ibid.; *Florida Times-Union,* April 10, 2007.

12 Interview with Ish Brant, September 24 and October 3, 2001; Interview with Billy Parker, September 20, 2001.

13 Interview with Rodney Hurst, by phone, August 26 and August 28, 1995; *Florida Times-Union,* October 23, 1993; *Florida Times-Union,* August 27, 2000.

14 Ibid.

15 Ibid.

16 "Racial Fury Over Sit-in," *Life,* September 12, 1960, 37; "Promise of Trouble," *Time,* September 12, 1960; *New York Times,* August 28, 1960; *Florida Times-Union,* August 28, 1960; *Florida Star,* August 28, 1960.

17 "Earl Johnson: Florida's Unsung Hero," *Florida Historical Quarterly,* vol. XLVI, no. 3-4 (July-October 1995), 71-74.

18 Ibid., 73.

19 *Florida Times-Union,* August 4, 1970.

20 Mims v. Duval County School Board, No. 4598-Civ-J, June 1971, 3; Kluger, *Simple Justice,* 748.

21 *Duval County, Florida Public Schools: A Survey Report* (George Peabody College for Teachers. Division of Surveys and Field Services, Nashville, Tennessee 1965), 207.

22 *Jacksonville Advocate,* February 16, 1980.

23 Ibid.

24 Ibid.; Scott, *The Education of Black People,* 4.

25 Interview with Ish Brant, former superintendent of public schools for Duval County, September 24, 2001.

26 Ibid.

27 Ibid.

28 Ibid.

29 *Florida Times-Union,* May 18, 2004.

30 Ibid.; *Mims v. DCSB,* 5.

31 *Mims v. DCSB,* 5-6.

32 Ibid.

33 Ibid.

34 *Florida Times-Union,* October 4, 1999.

35 *Mims v. DCSB,* 4.

36 Braxton v. Board of Public Instruction of Duval County Florida, 442 F. 2d 1339 (5 Cir. 1964).

37 Ibid.

38 *Florida Times-Union,* April 16, 2005; Abel Bartley, *Keeping the Faith: Race Politics and Social Development, 1940-1970* (Westport: Greenwood Press, 2000), 107; *Florida Times-Union,* February 17, 1964; *Florida Times-Union,* November 26, 1964.

39 *Mims v. DCSB,* 5.

40 Ibid.

41 Ibid., 7.

42 Ibid., 6.

43 Board of Public Instruction of Duval County Florida v. Braxton, 402 F. 2d 900 (5 Cir. 1968).

44 *Mims v. DCSB,* 4.

45 March 4, 1969 Dr. C. D. Hardesty, Yardley D. Buckman Present Status of Braxton et al v. B.P.I., United States District Court, Middle District of Florida No. 4598-Civil - J (Hon. William A. McRae, Presiding Judge), 9.

46 *Board of Public Instruction of Duval County Florida v. Braxton,* 7.

47 *Mims v. DCSB,* 7.

48 Ibid.

49 *Mims v. DCSB,* 5.

50 *Board of Public Instruction of Duval County Florida v. Braxton,* 8.

51 *Florida Times-Union,* May 16, 2004.

52 Ibid.

53 Ibid.

54 Ibid.

55 Kluger, *Simple Justice,* 762.

56 Jacksonville Branch, NAACP, v. Duval County School Board, Case No. 85-316-Civ-J-10C, 123-140.

57 *Florida Times-Union,* August 28, 1969.

58 Ibid.

59 Ibid.

Chapter Four

Moving Toward a Unitary System: The University of Miami's Desegregation Center Writes a Plan

A decade after the first *Brown* decision, many of the nation's school districts were still struggling to desegregate and achieve unitary status. In actuality, few other districts had put forth much effort to integrate their facilities. Most Southern school districts were more interested in delaying the integration process than in completing it. By 1968 there were a number of court cases mandating that school districts increase the pace of desegregation and create unitary systems. Throughout the South, there were still many school systems continuing to delay the inevitable, using various schemes to postpone or avoid desegregation. After 1964 the federal government actively pushed school districts to desegregate as part of its enforcement of the newly passed Civil Rights Act. The 1964 Civil Rights Act was designed to create an egalitarian society, removing the remaining legal obstacles to progress for racial minorities. Those who wrote the measure wanted to make sure that school integration would be one of the by-products of this legislation. Ending legalized segregation was an integral part of the grand scheme imagined by the Civil Rights Act.

Ending legalized segregation was the first step in ensuring an egalitarian society. Ground had to be made up where past discrimination had impeded the progress of minority groups. With the Civil Rights Act, the federal government made itself the arbiter of racial disputes. The Johnson administration saw itself as the champion of the underdog. The wording of Title VI of the Civil Rights Act clearly showed that. It stated:

No person in the United States shall, on the ground of race, color, or national origin, be excluded from participation in, be denied the benefits of, or be subjected to discrimination under any program or activity receiving Federal financial assistance.

Title VI gave the federal government a powerful weapon in its efforts to influence school districts, threatening districts with a loss of funding if they did not integrate. Each year the Health, Education and Welfare Department (HEW) issued guidelines rooted in the 1964 Civil Rights Act to help school districts measure their progress toward desegregation. Most Southern school districts failed to implement those guidelines. Duval County was one of the school districts that had clearly failed.[1]

By 1965 the federal courts were applying additional pressure on school officials to accelerate the pace of integration. In numerous rulings the courts demonstrated a determination to enforce the *Brown* decision and integrate the nation's public schools. School desegregation became a priority for the executive and judicial branches of government. One court decision demonstrated the high court's determination when it ruled in the *United States v. Jefferson County Board of Education* case. In this case, the court held that "school authorities are under the constitutional compulsion of furnishing a single integrated school system."[2] The court stated:

Negro children . . . have the "personal and present" right to equal educational opportunities with white children in a racially nondiscriminatory public school system. "The Brown case is misread and misapplied when it is construed simply to confer upon Negro pupils the right to be considered for admission to a white school." The United States Constitution, as construed in Brown, requires public school systems to integrate students, faculties, facilities, and activities. If Brown left any doubt as to the affirmative duty of states to furnish a fully integrated education to Negroes as a class, Brown II resolved that doubt. A state with a dual attendance system, one for whites and one for Negroes, must "effectuate a transition to a [unitary] racially nondiscriminatory school system." The two Brown decisions established equalization of educational opportunities as a high priority goal for all of the states and compelled seventeen states, which by law had segregated public schools, to take affirmative action to reorganize their schools into a unitary, nonracial system.[3]

The high court made it clear that the responsibility for integration could not be shifted to outside agencies. Boards had an affirmative responsibility to not just make integrated schools for black children available; they had to demolish the dual school system. In the same decision, the courts ruled that school districts had to make an adequate and reasonable start toward a new nonracial hiring policy for teachers, administrators, and other personnel. This new policy had to be in place by September 1966, after which state school districts were under court mandate to eliminate all vestiges of race as it related to the functioning of their schools. In essence the courts demanded an integrated unitary system where race was no longer a factor in making decisions.[4]

Moreover, the NAACP kept up the pressure on school systems, demanding that they fully integrate and create a unitary system. Jacksonville's NAACP had created a committee to push for educational reform. Eddie Mae Steward served as chairperson of the NAACP's Educational Committee. She became an expert on Duval County schools and a valued member of the NAACP. Steward was the first female president of Jacksonville's NAACP and later served as state president from 1973 until 1974. She described the attitude of the school system toward black education as "benign neglect. . . . They just weren't interested in educating black children." Eddie Mae Steward was born on October 12, 1938, in Callahan, Florida. However, she spent most of her formative years in Jacksonville. She graduated from Douglass Anderson High School before going on to Edward Waters College. During her early years, Steward was not an active civil rights fighter, but became inspired to join the civil rights movement after witnessing African American men being beaten by Klansmen on Ax Handle Saturday in August of 1960. Steward said that, "They were hitting mostly men, and these were people who had worked all day and had no knowledge of what was going on." Witnessing the savage beating of unarmed, innocent black men in her town by white men from outside of the city energized her.[5]

Eddie Mae then decided to do something about the injustices she witnessed in Jacksonville, her adopted city. Because she had small children, she was especially concerned about the educational inequities African American children faced. She became involved in school affairs when the school board assigned her children to attend the all-girls' Boylan Haven Academy. Boylan Haven had started out as an industrial arts school, opened in 1886 by the Women's Home Missionary Society for African American girls. Boylan was run by the African Methodist Episcopal Church, which opened a number of schools in the South during Reconstruction. By 1910 the school had moved into a three-story school building on Jessie and Franklin Streets. The school had undergone an $80,000 renovation by 1947, but saw substantial deterioration in subsequent years. The school was finally closed in 1959 and the students were shipped to other schools.[6]

As the school population increased, the school board took over the building and used it as an annex for nearby Matthew Gilbert Junior-Senior High School. In the fall of 1968, 194 Gilbert seventh-graders were shipped to makeshift classrooms in the old building. The school board thought that they were doing something good by moving the students into the old rotting building because it would keep them in the same area. School officials had come to believe they were the elected experts and knew what was best for the students. Board members had planned to spend $1.2 million to renovate Matthew Gilbert, so the Boylan Haven School was a good temporary solution to their problem. However, Judge William McRae blocked the Matthew Gilbert expansion plan because he wanted to see the report being conducted by the Florida School Desegregation Center at the University of Miami. In the meantime, the school board decided to send the children who would not fit into Gilbert into the Boylan Haven annex until the Desegregation Center finalized its report.[7]

This decision was clearly unacceptable to most African American parents because they viewed the school as unhealthy and unsafe. Any impartial observer could see that Boylan Haven was not a viable option. In the report the Miami Desegregation Center wrote, it described the school this way: "The condition and appearance of this structure are such as to make any reasonable approach to a sound education for junior high school children impossible." The irony was that the solution to the problem was obvious. The board could have easily transferred the 194 overflow students to the former Annie Beaman School just over two miles away. However, this would have required busing to achieve racial parity, and the board did not want to set that precedent. The board saw that the courts were beginning to use busing as a tool for desegregation, and although black students were routinely bused miles past white schools, busing black children to white schools was unacceptable. Eddie Mae Steward became the leader of a steering committee of concerned Gilbert parents who opposed sending their children to Boylan Haven. They agreed to protest the decision to the school officials and demand the board reconsider. On September 30, the committee demonstrated its anger when it boycotted the school. Instead of sending their children to Boylan Haven, the parents set up alternative classes run by volunteers and substitutes at Tabernacle Baptist Church. Despite the protest, the school board refused to back down.[8]

As the situation intensified, the NAACP threatened a citywide school boycott. This drew the attention of the press and local officials who all sympathized with the parents. Ron Martin of the *Jacksonville Journal* called the annex best suited as the site for a horror movie. The *Florida Times-Union* called the building "unfit by any standards as a place to send children to school." Steward even appealed to newly elected Jacksonville mayor Hans Tanzler. She convinced Tanzler to accompany her on a visit to the Boylan Haven annex. Tanzler was shocked by what he saw. He came away visibly moved by the experience. He described the school as disgusting and deplorable. He was quoted as saying, "I don't think anybody in the world would have any different impression." After three weeks of constant pressure, the school board finally relented and sent the students to Annie Beaman. After her victory over the school board, Eddie Mae Steward was catapulted into local prominence. She was emboldened by the victory and sought to conquer greater obstacles.[9]

As a leader on the NAACP's Educational Committee, Steward became ever more active on school equity issues. As the school board struggled to write an integration plan, the NAACP's Education Committee had come up with several plans which they argued would integrate the school system. According to Steward, "At that time, the NAACP was asking for a full discrimination suit. . . . We advocated . . . dividing the county into more districts and using natural boundaries to achieve that [desegregation]. Anybody in one district could go to [any] school in that district. We did not ask for a certain percentage of desegregation. . . . The most we were asking for, in terms of desegregation, was in one district with twenty percent desegregation."[10] Neither the school board nor the Desegregation Center seriously evaluated or considered the Educational Committee's plan. Superintendent Ish Brant referred to the NAACP plan as "unrealistic and biased." According to Brant it did not take into consideration the political realities which existed in the city. The Desegregation Center's Gordon Foster said the center was not in the habit of looking at plans until they had thoroughly investigated the school system. He also said the NAACP's plan was politically unworkable and did not adjust to the changing legal landscape.[11]

In Duval County, the school board had made limited progress in its efforts to achieve unitary status. As part of its delaying tactic, the school system had emphasized integration while ignoring the more glaring problem of creating a unitary system. It had become obvious to the courts and the NAACP that the school board needed help to move to unitary status. In response, Judge Bryan Simpson of the U.S. District Court advised the school board to request the assistance of experts located at the University of Miami's South

Florida Desegregation Center to help write a desegregation plan. The University of Miami's Desegregation Center could serve as a neutral party, writing a plan that provided an equal education for all of Jacksonville's children.[12]

The Desegregation Center began its work in 1965, when it was designated as the "first" federally funded assistance center established in the United States. Today, it is called The Southeastern Equity Center and has provided training and technical assistance with integration issues to school districts in Alabama, Florida, Georgia, Kentucky, Mississippi, North Carolina, South Carolina, and Tennessee since 1965. The center is funded by the Department of Education under the provisions of the 1964 Civil Rights Act. The work of the Equity Center is guided by the Region IV Equity Advisory Council, which is composed of the representatives of the State Chief School Officers of the eight states served by the center.[13]

The center continues to receive many requests for technical assistance as school districts and states strive to cope effectively with increased diversity; racial and ethnic tensions; desegregation; resegregation; integration; court-ordered unitary status; and the need to ensure that all children are provided scientifically research-based instruction that enables them to achieve high standards. The Equity Center continues to provide comprehensive direct assistance and training to hundreds of school districts as they deal with the challenge of creating, building, and sustaining culturally sensitive environments that provide equal access to a quality educational experience. The Southeastern Equity Center assists the school districts in Region IV.[14]

When Judge Bryan sent the school board to the Desegregation Center, he wanted its experts to look at Duval County's public schools and to pay special interest to administration, zone boundaries, feeder patterns, staff assignments, new school construction, and board practices, especially as they related to desegregation of its schools. By studying these areas, the court believed that they could more easily desegregate the system. Every level of the school board's planning, hiring, and administration had to be investigated to find residual patterns of discrimination and segregation.[15]

Shortly after Judge Bryan issued his order, Duval County Public School Superintendent Ish Brant wrote a letter to the director of the South Florida Desegregation Consulting Center, stating, "The Board of Public Instruction took action to formally request that the South Florida School Desegregation Consulting Center be invited to make the appropriate survey of desegregation progress in the school system. . . . Of course we will appreciate all the advice and counsel that your experience can afford us." This formal request was forwarded to Michael J. Stolee, the director of the center. It was clear from the beginning that the school system would have preferred to take another route. Branch was not optimistic that the Desegregation Center could write a workable plan but he felt he had no other choice but to follow the court's order. There was no unanimity among local residents about integration and little faith that a feasible plan could be developed.[16]

Each day local residents were reminded of how difficult it was to change local attitudes. The schools were one of the last bastions of Old South prominence. Parents and neighborhood organizations were willing to expend considerable effort to maintain the racial makeup of their schools. Schools were an important symbol of neighborhood pride and distinction. The city had already seen bombings, riots, and boycotts centered on educational equity issues. The NAACP leaders looked at most locally sponsored integration efforts with a jaundiced eye. The will to make the necessary changes was just not there. After years of fighting an entrenched power structure, NAACP leaders were weary of any proposals in which they had no say.

On October 2, 1967, Stolee wrote a response accepting the school board's request. In his letter, Stolee stated: "You may be very assured that we are very interested in working with you and your staff as well as with the Board of Public Instruction. Our philosophy is that we attempt to assist school people to solve problems occasioned by school desegregation without embarrassment, hostility, or preconceived notions concerning specific areas."[17] In late October, members of the Desegregation Center met with school officials and outlined the type of investigation needed. In November 1967 Stolee and his assistant director, Dr. Gordon Foster, began an intensive examination of the Duval County Public School System. The Desegregation Center initially conducted a comprehensive inspection of the policies and procedures of the school board designed to create a unitary system which catered to all students. Both the NAACP and school board agreed that the report the center submitted was in-depth and professional.

Gordon Foster, who supervised the investigation, came to Jacksonville with high hopes of developing a progressive, integrated school system. Foster was born in Cincinnati, Ohio, on May 17, 1918. He was a devoted investigator into everything educational, even as a youngster. He graduated from Oberlin College before going on to Miami University and Ohio State University for graduate work. He went to the University of Miami to work in their School of Education. There he learned the power of education to correct social ills. He was especially concerned with the unequal education that African American children received. Foster was impressed with Stolee and the efforts he was making to integrate schools. When Foster was given an opportunity to work for the Desegregation Center he immediately took advantage of it, moving his family to Florida and teaching in a university there. When he got to Jacksonville, he found a school board and superintendent who were both reluctant to make the radical changes needed to integrate the schools.[18]

The first part of the center's report looked at trends over the previous ten years. The Desegregation Center staff felt that it was important to understand the type and age of students who attended Jacksonville's public schools. Their report showed that the number of students in school in Duval County increased each year. Total school attendance in Jacksonville had increased by 32,204 students, or about thirty-six percent, from 1958 until1968. During the 1958-1959 school year, Jacksonville's school population stood at 88,637. By the 1967-1968 period, the school population had risen to 120,841. That increase corresponded with the general population increase in the region. Duval County's population was steadily growing during those years. Jacksonville's population had increased from 396,502 to 511,500 between 1955 and 1965. This represented a thirty-six and twenty-nine percent increase, respectively.[19]

The Desegregation Center conducted a precise grade-by-grade census of the students in Jacksonville's schools, to get an accurate count of percentages and numbers of white and African American students in each grade. In 1967 white students made up 72.3 percent of the student body in Duval County. Center investigators found that in the twelfth grade, white students made up 76.8 percent of the students, while in the third grade, whites represented only 69.8 percent of the students. This meant that whites were graduating at a higher rate than African Americans. This information was helpful in developing strategies for graduating more students.[20]

Graduation rates among African Americans had fallen below white graduation rates. The Desegregation Center investigated the high dropout rate in Duval County. This was a recurring problem, which had almost become endemic within the system. The school system had been investigating the dropout rate for some time. In 1963 the school board conducted a study on the dropout rate, "to determine the scope of the problem in the Duval County public school system, the causes for pupils' leaving school, and the probable implications of such causes for curriculum guidance and administration of the schools."[21] School officials felt that it was important to know why the voluntary withdrawal rate was so high. They hoped that they could fix the problem through curriculum changes or by some other means.[22]

During their investigation, the school board made a distinction between voluntary and involuntary withdrawals. Students who voluntarily withdraw from school usually do not attend another school. The students who were part of the involuntary withdrawals group usually re-entered the system either in Duval County or in some other school system. The school system had no data on dropout rates before 1963 or on dropouts before the sixth grade. The Desegregation Center investigators were surprised to find that the dropout rate among blacks and whites was the same. There was no distinct pattern of dropouts that could be traced along racial lines.[23]

After determining that the rates of dropouts were about the same, they looked at the reasons for dropping out of school. Almost half of the non-white students who voluntarily left school during the 1965-1966 school year, the only year for which data is available, left because of truancy or excessive absences. The percentage of whites who left for that reason was only 15.5 percent. Even though there were few differences in rates of dropouts, there were differences between why African Americans and white students left school.[24]

The number one reason why white kids said they left school was a lack of interest. There were fifty-four non-white students who left school because of pregnancy. Another thirty-one left to get married. There were only fourteen white students who left because they were pregnant, but 224 left because of marriage. There was no data on how many of those marriages were the result of unplanned pregnancies. The rates for those leaving because of behavioral problems and financial reasons were also about the same for blacks and whites.[25]

The Desegregation Center also looked at retention and promotion rates. In Duval County, majority black schools had a higher retention rate than majority white schools. In the first five grades, there was no significant difference in retention rates among African American and white children. In grades seven through twelve, the data were not so clear. In grades seven through nine, the retention rate among African Americans was much higher than among whites. The retention range for whites was .8 to 5.9 percent, while among African Americans it was 12.2 to 27.8 percent for the years 1962 through 1967.[26]

The retention rate for African Americans in grades ten through twelve was higher than for whites. The disparities were not nearly as high as they were for grades seven through nine. The range was from 2.6 percent to 12.3 percent for whites and 6.0 percent and 26.2 percent for African Americans. The practice of social promotion was not universally followed. Administrators and teachers made retention decisions based on a number of factors, including profitability to the student, number of times retained, and teachers' recommendations.[27]

The report also looked at age distributions among students in specific grades. Researchers found that there were actually higher percentages of whites who were overage for their grades than non-whites. The first part of the survey committee's report investigated population, voluntary withdrawals, retention, and average age per grade. The investigation looked at how race affected each of these areas. With this information in hand, the Desegregation Center began preparing its plan. Initially, the Desegregation Center made a number of preliminary conclusions. The most significant racial difference researchers found was that the dropout rate among African Americans was much higher than that of whites. African Americans left school after their legal obligation for school attendance ended. The conclusion the researchers came to was that "These figures indicate very clearly that Negro students are dropping out of school much more rapidly than their white counterparts as soon as they reach the traditional junior high drop out age level."[28]

The next part of the study looked at faculty allocations and qualifications. During the 1967-1968 school year, the Duval County Public School System employed about 5,500 teachers. To get information about teachers, the Desegregation Center relied on formal surveys. 5,394 of the teachers surveyed returned their survey questionnaires. The center got teachers' names from principals, directors of personnel, staff members, the teachers themselves, and inspection of personnel files.[29]

Duval County recruited its staff from Southern states east of the Mississippi. Many of the policies used to recruit teachers were based on the segregated nature of the school system. White teachers were recruited to teach at white schools and black teachers were recruited to teach at black schools. After the successful challenge to segregation in the early 1960s, the school board was forced to change its recruitment and transfer policies. Each teacher applying for employment in Duval County had this statement appended to their application: "Duval County is a racially desegregated school system and members of its staff are subject to assignment in the best interest of the system and without regard to race or color of the particular employee."[30]

However, for school board officials, it was obviously in the best interest of the system to assign white teachers to all-white staffs and African American teachers to all-African American staffs. Of the more than 5,000 teachers in the system, fewer than seventy-five were assigned to schools where their race was in the minority. There was only one school which had white teachers assigned to a predominantly African American school. Grand Park Elementary School had ten African Americans, one Indian, and seven white teachers. The school was experiencing student turnover; for the first time, African Americans became the majority as white students transferred to other schools in the district or to private schools.[31]

Primarily because of NAACP pressure, the school system had overcome its discriminatory salary schedules. Since the 1930s, the NAACP had been filing lawsuits challenging the dual pay scales used by school systems. As a result, Southern school systems had changed their behavior and offered a single pay scale. Teacher salaries were based on three criteria: years of service, degree held (certificate rank), and responsibilities beyond the normal school day. There were several Duval County teachers whose salaries were inconsistent with the salary schedule. However, there was no racial component associated with this because both African Americans and whites had similar inconsistencies.[32]

Duval County teachers were paid from a base salary of $5,000 a year, multiplied by a complex index based on years of experience, rank, and extra-school day responsibility. A beginning teacher with a four-year degree would receive 106 percent of the beginning salary, or $5,300. A high school teacher with a master's degree and thirteen years of experience received 193 percent of the $5,000 base pay, or $9,650. After a careful examination of teacher salaries, the Desegregation Center could not detect any race-based salary discrimination within Duval County. The years of struggle and lawsuits from the NAACP had forced the school district to equalize pay and standardize the pay scale.[33]

The Desegregation Center was also interested in the makeup of the Duval County Public School System. They studied the school distribution and the structure of the curriculum and grades. Duval County operated ninety-five elementary schools; twenty-six secondary schools; three combination elementary and junior high schools; and three vocational and/or adult schools. Regardless of the level of student integration, schools could be easily classified as either African American or white simply by looking at the faculty and staff. Schools that had desegregated staffs generally only had one, two, or three African American teachers. The vast majority of faculties at Jacksonville's schools were either one hundred percent African American or one hundred percent white. Elementary schools had done the most work in desegregating. There were thirty-two African American teachers assigned to predominantly white schools. There were only fifteen African American teachers assigned to predominantly white secondary schools while four were assigned to combination elementary-secondary schools. There had been no serious effort made to desegregate the vocational or technical school faculties.[34]

Several obvious observations were made about faculty integration after the initial review. First, percentage-wise, there was little faculty desegregation taking place in Duval County. Second, with one exception, there were no white teachers in predominantly African American schools. Finally, there were no African American administrators in predominantly white schools. The little integration that had occurred had been spontaneous, with little discernible coordination. It was clear that the school district did not have a workable plan for integrating the faculty and staff.[35]

A similar condition applied to the district's school resource officials, of whom twenty-four percent were African Americans. These officials worked from the county office but traveled to various schools to provide administrative and instructional services. They taught courses like driver's education, art, music, and physical education. White resource officials were assigned to white schools and African American resource officials worked at African American schools.

A review of the teachers in the Duval County Public School System shows that there was no difference in qualifications between African American and white teachers. African American teachers were just as prepared as white teachers, if not more so. The same held true for the county resource officials. African Americans who held those jobs were just as competent as whites who held the same positions.[36]

Out-of-field assignments for African American and white teachers did have a racial component. Someone with an out-of-field assignment is a person who is teaching in a specialty other than their area of certification by the state. Of African American teachers, sixty-one, or four percent, were working out of field. White teachers had a substantially higher out-of-field ratio. There were 375 white teachers, or ten percent, working outside of their specialty. The vast majority of out-of-field teachers were in the elementary schools. The school system had difficulty finding special education teachers and guidance personnel. On the high school level, there was a problem finding math and science teachers, so a significant number of teachers were working outside of their original field to fill these positions.[37]

There were few differences in teaching experience based on race. A credentials check found that forty-eight percent of African American elementary teachers had at least ten years of experience. The same study found that fifty percent of white teachers had ten or more years of experience. On the high school level, twenty percent of the African American teachers had between one and three years of experience and forty-seven percent had ten or more years of experience. For white teachers, the numbers were similar. Twenty-five percent of white teachers had one to three years of experience while thirty-nine percent of white teachers and administrators had ten years or more of experience.[38]

Next, the Desegregation Center looked at the courses of study undertaken by the Duval County school students. By 1967 Jacksonville's public schools had been studied by a number of professional organizations, including local educators; the Florida State Department of Education; the Southern Association of Colleges and Schools committees; and the George Peabody College for Teachers Division of Surveys and Field Services staff. Each study commission found the same two problems. One consistent complaint was that the city did not allocate enough resources to adequately fund the schools and solve the system's problems. The other issue was a lack of positive leadership in both the school system and the city.[39]

The center also investigated the impact of the district's dual system. The Duval County Public School System was organized on a 6-3-3 basis. This was the recommendation of the Peabody Survey, which proposed that all Florida schools adopt this pattern. The 6-3-3 pattern means that schools have six grades of elementary study, three grades of junior high or middle school study, and three years of high school study. However, Jacksonville had not completed the process. There were several schools, affecting nearly 7,000 children, that did not fit into this pattern. Of that number, 4,873 children were African American and 1,926 were white. There were four African American schools that did not follow the model. Two of these had grades 1-3, and 4-6, respectively. The center suggested that developing a unified 6-3-3 system would go a long way toward improving racial balance in Duval County.[40]

The Desegregation Center also recommended that efforts be made to integrate the faculty. They argued that utilizing special primary and middle schools could be an effective tool for integrating the school system and the faculty.

The school year in Jacksonville was 180 days long for students and 194 days for teachers. The school day ran for either six and one-half hours or four hours. Schools with double sessions were the four-hour schools.[41] Despite the progress the school system had made, there were still 2,274 students who were attending schools with double sessions. Of those 2,274 students, 1,627 were African American. The Miami Desegregation Center recommended the full utilization of all elementary school space to end the dual sessions immediately. They also recommended using suitable housing to conduct kindergarten classes in order to make more room available for elementary classes.[42]

Another area of concern for the Duval County Public School System was class size. On the elementary level, Jacksonville's classes ranged in size from sixteen to forty-three students. In sixty-three of the one hundred elementary schools, the administrators reported thirty-three or more students in a class. There were seven schools that reported elementary classes of forty or more students. Only fifty of the one hundred elementary schools in Jacksonville had achieved a thirty or fewer class size average.[43] Only one of the classes with forty or more students was in an African American school. Only nine of the twenty-three African American schools reported class sizes of thirty or more students. Class sizes between African American and white schools were equal.[44]

The county had made progress in creating seventh-, eighth-, and ninth-grade junior high schools throughout the system. There were only nine schools that remained outside the junior high pattern, of which five were African American. The county superintendent's office had established a one to twenty-six teacher-student ratio for junior high schools. By 1967 the school system had reached this goal. There were still several schools that had classes with thirty-five or more students in them. There was no evidence of African American schools having larger classes.[45]

The school system wanted a twenty-six to one student-teacher ratio on the secondary level also. There were seventy high schools in Jacksonville. Of those, ten conformed to the 10-12 grade pattern. There were three schools with grades 9-12, three with 7-12, and one that had grades 1-12. There were some schools that kept class sizes under twenty-six, and others that had more than thirty-five students in their classes. It is obvious that the differences were not race-based.[46]

The recently completed Peabody Study had suggested that Duval County change its junior high school requirements and move from a six-period day to a seven-period day. Students were required to complete three years of study in English, mathematics, science, social studies, and physical education. The sixth period was used for art, music, home economics, or shop. In the eighth and ninth grades, students could use that period for foreign languages, orchestra, band, journalism, library science, typewriting, general business, or reading.[47]

The Desegregation Center also investigated to see if differences existed between African American and white schools on curriculum and the time spent on subject areas. They reported, "No major difference was found in the curriculum offered at white and Negro schools, nor was there a definite pattern of differences in the time allocated to particular subjects." There were obvious variations based on how they structured their curriculum and subject areas. Some schools spent more or less time on certain curricular areas than others. There were several African American schools that were in dire need of a reading specialist to do remedial work with students. Schools with large numbers of disadvantaged students needed diagnostic, remedial, and developmental services for some of these students.[48]

Even though there were no differences in the curriculum or amount of time allocated for study between African American and white schools, there were clear differences in how teachers approached these subjects. The teacher surveys confirmed the belief that more African American personnel were needed in supervisory and specialist positions. School board officials recognized this problem and attempted to recruit African Americans to these positions, but low salaries and other factors thwarted their efforts. The Desegregation Center suggested that effective teaching techniques be studied and shared with other schools along with instructional material. There should also be a special effort made to recruit African Americans in some curriculum areas.[49]

In December 1970 a hearing was held in which Judge William McRae, responding to the changing legal landscape, ordered the school board to move to a unitary system, eliminating all vestiges of the dual system by February 1, 1970. The court ordered the Desegregation Center to modify its original plan to meet the accelerated schedule, and said, "This plan is to be the guidance of the Court and of the parties in this action in further proceedings, and it is to take into consideration this court's concern that students classed as non-transported be allowed, in the school board's discretion, to attend neighborhood school."[50]

There were two factors that hampered the work of the Desegregation Center. They did not have pupil spot maps by race, so they had no way of knowing the race of students, nor where they lived. Also, there was no strict enforcement of attendance policy for prescribed attendance zones. There were several areas where students who lived in an attendance zone did not attend the schools in their zone.[51]

By 1970 Jacksonville had 134 separate schools that made up the public school system. There were 100 elementary schools, eighteen junior high schools, and twelve senior high schools, with one combination elementary-junior high and three combination junior-senior high schools. There were 121,498 students, of whom 34,168, or 28 percent, were African American. Of the 101 elementary schools, fourteen were all African American, five were 99 to 99.9 percent African American, and two were 90 to 98.9 percent African American. Of the twenty-one junior high schools with grades seven through nine, four were all African American and one was 90 to 98.9 percent African American. There were fifteen senior high schools with grades ten through twelve, of which three were all African American and one 90 to 98.9 percent African American. There was also one all-African American junior-senior high school.[52]

In 1970, nearly sixteen years after the *Brown* decision, Jacksonville still operated twenty all-African American schools. Approximately 84.3 percent of African American elementary students attended schools that were 90 percent African American. On the junior high level, the percentage was 65.2, and on the high school level, it was 77.6. The school system had spent most of its time and money on equalizing education, as opposed to integrating it. Still, many schools had been refurbished, most of the faculty had been integrated, and there was a working system of accountability.[53]

By 1970 the school board did have a policy that principals should reflect the dominant group at each school. Predominantly African

American schools had African American principals and predominantly white schools had white principals. The Desegregation Center recommended that the school board change that policy, arguing that it represented a dual structure. Principals, like teachers, were professionals who should be able to perform their duties in a school of either race. It was also recommended that at least one African American counselor be assigned to each junior and senior high school. The center also recommended that the school board increase the number of qualified African American administrators in responsible positions, both at the central office level and within individual schools.[54]

Finally, the Desegregation Center suggested changing the school classification system. By identifying African American schools with the number 100 and above, and white schools with numbers less than 100, the system maintained a dual structure. The center suggested that the school numbering code be discontinued. This would be a really visible symbol of the changed structure. With the exception of three schools, all of the schools in Duval County were easily identifiable by their numbers. The Desegregation Center argued that some might interpret this numbering system as a remaining vestige of the dual system.

As 1970 came to an end, The Duval County Public School System was on its way to establishing a unitary status. However, within a few years, the black community realized that a good start was a long way from a finished process.[55] The school system had gone only as far toward desegregation as the law and the federal government had compelled them to do. Though they publicly claimed to be pursuing integration, they continued to be unwilling to make the tough choices to bring it to pass. There is no doubt that, although the new superintendent and school board that came after consolidation were much more willing to make changes, they were not yet ready to answer the legal challenges introduced by the NAACP. Therefore, the changes that occurred during the early 1970s were only the opening salvos, and not the end of the war. Those who were fighting for a unitary integrated school system would have many more battles before they could sleep.

Notes

1 *A Report to the Duval County Board of Public Instruction: Florida School Desegregation Consulting Center University of Miami* (Coral Gables: University of Miami, 1968), 2.

2 United States and Linda Stout et al. v. Jefferson County Board of Education et al., 372 F.2d 836 (5 Cir. 1966), 1.

3 Ibid., 1.

4 *Miami Desegregation Center Report,* 2.

5 *Jacksonville Skirt!,* January 17, 2011.

6 Judith Poppell, "The Desegregation of a Historically Black High School in Jacksonville, Florida." (PhD diss., University of North Florida, 1988), 33; "Jacksonville Looks at Its Negro Community: Brief Report of the Bi-Racial Follow-Up Committee." Jacksonville Bi-Racial Fellowship, March 1948, 51.

7 *Florida Times-Union,* December 9, 2005.

8 "October 15, 2003: Congresswoman Brown Announces Passage of Eddie Mae Steward Postal Bill," *Florida Times-Union,* May 28,1999.

9 *Florida Times-Union,* December 9, 2005.

10 Interview with Eddie Mae Steward, June 24, 1998, as cited in Poppell, "The Desegregation of a Historically Black High School," 108.

11 Interview with Ish Brant, October 3, 2001; Interview with Gordon Foster, February 16, 2010.

12 *Miami Desegregation Center Report,* 3.

13 http://www.southeastequity.org/

14 Ibid.

15 *Miami Desegregation Center Report,* 3.

16 *Miami Desegregation Center Report,* 4; Interview with Brant, September 24, 2001.

17 *Miami Desegregation Center Report,* 5.

18 Interview by phone with Gordon Foster, September 1, 2010.

19 *Miami Desegregation Center Report,* 10; Abel Bartley, *Keeping the Faith: Race, Politics and Social Development in Jacksonville, Florida 1940-1970* (Westport: Greenwood Press, 2000), 5.

20 *Miami Desegregation Center Report,* 17.

21 Ibid., 22.

22 Ibid.

23 Ibid., 22-25.

24 Ibid., 26-28.

25 Ibid.

26 Ibid., 31.

27 Ibid., 30.

28 Ibid., 37.

29 Ibid., 38.

30 Ibid., 38-39.

31 Ibid., 39.

32 Ibid.

33 Ibid., 40.

34 Ibid., 41.

35 Ibid.

36 Ibid., 44.

37 Ibid., 45.

38 Ibid., 47.

39 Ibid., 55.

40 Ibid., 61.

41 Ibid., 62.

42 Ibid., 63.

43 Ibid., 64.

44 Ibid., 65.

45 Ibid., 68, 69, 70.

46 Ibid.

47 Ibid., 79.

48 Ibid., 75, 76.

49 Ibid., 78.

50 Revised Desegregation Center Plan, 3.

51 Ibid.
52 Ibid., 3, 4.
53 Ibid., 4, 5.
54 Ibid., 12.
55 Ibid., 12-13.

Photographs

Pictured above is the earliest known photograph of the first faculty of Stanton High School standing in front of the original building sometime in the 1870s or 1880s. Stanton had its beginnings in elementary-level education. Under the administration of J. C. Waters, the first principal, and D. W. Culp, who followed as principal, the school had six grades and became known throughout the state of Florida for high educational standards.

From the book *Stanton Campus History Series.* Courtesy of the Jacksonville Public Library.

FAVORITE EXPRESSIONS OF THE FACULTY.	
Mrs. M. B. McLendon	"There is only one way for intelligent people to do things, and that's in an intelligent way."
	"Well—"
Mrs. C. C. Lewis	"Say girls!"
	"No no! child you ought know better."
	"Common sense ought tell you better."
	"Whose making that undertone."
Mrs. W. G. Watt	"P'raps."
	"Don't come straggling in my class you don't do it in any other class."
	"Have you got a book?"
	"Have you got a book?"
Mrs. M. E. Lowe	"I would not expect that of my Senior girls."
Mrs. O. H. Bryant	"Hush girls."
Miss H. C. Chaplin	"Yes that's right."
Miss N. A. Espy	"Lets have it quiet please."
Prof. J. N. Wilson	"One—two—three—B-r-e-a-k."
Mr. R. E. Payne	"Ugh, ugh."
	"Is that true?"
	"I don't see why you couldn't get that."
Mr. F. M. Moton	"Lets be sociable."
	"Don't frown so Inez, Nellie."
Miss C. K. DeVaughn	"You'll have to go out."
	"Well now."—"There."
Mr. C. Calhoun	"Get to work boys."
Mrs. A. B. Coleman	"Keep quiet."
	LILLIAN ANDERSON, Class of '24.

The Stanton faculty for grades 1 through 12 is fondly remembered in the 1924 yearbook, with examples of favorite expressions of these teachers as heard by the students.

This picture features the faculty for the years 1925 to 1926. Although everyone can not be identified, this photograph includes A. Stewart, Mr. and Mrs. Beachemp, Mrs. Grant, Mrs. Harbin, Mr. Payne, Mrs. Watt, Mrs. Grant, Ms. Baldwin, Ms. Hayes, Mrs. Butler, Mrs. Johnson, Mrs. Meyers, Mrs. Payne, Mrs. Black, Mrs. A. Payne, and Mrs. Lewis.

From the book *Stanton Campus History Series*. Courtesy of the Jacksonville Public Library.

Adult education geography class at Stanton High School, March 1935. State Archives of Florida, *Florida Memory.*

Adult education sewing class at Stanton High School, March 1935. State Archives of Florida, *Florida Memory.*

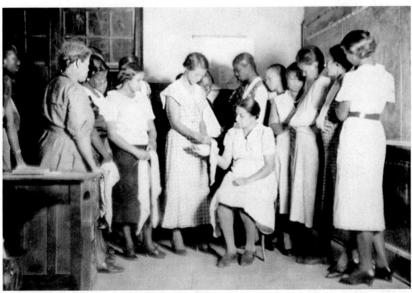

Adult education first aid class at Stanton High School, March 1935. State Archives of Florida, *Florida Memory.*

Pearlie Cobb Scarborough and Thomas Morris graduating from Stanton High School in Jacksonville, 1935.

Abel A. Bartley

PROF. F. J. ANDERSON, PRINCIPAL

CHARLES D. BROOKS, ASST. PRINCIPAL

MISS EMMA LEE TURNER, DEAN OF WOMEN

From the Stantonian Yearbook 1942. Courtesy of the Jacksonville Public Library.

THE STANTONIAN

MRS. KATHRYN H. BLANCHARD,
SECRETARY

MRS. MARTHA B. McLENDON, LIBRARIAN

From the Stantonian Yearbook 1942. Courtesy of the Jacksonville Public Library.

THELMA H. JONES
B.S., Florida A. & M. College
VIVIAN O. ELLIS
B.S., Florida A. & M. College; Advanced Work, Chicago University
RAYMOND S. MILLER
B.S., Florida A. & M. College
CORIETTA P. NELSON
B.S., Tuskegee Institute; M.A., Columbia University
A. HALEY ROBINSON
B.S., Florida A. & M. College
LUCILLE G. COLEMAN
B.S., Florida A. & M. College; M.A., University of Iowa
CLAUDE O. HILLIARD
B.S., Florida A. & M. College
MARTHEENIA GUNN
B.S., West Virginia State College
WILLIAM THEODORE HARPER
A.B., Florida A. & M. College
JERUSHA L. CRAWFORD
A.B., Atlanta University

From the Stantonian Yearbook 1942. Courtesy of the Jacksonville Public Library.

ALICE L. GRIFFIN
A.B., Florida A. & M. College
DORIS AVERY GREENLEE
A.B., Morris Brown College
COATSIE G. JONES
A.B., Florida A. & M. College
AMY S. CURRIE
B.S., Florida A. & M. College
DAISY A. DUNCAN
A.B., Florida A. & M. College
THERESA S. WILLIAMS
A.B., Florida A. & M. College
WILLIAM H. MATHIS
B.S., Florida A. & M. College
JOHN H. MORRIS
A.B., Florida A. & M. College
MINNIE C. CAVE
Ph.B., Claflin College
LUCILE BUTLER
A.B., Howard University Hampton Institute; University of Michigan

From the Stantonian Yearbook 1942. Courtesy of the Jacksonville Public Library.

THE STANTONIAN

ADMINISTRATION, DEPARTMENT HEADS AND FACULTY

PRINCIPAL
Professor F. J. Anderson
DEAN OF BOYS
C. D. Brooks
DEAN OF GIRLS
E. L. Turner
COACH
James P. Small
LIBRARIAN
Martha B. McLendon
SECRETARY
Kathryn H. Blanchard
ENGLISH DEPARTMENT
Amy S. Currie
MATHEMATICS DEPARTMENT
C. P. Nelson
COMMERCIAL DEPARTMENT
C. O. Hilliard
SCIENCE DEPARTMENT
R. S. Miller
HISTORY DEPARTMENT
Lucille G. Coleman
LANGUAGE DEPARTMENT
Minnie C. Cave
HOME ECONOMICS
Fannie Rooks
MANUAL TRAINING
Frank W. Hamilton
DIVERSIFIED CO-OPERATIVE TRAINING
Edward Benthone
MUSIC DEPARTMENT
W. T. Harper

HOME ECONOMICS DEPARTMENT
Helen James
Ondria King
Mary Barnett
HISTORY DEPARTMENT
Mamie Butler
Myrtia Harrison
Theresa Williams
C. D. Brooks
ENGLISH DEPARTMENT
Coatsie Jones
Maggie Carter
Emma Martin
Daisy Duncan
Vivian Ellis
Alice Griffin
Sadie Wilson
Doris A. Greenlee
PRINTING DEPARTMENT
W. H. Mathis

MATHEMATICS DEPARTMENT
Jerusha Crawford
Vivian Ellis
T. H. Jones
Theresa Williams
SCIENCE DEPARTMENT
George Nairn
Harriett Schell
J. P. Small
M. H. Barnett
LANGUAGE DEPARTMENT
Alvin McFarland
Ila Williams-Thomas
J. H. Morris
MUSIC DEPARTMENT
William T. Harper
COMMERCIAL DEPARTMENT
Annie Robinson
M. J. Gunn
DIVERSIFIED CO-OPERATIVE TRAINING
Edward Benthone

From the Stantonian Yearbook 1942. Courtesy of the Jacksonville Public Library.

Mr. Ishmael "Ish" Brant, Superintendent of Schools, Duval County Board of Public Instruction, 1957-1969.

Dr. Irving E. Scott, named Director of Negro Education for the Duval County School System in 1953.

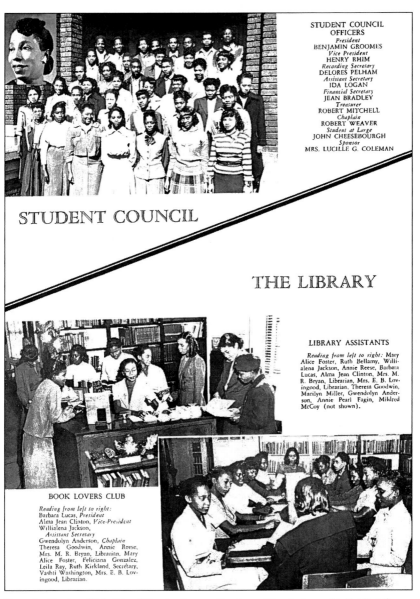

STUDENT COUNCIL
OFFICERS
President
BENJAMIN GROOMES
Vice President
HENRY RHIM
Recording Secretary
DELORES PELHAM
Assistant Secretary
IDA LOGAN
Financial Secretary
JEAN BRADLEY
Treasurer
ROBERT MITCHELL
Chaplain
ROBERT WEAVER
Student at Large
JOHN CHEESEBOURGH
Sponsor
MRS. LUCILLE G. COLEMAN

STUDENT COUNCIL

THE LIBRARY

LIBRARY ASSISTANTS

Reading from left to right: Mary
Alice Foster, Ruth Bellamy, Willi-
alena Jackson, Annie Reese, Barbara
Lucas, Alma Jean Clinton, Mrs. M.
R. Bryan, Librarian, Mrs. E. B. Lov-
ingood, Librarian, Theresa Goodwin,
Marilyn Miller, Gwendolyn Ander-
son, Annie Pearl Fagin, Mildred
McCoy (not shown).

BOOK LOVERS CLUB

Reading from left to right:
Barbara Lucas, *President*
Alma Jean Clinton, *Vice-President*
Willialena Jackson,
Assistant Secretary
Gwendolyn Anderson, *Chaplain*
Theresa Goodwin, Annie Reese,
Mrs. M. R. Bryan, Librarian, Mary
Alice Foster, Feliciana Gonzalez,
Leila Ray, Ruth Kirkland, *Secretary*,
Vashti Washington, Mrs. E. B. Lov-
ingood, Librarian.

From the Stanton High School Yearbook 1951. Courtesy of the Jacksonville Public Library.

Abel A. Bartley

OUR PRINCIPAL

PROFESSOR CHARLES D. BROOKS

I should like to extend sincere congratulations to the First Graduates of the New Stanton Senior High School. Certainly this represents a signal honor. No other class in the history of Stanton has had the privilege of graduating under such ideal conditions. This is an honor which should remain dear to you "From Here to Eternity." As you move further into adulthood, it is hoped that you will become integrated in community life and make contributions to its growth, which will bespeak the excellent opportunities afforded you.

In you shall be entrusted the responsibility of upholding the standards of leadership, scholarship and efficient performance of duty characteristic of Stanton graduates.

I commend Mr. I. E. Bryan and his Annual Staff for the diligent spirit shown in perfecting this publication.

MRS. G. C. BOWENS
Secretary

Secretary to Mr. Brooks, she is charming, efficient, and energetic.

From the Stanton High School Yearbook 1954. Courtesy of the Jacksonville Public Library.

From the Stanton High School Yearbook 1954. Courtesy of the Jacksonville Public Library.

From the Stanton High School Yearbook 1954. Courtesy of the Jacksonville Public Library.

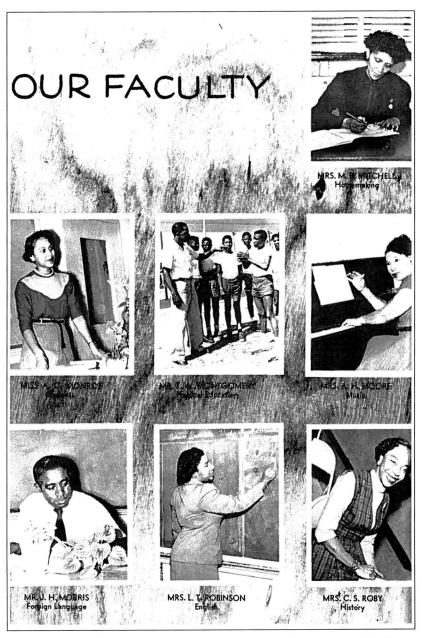

From the Stanton High School Yearbook 1954. Courtesy of the Jacksonville Public Library.

The picture at left features Floyd J. Anderson, a principal of "Old Stanton" during the 1930s and 1940s. This photograph appeared in the 1940 and 1941 yearbooks, which he personally autographed for one of his students. During his administration, Stanton's rigorous high academic standards grew as Stanton became a high school exclusively. In the photograph below is Principal Anderson, in the first row at far left, and faculty members in 1937. Many of the faculty pictured here continued to teach at Stanton far into the 1970s. Some went on to become principals and administrators at other local schools as well.

From the book *Stanton Campus History Series*. Courtesy of the Jacksonville Public Library.

Tolbert A. Jackson was a faculty member at Stanton in the 1940s and 1950s. He taught English but was also involved with music and band direction. He left a lasting impression on the school as the writer of the alma mater, the school song. He was often the advisor for the yearbook, and he started the school newspaper, the *Stantonian*. He is pictured here in a dedication page from the class of 1961.

This picture features I. Emerson Bryan, a faculty member who was a key contributor to the school's yearbooks and historical records as he served as a primary photographer for the school. He was the yearbook advisor from 1947 through the 1960s. Stanton's yearbooks had the distinction of being rated among the top high school annuals. He also served as chairman of Stanton's industrial arts department in the 1960s, known to be one of the best departments in the state.

From the book *Stanton Campus History Series*. Courtesy of the Jacksonville Public Library.

In the 1952–1953 school year, Jessie L. Terry served as the last principal of Stanton Senior High School, No. 101—now referred to as "Old Stanton" on Ashley Street. He had served since the late 1940s, following the administration of F. L. Anderson. Terry was noted for his democratic leadership style and relationships with his staff. He put emphasis on strong bodies, alert minds, and moral obligation to self, one's fellow man, and one's divine creator. He is pictured here in 1953.

From the book *Stanton Campus History Series*. Courtesy of the Jacksonville Public Library.

In 1953, the Stanton Senior High School name was transferred to its current location on Thirteenth Street and was renamed New Stanton Senior High School. Charles D. Brooks, pictured above in 1954, who had served as assistant principal of Stanton Senior High ("Old Stanton"), was the first principal of this new school until 1969. Known for wanting respect over popularity with the students, Brooks is remembered as a stern yet compassionate man, one who cared about his students. Brooks has stated he is most proud of the fact that many of the prominent businesspeople in the Jacksonville community completed school under his administration. Brooks believed in providing a good education to African American students during a time of segregation and inhumane treatment. One of his proudest moments as principal was in 1953, when the Florida Department of Education cited Stanton as one of the finest schools in the state. He is seen in the photograph below talking with a staff member in 1968.

From the book *Stanton Campus History Series*. Courtesy of the Jacksonville Public Library.

New Stanton High
School had two assistant
principals from 1953 to
1969, Charles F. James
and Elwood J. Banks
(pictured here in the
1950s). Banks was the
assistant principal up
through the 1960s. Banks
was also known as the
"Voice of the Blue Devils,"
as he was the play-by-play
announcer for all Stanton
football games and pep
rallies during this era.
Many students recall his
"mighty voice" over the
airwaves at such places as
the Durkeeville Ballpark
and the East-West Classic
at the Gator Bowl.

In the early 21st century, Thomas
Crompton Jr., a former mathematics
teacher at New Stanton, produced
an original book of memories
about the faculty and staff of New
Stanton from 1953 through 1969.
Full copies of this original book
may be found at the Jacksonville
Public Library–Downtown Branch
in the African American historical
section. Pictured here is a sample
page from this original book
featuring Crompton's photograph.
(Courtesy of Thomas Crompton Jr.)

From the book *Stanton Campus History Series*. Courtesy of the Jacksonville Public
Library.

Chapter Five

Disaccreditation, Delay, and Boycotts: Education in the Age of Chaos.

Duval County

By the mid-1960s, Jacksonville faced serious political, economic, educational, and racial issues. The local government was in flux as political leaders were arrested, public high schools were disaccredited, city services were in decline, and civil rights protestors were picketing downtown businesses. African Americans engaged in direct-action campaigns aimed at the businesses and institutions that continued to segregate and discriminate against blacks. To force the school district to address the racial inequities, the NAACP organized a controversial school boycott. Many of the problems that had surfaced during the 1950s demanded action. Jacksonville's leaders had put the economic and social welfare of the city in jeopardy by ignoring chronic concerns and yielding to expedient solutions to critical dilemmas. The city's educational problems were directly related to its political and racial problems. No single issue could be solved until city officials fixed the others.

During the 1960s, Jacksonville and Duval County suffered from a disjointed and chaotic governmental structure. The government's problems fed a general malaise, which permeated nearly every aspect of city life. Several problems shocked local residents and helped forge a movement to reform the government and improve the schools. Following a familiar pattern, Jacksonville had suffered a series of difficulties, which now pushed local residents to seek reform in local government. Since the 1880s, residents of Jacksonville and Duval County had been trying to create a government that provided accountability and served all citizens equally. Local politicians had proven incapable of efficiently governing the city. Elected officials found themselves in a protracted struggle with business interests that battled them on reform measures. A pattern of scandal and reform had characterized Duval County's political landscape since the 1880s.[1]

During the post-Civil War period, Jacksonville emerged as a major focal point of St. Johns River trade and commerce and also as one of Florida's most popular tourist destinations. As the tourist industry grew, the demands on local government increased. Jacksonville's urban center required resources and public facilities to feed the growing demand. Urban development required street lights, roads, sewage systems, and clean water sources. The city did not have enough money to fund these necessities. However, a number of moderately prosperous suburbs surrounded Jacksonville. These suburbs attracted people of means who could be taxed to underwrite the necessary improvements.[2]

The residents of these suburbs were reluctant to fund Jacksonville's urban development, even though their livelihood often depended on the tourists who visited Jacksonville. To raise the necessary funds to modernize city services, city leaders floated a bond. However, city officials could not raise enough money through bonds to fund all the needed improvements. Several local officials recommended annexation of profitable suburbs, abolition of existing governmental structures, and the creation of a consolidated government. However, at that time, local residents were not ready for such a change and rejected this plan.[3]

By the early 1880s, Jacksonville had more than 20,000 residents, but the government was still not functional. Jacksonville's population declined temporarily when many residents abandoned the city after a smallpox epidemic. In addition, Jacksonville had a serious fire problem, since the city refused to invest in fire equipment or pay adequate funds for a fire department. The result was a series of devastating fires, which had insurance agents threatening to stop insuring Jacksonville property. The tourist industry began to dry up as investors in Tampa, St. Augustine, and other cities built luxury hotels that attracted wealthy vacationers. Furthermore, the poor condition of Jacksonville's port hampered the city's progress. A sandbar at the mouth of the St. Johns River frequently blocked shipping, leaving ships locked on the river for weeks. The city's conservative leadership refused to fund necessary port improvements or dredging projects, which could have opened the city to more shipping.[4]

Jacksonville's leaders' refusal to act effectively paralyzed the city and hampered economic development. This stagnant government stymied economic growth and left the city in decline. Those in the business community refused to allow government to imperil the city. Colonel Jaquelin James (J. J.) Daniel, head of the Board of Trade, which was established in 1884, pushed the city to make the necessary changes to restart Jacksonville's economic growth. The Board of Trade, which evolved into the present-day Chamber of Commerce, helped firemen get better wages, paved streets, built sidewalks, and improved the river and port. The members also helped to achieve better relations with other parts of the city. Board members successfully bargained for better rail, telephone, and steamship rates for Jacksonville merchants. They sponsored beautification projects and supported improved community morality campaigns.[5]

The Board of Trade's activities did not end there. In 1885 Floridians wrote a new state constitution, which gave Jacksonville new powers over the suburbs to abolish boundaries and create a consolidated government. This allowed the local residents to vote out some of the more ineffective leaders and replace them with people more receptive to the business community. In 1887 a grand jury investigation into the local area found appalling conditions in Duval County. The investigative committee looked at schools, roads, and bridges. The members were especially critical of the educational facilities in the city. The schools had no sanitary or toilet facilities. Many of the schools were just wooden shacks. Bridges and roads had been neglected and were left in a deplorable state. Conditions in the African American community were the worst.[6]

The Board of Sanitary Trustees warned that Duval County needed to clean the city's marshes, garbage piles, and polluted waterways or the city could face an epidemic. Local officials ignored the warnings and refused to act. When a yellow fever epidemic hit the city in 1888, killing 427 of the 4,704 people living in

Jacksonville, the Board of Sanitary Trustees said, "We told you so." According to historian Richard Martin, "The disease killed a score of the city's most effective leaders, caused a decline in population, started a county-wide economic recession of several years, and marked the end of Jacksonville's domination of the tourist business in Florida."[7] Jacksonville's government was incapable of handling the city's problems. Local leaders depended on private enterprise and local citizens to make critical changes and deal with pressing problems. Local government had power only in Jacksonville, even though many of the problems required regional support. Many of the people who depended on the city for a livelihood resided in the county, and were unwilling to finance projects that benefited the city itself.[8]

Nevertheless, Jacksonville continued to have steady population growth but little coordinated development. The city never lived up to its potential because the government remained incapable of solving problems. From 1888 until 1917, local residents talked about reforming the government and annexing profitable parts of the suburbs, but with few results. In 1917 Jacksonville revised its charter and, between 1917 and 1931, the city repeatedly reformed the government, strengthening the power of the mayor; abolishing boards and commissions; creating an elected city council; and forming an elected commission. However, these changes were mostly cosmetic and the city government continued to disappoint local residents.[9]

In 1918 and 1923, proposals were floated by several organizations to abolish local government and create a consolidated city-county government. A 1931 scandal rocked the local government when a grand jury indicted seventy-five public officials. Among those indicted were school board members; a school superintendent of maintenance and building; a deputy sheriff; a former constable; and a number of justices of the peace. All were charged with malfeasance in office for accepting bribes. Local residents were shocked and once again saw reform as the answer.[10]

After several citizens appeared before city council and attempted to question spurious items in the local budget, council members used their allies and friends to shout them down. Those citizens who spoke out were furious and met to plan for other action. A new committee was established, which once again investigated ways to make government work better in Jacksonville. On September 2, 1931, a group of 150 prominent citizens met in the Seminole Hotel and formed the Better Government Association. Al C. Ulmer, a prominent real estate investor, headed the group. The Better Government Association launched an intensive investigation into city and county government. Not long after the association's members began their investigation, indictments were handed down. Once again government reform was in vogue in Jacksonville. Local residents voted to annex South Jacksonville, a community of 5,658 residents. After the excitement subsided, and with the disaster averted, the Better Government Association was dissolved.[11]

However, disaffection continued. In 1934 several people supported a state constitutional amendment which authorized consolidating city and county governments in Duval County. The amendment passed by large margins in both the city and the state. C. Daughtry Towers, a local lawyer who championed governmental reform, headed the City-County Consolidation League, which promoted consolidation. Towers and his organization recommended merging city and county tax assessment and collection under a single officer; creation of a unified legal department; reorganization and consolidation of county courts; consolidation of the local police and sheriff's departments; combining the city council and county commission into one administrative unit; and merging city and county jails, charities, accounting departments, engineering, and voter registration processes.[12]

Towers predicted that, "The merger will eliminate duplication of offices, and cost of local government will be reduced by approximately $500,000."[13] A plan was written and submitted to city and county officials, who went on record as favoring the proposal. The charter revisions were submitted to the state legislature where they were debated and substantially changed. The judiciary was to remain separate, the school superintendent was to remain an elected official, and the commission was expanded from three members who could appoint department heads, to five members with no appointment powers. Local citizenry rejected the revised plan. Then a well-organized anti-consolidation movement was organized to defeat the consolidation proposal. The opponents of consolidation planted suspicion about the proposal and those who supported it. Anti-consolidationists generated so much doubt that when the June 18, 1935, referendum was held, only 16,674 of the city's eligible 26,000 voters went to the polls. Even with this small participation, the results were decisive and the proposal was defeated 9,499 to 7,115.[14]

During the 1950s and early 1960s, Jacksonville's population expanded as migrants from every region of the country relocated to the city. The city experienced a building boom during the 1950s, which dramatically transformed the urban landscape and created a modern, progressive-looking city. The Jacksonville Chamber of Commerce hawked the city to potential investors as the Gateway to the New South. They especially marketed the St. Johns River as a playground to the boating and yachting set. However, they realized that the city still had serious problems. The schools were in a deplorable state, nearly thirty percent of the city was urban slums, and the government was racked with scandal. There was little chance that Jacksonville would attract investment until it fixed these problems.[15]

The 1960 census returns showed a city in decline. Jacksonville was rapidly losing its population base to its developing suburbs. In an effort to reverse this downturn, the business community reintroduced the notion of consolidation, or annexation. However, local citizens immediately rejected this solution, as annexation would have expanded a corrupt, ineffective, and dysfunctional local government into the suburbs. No one wanted Jacksonville's current government. Journalists who investigated Jacksonville's local scene immediately saw the problems with the government. A Memphis journalist remarked that Jacksonville was the only city with a city council and a city commission, each with its own divergent view of what was best for the city. African Americans and local government employees served as the deciding vote in the city.

They were constantly negotiating with the government for improved conditions, often to the detriment of the city at large.[16]

Measured against comparably sized cities, Jacksonville had the most full-time employees and the highest monthly payroll of any city in the nation. Each month, $1,499,616 was spent on city employees. These city employees represented a powerful voting block that had an interest in maintaining the status quo. The result was very little action, even when scandals rocked the government. In 1960 large amounts of money were embezzled from the Police Credit Union; in addition, funds were misused in the office of the County Clerk of Criminal Courts. Although there were efforts to push an annexation measure after these revelations, they did not get very far.[17]

Governmental problems seemed to undermine the tremendous progress Jacksonville had made in other areas. The so-called Jacksonville Story advertised the urban transformation which had hit the city. The story highlighted the tremendous physical revitalization of Jacksonville's downtown area. During the preceding years, Jacksonville had built a civic center, county courthouse, and city hall; beautified and expanded the port area; and reconstructed the skyline. The city also profited from the municipally owned power station. The Jacksonville Electric Authority provided the government's general fund with $169.4 million in additional revenue between 1946 and 1965.[18]

For Jacksonville city residents, annexation again seemed like the obvious answer to their problems. Jacksonville had to provide city services to a rapidly expanding metropolitan population of more than 500,000 from a local urbanized population of 200,000 people. More than 5,000 of the city workers lived in the county where they paid no city taxes. Therefore they had no voice in the governmental affairs of the city where they worked, and no tax obligation to the people who paid their salaries. A January 1963 referendum on annexation failed as county residents rejected the effort, even while city residents voted heavily in favor of the proposal.[19]

After the proposal failed, there was open talk about the prospect of Jacksonville's becoming a majority black city. The specter of having a black mayor of the city frightened many disengaged whites. By then African Americans made up forty-four percent of the local electorate. People with higher incomes and better education continued to flee the city. The reality that Jacksonville was growing poorer, darker, and less educated pushed many formerly undecided people to think about radical proposals. In November 1964 county residents once again rejected an annexation proposal while city residents once again supported the measure.[20]

During the period of 1965 through 1966, local television stations worked to influence public opinion in the direction of consolidation. Claude Yates, a Jacksonville business executive, brought community leaders together and drew up a consolidation proposal. Yates gained critical support from Bill Groves, the WJXT TV News and Public Affairs director. WJXT was the most-watched local station in the area. The push from the local media, coupled with the scandals in local government, helped move public opinion in favor of major governmental reform. A commission was put together to study the problem and offer recommendations. The study commission issued its recommendations in January 1967 in a published document, *Blueprint for Improvement*. In this document they recommended abolishing the existing structures and consolidating city and county government. They also called for a strong mayoral position with a city council elected from wards and also with at-large seats. Once published, this 179-page document was made available to the general public.[21]

There was considerable debate over the proposal, with almost immediate opposition. Several people disagreed with the idea of a strong mayoral position. Others opposed consolidation, and several voiced concern about the loss of elected officials. Some were against the proposal because they had benefited from the old system. African Americans opposed it because they saw it as a scheme to undermine blacks' political aspirations. However, as more people watched the deteriorating situation, they began to support the proposal. The fear of changing the governmental structure was eventually outweighed by the need for a more efficient and effective government. Jacksonville was growing up and it needed a mature, competent government to reach its potential.

Slowly, pro-consolidationist forces were able to seize the day and create a multi-racial coalition of concerned citizens to support the change in governmental structure. Public opinion also began to congeal around the idea that the present structure of government was unhealthy. The need for government reform was so obvious to anyone who had suffered under the old system that, by the time of the election, the results were anti-climactic. On August 8, 1967, 81,457 local residents went to the polls to vote on the consolidation measure. The voters overwhelmingly supported consolidation by almost a 2 to 1 margin, with 52,482 voting for it and 28,873 voting against it. This vote created the largest city in the United States. Consolidation opened new opportunities for taxing, and also helped forge county-wide planning and strategy.[22]

With the government crisis solved, city officials now turned their attention to the school crisis. No one was shocked when, on November 30, 1964, the Southern Association of Colleges and Schools (SACS) voted to revoke accreditation from Jacksonville's fifteen public high schools. For nearly a decade the organization had been warning and threatening Duval County about its deteriorating school situation. The primary reason for their decision was the low level of spending on schools. The lack of funds had led to inadequate upkeep of buildings; insufficient textbooks and facilities; and a serious lack of administrative planning and organization. The disaccreditation crisis awakened many local residents from their apathy and caused them to take these long-neglected educational issues seriously.[23]

The Florida Commission of SACS had warned Duval County residents that they needed to spend more on education. When their warnings were ignored, SACS recommended that the fifteen public schools in Duval County be disaccredited. SACS' full committee met in Louisville, Kentucky, in November to consider the recommendation. Jacksonville's business and political leaders traveled to the meeting and made an impassioned plea to save the schools, but their arguments were to no avail. The association voted to remove accreditation from the schools.[24]

Though the basic problem with Jacksonville's schools revolved around financing, that issue was tied to social policies that had undermined efforts to reform education. Since the 1950s, Jacksonville had been facing a calamity that local officials chose to ignore. Jacksonville's population had increased rapidly during the 1950s and early 1960s. Although the central city was not growing as quickly, other parts of the community were exploding. The city's schools were becoming overcrowded, but local residents were more interested in protecting a property tax assessment system that artificially deflated the value of property, creating limited revenue for school spending.[25]

By the mid-1960s, twenty-one percent of Duval County's population was made up of school-aged children. Jacksonville had the largest youth population in Florida when compared with Florida's nine other largest cities. However, Jacksonville's citizens refused to adequately fund their schools. Jacksonville's residents had a disposable income of $1,817 per capita in 1961, which was the fifth highest in the state. Nevertheless, the per-pupil spending was only $253.04, the lowest in the state. Also, many teachers taught subjects they were not qualified for. Teachers in Duval County faced deplorable conditions, including overcrowded classrooms; unpaid overtime for extracurricular activities; no designated school time for preparation and grading; and inadequate instructional material and equipment. Added to these problems were the low wages teachers received. Duval County had the lowest teacher salaries in the state. Seventy-five percent of the male teachers, who made up twenty-five percent of the teaching force, had to work a second job just to sustain their families. As a result, the county school system had a high teacher turnover rate.[26]

The low level of spending was part of a general neglect of education in the state. Duval County students faced large classes with high student-teacher ratios. The equipment used in the classrooms was generally outdated and of poor quality. Students often had to share or go without textbooks. There were few laboratories and limited audio visual equipment, and the libraries were under-staffed, underfunded, and under-resourced. No one was really shocked to learn that Duval County had one of the state's highest dropout rates. Only sixty percent of the county's seventh graders graduated from high school. Students who took the college placement exam often did worse than the rest of the state. Educational problems in the white community were magnified in the African American community.[27]

Under Florida's constitution, everyone received a $5,000 homestead exemption, meaning that the first $5,000 of assessed value on all homesteads was exempt from taxes. The law assumed that the property would be assessed at fair market value. However, to curry favor with voters, many of Florida's counties, including Duval, did not assess their properties at full value. A 1955 study of property assessments in Duval County found that properties were being assessed at an average of 41.46 percent of true value. In 1964 the Duval County Taxpayers Association put the value at 30.52 percent. This low assessment, coupled with the homestead exemption, practically eliminated property taxes for most of Duval County's homeowners.[28]

For example, a $15,000 home assessed at 30 percent of value, or $4,500, escaped property taxes altogether. The Duval County Taxpayers Association estimated that 60,000 of the 93,500 homesteads in Duval County were totally exempt from property taxes. The remaining properties were being taxed at high millage rates to bring in the absolute minimum funds necessary to run the schools and other county agencies. State law capped school tax millage at 20 mils for schools. That meant that only $20 for every $1,000 of assessed value could be used for education. The lower the assessment of property values, the less money officials had to fund schools. This was the situation that had led to the decision of the SACS to remove accreditation from the county's schools.[29]

Several ad hoc committees attempted to solve the tax problem. However, they were all doomed to failure because few people were interested in proposals which raised their taxes. In 1964 school board member Ray David challenged incumbent tax assessor

Ralph N. Walter for the Democratic candidacy. David argued that the county had to expand the tax burden by increasing the assessment ratio. He was vehemently attacked by Walter, who ran newspaper ads claiming that David was trying to abolish the homestead exemption. Walter's arguments swayed the electorate, who were not interested in having their homes taken off the homestead exemption list. Walter swamped David in the primary election and then easily defeated his Republican opponent.[30]

In October 1963 a group of concerned local citizens formed a new organization called the Taxpayers Association. Prime F. Osborne, a local railroad executive, headed the group, which was mainly a coalition of businessmen and "good government" types. The group had grown concerned about the impending loss of accreditation by the schools due to a lack of funding. They wanted to develop a more equitable taxing system to provide the school system with more funds. They hoped to use the courts to force the county officials to fairly assess property values. They began their work by engaging in a thorough investigation of county assessment ratios. After completing their work, they filed suit against Walter, accusing him of violating state law by not assessing property at a "just valuation."[31]

The case went to court in December 1964 before Circuit Judge William Durden, who listened carefully to the arguments before delivering a landmark ruling in January 1965. Durden ruled that Walter had acted illegally by "systematically, deliberately, and intentionally under assessing real and personal property at a steadily decreasing ratio of its true value."[32] He ordered that property be assessed at full cash value. This case transformed the way taxes were assessed in the state thereafter.

In March 1965, the Duval County School Board funded an exhaustive 336-page study compiled by the Division of Surveys and Field Services of George Peabody College of Teachers. This so-called Peabody Report made extensive use of interviews, school visits, and a mountain of printed data to make its conclusions. The report carefully outlined the problems facing the Duval County Public School System, which it blamed directly on the funding crisis. The writers of the report recommended a complete overhaul of the tax system. The report also implicated the dysfunctional government in the school crisis. It mentioned the lack of home rule, the overabundance of elected officials, the diffused authority, and the independent Budget Commission.[33]

The Peabody Report also placed blame on the school system, which was dominated by the powerful Jacksonville political machine. The schools had become too embroiled in the political process. There were charges of solicitations for campaign funds by school personnel, rebates for teacher appointments, politically motivated personnel assignments, and duplicity in school construction. The report concluded that, "It would appear, while the degree of validity is indeterminable, that the school system has not been free of entanglements with and interference from the political community."[34]

The Peabody Report recommended that the 1964-1965 Duval County school budget be increased from $33.5 million to well over $50 million. Reevaluation of property created a huge local tax base. Due to the reassessment of taxable property, Duval County's tax base rose from $523 million to $1.66 billion. The number of homes totally exempt from property taxes was reduced from 63,715 to 15,179. With increased funding, the school accreditation crisis could be solved.[35]

By 1964 Duval County's public school system had made remarkably little progress toward integration. African American children were still locked in separate and unequal schools, often taught by teachers who were underqualified for their positions. One of the most damaging charges was the claim of job buying. There was evidence that teachers were buying their jobs by offering a kickback to officials for job consideration. African American leaders constantly warned school officials that they would not allow these horrific conditions to continue without a response. The NAACP, which had filed the original case challenging segregation, was under the leadership of Rutledge Pearson, an eighth-grade school teacher. Because of his teaching position, Pearson was somewhat limited in what actions he could pursue. Pearson understood the precarious position he was in, so he relied on other civil rights entities to lead the efforts.

The Ministerial Alliance, under the leadership of James Dailey, allied itself with the NAACP and took the lead in pressing local officials to improve conditions. The Citizens Committee for Better Education, an African American political action organization, was also instrumental in coming up with solutions to Jacksonville's educational problems. Just a few months earlier the Southern Association of Colleges and Schools had taken accreditation from all fifteen of Jacksonville's local high schools. Dailey and his cohorts worked closely with Pearson on an effort that would presumably demonstrate the frustration local African American residents felt.

They knew that Jacksonville had recently been the scene of ugly racial conflicts as NAACP-sponsored demonstrations turned violent. Local officials reacted with a hard hand to stop the demonstrations, which were timed to embarrass longtime mayor William Haydon Burns's bid for the Florida governor's office. Despite the demonstrations and the violence they produced, Burns won a lopsided victory. Burns later actually used the disturbances to bolster his leadership credentials.[36]

With these recent conflicts in mind, the NAACP and the Ministerial Alliance searched for a response. Jacksonville's African American community was fed up with the school board's empty promises of action on their complaints. As the school board contemplated opening the newest school on Moncrief Road, they envisioned it being used by sixth, seventh, and eighth graders. The school was scheduled to be opened on December 7, 1964. African Americans wanted it reserved for black high school students, but school board officials ignored their demands. Dr. Andrew Robinson, a thirty-five-year-old Jacksonville native who had graduated from Florida A&M University and had a PhD from Columbia University, was assigned as the new school's principal. The 2,000-student-capacity school was built at a cost of $2 million and was modeled on the new Fletcher High School in the Beaches community. The Moncrief Road school had a trade and industrial area, which Fletcher did not have. When it opened, this new school was referred to simply as School No. 165.[37]

In several cities of the North and South, frustrated parents had used school boycotts to protest unpopular school actions. On December 7, 1964, 17,000 of the 31,000 African American students in Jacksonville stayed away from school in a well-coordinated boycott of local schools. The students were protesting the overcrowded conditions. This was an NAACP-inspired response to the lack of action on the part of the school board.[38]

The school boycott shocked local residents and divided the African American community. Dr. Martin Luther King had praised boycotts in other areas but many believed that it was wrong for students to miss class time. The Duval County school boycott lasted two days and cost the school system an estimated $135,000. Rutledge Pearson and Wendell Holmes were the organizers of the school boycott. They had been vocal supporters of the disaccreditation decision by SACS and wanted to do something bold to get the school board's attention. According to Pearson, the boycott was aimed "at calling official notice to some nine listed inequities in the school setup, but also as a protest against official apathy concerning Negro problems generally." Wendell Holmes called the boycott because of the school board's recalcitrance and its failure to address African American concerns.[39]

The boycott became a controversial issue in the African American community. Several black leaders expressed outrage at the thought of keeping children out of school. Frank Hampton, a longtime activist, opposed the boycott. Though he sympathized with the cause, he said, "Some of these kids should be in school 24 hours a day. And some of those who advise them to stay out should be in school, too." Another African American called the boycott, "an evil against the children," because of the loss of school money. "We have lost between $25,000 and $30,000 from what was a poor budget already."[40]

Others in the African American community supported the boycott and understood its significance. Margaret Wright, the Parent Teachers Association president at an African American elementary school, complained, "I once made 4,000 candied apples in one week to buy equipment . . . which the county should have provided." She also recounted how she begged in the neighborhood for $542 to build a sidewalk for the school. She kept her children out of school and urged others to do the same. Wright referred to her decision as "a silent protest." She saw the boycott as a just response to an intolerable situation.[41]

The school board pressured Pearson and others to end the boycott. Dr. Herman Fricke, chairman of the SACS Florida Committee that had first recommended that Duval schools lose accreditation, blasted boycott leaders for what he saw as exploitation of students. He called boycott organizers irresponsible and accused them of making a bad situation worse. He estimated that each $5,000 lost would cost one teacher's job. Although his organization reportedly found no evidence to support the African American community leaders' claims of discrimination in allocating funds for schools, Fricke still recommended that the Duval County School System lose its accreditation.[42]

Wendell Holmes responded by asserting that segregation itself produced inequalities. He expressed shock that Fricke's committee found no inequities in the system. "We would welcome the opportunity to meet with any officials or professional groups to discuss these matters," declared Holmes, "for we know that we can responsibly substantiate these claims." Pearson said the boycott was fair play because Jacksonville's African American high schools had met accreditation standards. In speaking to whites about the loss of accreditation, Pearson said, "Now you know how it feels." On December 10, 1964, the boycott ended. Since the Florida Minimum Foundation Program paid $2.11 a day for each child, the three-day boycott cost Duval County at least $75,000.[43]

The school board reacted with outrage toward the boycott. The board hounded Pearson and attempted to fire him from his teaching job. When this failed, board members saw to it that both Pearson and Holmes were arrested and charged with contributing to the delinquency of a minor. The charges did not stick as the NAACP sent counsel to represent the men. As the era closed, the

NAACP had made several inroads into the legalized discrimination of the local school system. Though the numbers were still very low, African Americans had made the point that after more than ten years, they were not tired.

Notes

1 Richard Martin, *Consolidation: Jacksonville; Duval County: The Dynamics of Urban Political Reform* (Jacksonville: Crawford Publishing Company, 1968), 17.
2 Ibid., 5-6.
3 Ibid.
4 Ibid., 9-10.
5 Ibid., 10.
6 Ibid., 11.
7 Ibid., 12
8 Ibid.
9 Ibid., 17.
10 Ibid.
11 Ibid., 16-17.
12 Ibid., 18.
13 Ibid., 19.
14 Ibid., 19-21.
15 Ibid., 41-43.
16 Ibid., 44.
17 Ibid., 44-45.
18 Ibid.
19 Ibid., 45.
20 Ibid., 46.
21 Ibid., 96.

22 Abel Bartley, *Keeping the Faith: Race Politics and Social Development in Jacksonville, Florida 1940-1970* (Westport: Greenwood Press, 2000), 147; *Florida Times-Union,* August 9, 1967; "A Cure for City Blight–The Jacksonville Story," *US News and World Report,* January 3, 1972, 25.

23 Damon Miller, "Jacksonville Consolidation: The Process of Metropolitan Reform" (senior thesis, Princeton University, 1968), 45.

24 Ibid., 49.

25 Ibid., 45.

26 Ibid., 46; James B. Crooks, "Jacksonville Before Consolidation," *Florida Historical Quarterly,* vol. LXXVII, no. 2, Fall 1998, 156.

27 Crooks, "Jacksonville Before Consolidation," 152-155.

28 Miller, "Jacksonville Consolidation," 46.

29 Ibid., 47.

30 Ibid., 47-48.

31 Ibid., 48; Crooks, "Jacksonville Before Consolidation," 156.

32 *Florida Times-Union,* June 6, 1965.

33 Miller, "Jacksonville Consolidation," 50.

34 Ibid., 49; *Duval County Public Schools A Survey Report: Division of Surveys and Field Services* (George Peabody College for Teachers, Nashville, Tennessee, 1965), 10-11.

35 Miller, "Jacksonville Consolidation," 51.

36 Irvin D. S. Winsboro, *Old South, New South, or Down South?: Florida and the Modern Civil Rights Movement* (Morgantown: University of West Virginia Press, 2009), 188-192.

37 Judith Poppell, "The Desegregation of a Historically Black High School in Jacksonville, Florida." (PhD diss., University of North Florida, 1988), 91-93.

38 *New York Times,* December 9, 1964.

39 *Pittsburgh Courier,* December 19, 1964.

40 *Jacksonville Journal,* December 8, 1964.

41 *Jacksonville Journal,* December 10, 1964; *Pittsburgh Courier,* December 19,1964.

42 *Jacksonville Journal,* December 10, 1964.

43 Ibid.; *Pittsburgh Courier,* December 19, 1964; *Jacksonville Journal,* December 10, 1964.

Chapter Six

No Time for Delay: The 1970s and the
Move Toward Full Integration

The late 1960s and early 1970s were periods of flux for those involved in school desegregation suits. The political and legal landscape shifted abruptly as the courts continuously refined their school desegregation opinions and increased pressure on local school boards to completely desegregate their systems. Meanwhile, a political shift fueled a retreat by federal officials on civil rights issues as Richard Nixon-inspired conservatism replaced the liberalism of the John F. Kennedy and Lyndon B. Johnson eras. The 1960s began with the Kennedy administration compelling southern universities to integrate. This was followed by the period between 1965 and 1968, when the Johnson administration pressured school districts to comply with federal court-ordered school desegregation rulings. During the Johnson administration, the Justice Department utilized lawsuits, sanctions, and threats of shutting off federal funding to push recalcitrant school districts to move forward with the process of desegregation. Many people were impressed with the way the Johnson administration compelled school districts to change their operations. One commentator observed, "Just a few years of intensive enforcement was enough to transform Southern school districts and to create much stricter and clearer desegregation standards."[1] In Duval County, Florida, the promise of change never equated with the reality of black life. Duval County's school officials proved to be savvy foes who worked effectively to maintain segregation despite federal pressure.

With support from President Johnson, school integration became a federal priority as the government pushed the implementation of the *Brown* decision. These efforts were greatly improved when, over boisterous Southern objections, President Johnson nominated Thurgood Marshall, the former lead counsel of the NAACP and the architect of the winning strategy in the *Brown* case, for the high court on June 13, 1967. A heated debate followed the nomination as Marshall was thoroughly scrutinized by conservatives, racists, and Republican groups, all of whom expressed objections to his appointment. Marshall was confirmed on August 30, 1967, with a 69-11 vote. The seventy-eight days between the nomination and Senate confirmation was an unusually long period and allowed his opponents time to express their concerns. "It was a much longer process than usual because the Southern senators, again were still out to embarrass the nominee." Stephen Carter noted, "When a black nominee is controversial, the battles seem far more bitter than when the controversial candidate happens to be white."[2] Marshall's appointment was a major victory for African Americans, who now had a symbolic representative on the nation's highest court. Liberal forces cheered these efforts, while conservatives blasted the federal government for overstepping its bounds and interfering with local issues. Angry Southern politicians led an exodus of white Southerners from the Democratic Party and into the Republican Party, where they pushed an increasingly conservative agenda that deemphasized social justice issues and championed limited government. During the 1968 presidential contest, racial issues once again emerged as a point of contention between the two parties.[3]

Many Americans saw 1968 as a transformative year which rearranged the nation's political and racial landscape. The tragic events of that year helped usher in a conservative era that continues to reverberate throughout our society. As *Time* magazine noted:

Nineteen sixty-eight had the vibrations of an earthquake about it. America shuddered. History cracked open: bats came flapping out, dark surprises. American culture and politics ventured into dangerous and experimental regions: uplands of new enlightenments, some people thought, and quagmires of the id. The year was pivotal and messy. It produced vivid theater. It reverberates still in the American mind.

Nineteen sixty-eight was tragedy and horrific entertainment: deaths of heroes, uprisings, suppressions, the end of dreams, blood in the streets of Chicago and Paris and Saigon, and at last, at Christmastime, man for the first time floating around the moon.[4]

With the Vietnam War straining the financial and social foundations of the nation, many were still shocked when President Johnson announced that he would not seek a second term as president. His announcement closed the door on the era of hope generated by his ambitious War on Poverty and emphasis on civil rights. The massive transformation of the federal government begun by President Franklin Roosevelt and his New Deal of the 1930s was over, as the conservative backlash once again impacted black rights just as it had done one hundred years earlier. On April 4, Dr. Martin Luther King Jr. was assassinated in Memphis, Tennessee. His death symbolically ended the civil rights era and signaled the period of retreat on civil rights by federal authorities. On June 6, Robert Kennedy was assassinated in Los Angeles, California. His death ended America's fascination with Camelot and the idealism of the Kennedy years. The Kennedys were perceived as champions of the poor and oppressed. With the death of Bobby Kennedy, many wondered who would take up the progressive mantle.

Republican presidential candidate Richard Nixon pounced on the opportunity to capture Southern votes. Nixon felt that he could take advantage of the chaos caused by the many social justice movements. He formed an unlikely alliance with conservative South Carolina senator Strom Thurmond, the former Dixiecrat candidate, to capture the disaffected white Southerners who had once voted for the Democratic Party. Nixon saw a coming revolt of Southern politicians. He met with frightened Southern Republicans on August 6, 1968, in a hotel on Miami Beach to assure them that, if elected, his administration would oppose forced busing and would support freedom of choice plans, a favored delaying tactic used by Southern school districts. Evidence clearly showed that freedom of choice plans did not work because white parents refused to send their children to black schools and African American parents were afraid to send their children to white schools. Finally, Nixon assured them that he would not cut off federal funds to school districts that refused to desegregate.[5]

Nixon saw school integration as a political issue he could manipulate to his advantage. He straddled the fence on school integration, arguing, "I believe that the decision was a correct one, but while the decision dealt with segregation and said that we would not have segregation, when you go beyond that and say that it's the responsibility of the federal government, and the federal courts, to, in effect, act as local school districts in determining how we carry that out, and then to use the power of the Federal Treasury, to withhold funds or give funds in order to carry it out, then I think we are going too far."[6] As Richard Kluger wrote, "Nobody could mistake Richard Nixon for a friend of America's people of color. . . Toward the hopes of African Americans, Nixon generally turned a cold shoulder." Early in his administration Nixon ordered that desegregation plans be, "developed in method and content in such a manner as to be inoffensive to the people of South Carolina"–and every other Southern State.[7]

After 1968 federal government support for school integration slowed significantly as President Nixon took office highlighting the white backlash against the perceived gains of African Americans in the civil rights era. Ignoring the lack of progress on school desegregation fifteen years after the *Brown II* decision, Nixon argued that the process was going "too far, too fast" and promised that his administration would do what it could to slow it down. Nixon told reporters in a news conference, "There are those who want instant integration and those who want segregation forever. I believe that we need to have a middle course between those two extremes." This recalcitrance helped reenergize controversial politicians, such as George Wallace of Alabama, who engaged in purely racial politicking which emphasized opposition to school integration. Wallace courted conservative whites frightful that their children would be subjected to "ghetto conditions" as they rode school buses. The change in tone from the federal government encouraged those who wanted to resist integration. Though President Nixon publicly supported integration, he was not above using racial issues to court Southern support. Therefore, the late 1960s were a period of retreat on school integration by the federal government. Nevertheless, in Jacksonville, this period opened a season of progress unlike any other seen before for school desegregation.[8]

In 1969 the Supreme Court entered a new era as Warren Burger, a "conscious conservative," replaced liberal Earl Warren as chief justice. Burger, a Nixon appointee, was supposed to usher in a new age and direction for the high court. Nixon hoped that efforts to integrate school districts would slow with this change in leadership. He clearly wanted to set a new conservative tone on all issues, especially racial ones, by promoting Burger. This could best be accomplished by ending the nearly twenty-year liberal domination of the high court established by the Democratic administrations of the 1930s. Taken as a whole, Nixon's appointments to the Supreme Court were expected to set a different tenor from that of the 1950s and 1960s Warren Court. Harry Blackmun, who joined the high court on June 9, 1970, was considered a credentialed conservative. However, during his twenty-four years on the court, he shifted to the left and authored some of the most famous liberal decisions, including the controversial *Roe v. Wade* decision legalizing abortion.[9]

Lewis Powell, who joined the high court on January 7, 1972, was also considered a conservative, but became one of the court's most notorious centrists during his term. He delivered the deciding vote in the controversial 1978 *Regents of the University of California v. Bakke* case, which outlawed quotas but maintained the principle of affirmative action, allowing race to be used as a factor in making decisions for college admissions. Both men were considered enlightened moderates who wanted to enforce the law. However, William Rehnquist was an unapologetic conservative who had initially opposed the court's position in the *Brown* case. He had written a controversial memo to Justice Robert Jackson arguing in favor of maintaining *Plessy* when he was a young intern working for the high court. According to *Time* magazine, "In the memo, he had argued that the separate but equal doctrine laid down by the Supreme Court in 1896 was 'right and should be reaffirmed.'" Rehnquist wrote, "Appellants seek to convince the Court of the moral wrongness of the treatment they are receiving. I would submit that this is a question the Court need never reach. . . . If this court, because its members individually are 'liberals' and dislike segregation, now chooses to strike it down, it differs from the McReynolds court only in the kinds of litigants it favors and the kinds of special claims it protects."[10] Rehnquist joined the Supreme Court on January 7, 1972. He anchored a conservative block on the court that dominated much of the last two decades of the 20th century and significantly slowed progress on school equity issues. In 1986 President Ronald Reagan appointed Rehnquist chief justice of the Supreme Court, where he continued to serve as a conservative bulwark until his retirement on September 3, 2005. Despite its conservative bent, the court continued to speak with one voice on school desegregation matters. The process had to go forward and the delays had to end.[11]

Although the Nixon administration demonstrated an unwillingness to pressure school districts to make bold moves toward desegregation, and actually encouraged resistance to school busing, the courts held their ground. Nixon told reporters, "I do not believe that bussing to achieve racial balance is in the interests of better education." He went on to say that his administration would not use busing to integrate schools that were, "segregated not by law but by housing patterns." Though Nixon was willing to delay integration, the courts were unwilling to accept delays. When the Burger court made its decision in the 1969 *Alexander v. Holmes County (Mississippi) Board of Education* case, the justices defined the term "deliberate speed." This case involved an appeals court allowing a Mississippi school district more time to implement a desegregation plan. "The Court made it clear that the deliberate part of that phase had expired . . . they held that the obligation of every school district is to terminate dual school systems at once and to operate now and hereafter only unitary schools." On December 1, 1969, the United States Court of Appeals rendered its decision in the *Singleton v. Jackson* case. Following the dictates of the U.S. Supreme Court in the *Alexander v. Holmes County (Mississippi) Board of Education* case, the federal courts ruled that school districts had to begin operating unitary systems immediately, ending the numerous delaying tactics used by local school boards. The courts said that, "converting to a unitary system (involves) basically the merger of faculty and staff, students, transportation, services, athletics, and other extra-curricular school activities." Therefore, after more than fifteen years, the school districts had to desegregate.[12]

This renewed action by the courts inspired the NAACP to push the courts in Duval County to move forward. The court of appeals directed that the conversion to a unitary system take place in two steps. The first step had to be accomplished by February 1, 1970. It involved the desegregation of faculty and other staff so that the ratio of African American to white teachers in the schools was thirty percent to seventy percent. The second step involved creating student attendance plans that merged student attendance bodies into a unitary system by the beginning of the 1970 fall term. On December 30, 1969, Judge William A. McRae ordered the reassignment of teachers and staff to achieve a ratio of seventy percent to thirty percent white to African American in each Duval County school. In a later decision, he ordered the University of Miami Desegregation Center to review the school board's plan and determine the best course of action.[13]

On August 4, 1970, Judge McRae announced that the school board had to first desegregate the twenty-seven African American schools to reach unitary status. On August 6, he ordered the desegregation of every African American elementary school with an attendance zone next to a predominantly white school. They were to use pairing and clustering techniques previously approved by the court of appeals to accomplish this goal. However, Judge McRae's order ignored the eighteen African American schools in the city's core.[14]

The school board appealed the decision to the Fifth Circuit Court of Appeals. The plaintiffs counter-appealed, asking that the court apply the same integration techniques to the eighteen inner-city African American schools not covered by the previous order. While the appeals were pending, the Supreme Court rendered its decision in the *Swann v. Charlotte-Mecklenberg* case. This case involved the school system serving Charlotte, North Carolina, which was the largest city in North Carolina. The Charlotte-Mecklenburg School System, which included the city of Charlotte, had more than 84,000 students in 107 schools during the 1968-1969 school year. Approximately twenty-nine percent, or 24,000, of the students were African Americans, of whom about 14,000 attended twenty-one schools that were at least ninety-nine percent black.[15]

At the commencement of this litigation, the school district was being run under a desegregation plan approved by the district court in 1965. The surrounding Mecklenburg County made it the largest school district in the state, with a twenty-nine percent African American enrollment. African American parents sued, arguing that the school district had not actually desegregated. The district court drafted a comprehensive plan which called for pairing of schools, gerrymandering of school districts, and increased busing to integrate the schools. In April 1971 the U.S. Supreme Court demanded the plan be implemented. They argued that neighborhood schools were not sacrosanct. The high court stated that strange, awkward, and inconvenient remedies might be required to eliminate the vestiges of school segregation. They went on to argue that the opposition to school busing was a red herring, especially when one considered that forty percent of all school-age children were already being bused. The opposition to busing was essentially an opposition to integration.[16]

The courts, seemingly tired of the constant delays, ordered the immediate integration of public schools. The decision mandated the elimination of dual school systems and ordered school districts to establish unitary systems at once. The Supreme Court reiterated its pronouncement in *Green v. County School Board* that, "The burden on a school board today is to come forward with a plan which promises realistically to work . . . now . . . until it is clear that state-imposed segregation has been completely removed and racial discrimination is eliminated root and branch."[17] The *Green* decision was important because the courts ordered that the school district act immediately to formulate a plan which had neither black nor white schools, just simply schools.[18]

The *Charlotte-Mecklenberg* case made it clear that the courts would not allow any one-race schools in a unitary system unless the schools could "satisfy the court that their racial composition is not the result of present or past discriminatory action." The courts also made it clear that, in a school district like Duval County which had a history of racial segregation, the presumption would be against the legitimacy of substantially one-race schools. In other words, the courts would not take the school board's word for it; the board had to prove the segregation was a result of circumstances outside of its control.[19]

The Jacksonville NAACP immediately went back to the courts to seek relief after lawyers read the *Mecklenburg County* decision. With city-county consolidation in 1967, Duval County's school system became the thirteenth largest school district in the nation. After city-county consolidation, Jacksonville, with 840 square miles of area, was the largest city in America. It was now two-thirds the size of Rhode Island. Jacksonville also had a long, ugly history of racial discord. In addition, most of the African Americans were centralized in and around the urban core.[20]

During the 1970-1971 school term, the Duval County Public School System had 122,549 students, of whom approximately seventy-two percent were white and twenty-eight percent were African American. The school system consisted of one hundred elementary schools, twenty-two junior high schools, one junior-senior high school, thirteen senior high schools, and one technical high school. There were eighteen schools identified as African American. They consisted of twelve elementary schools, four junior high schools, and two senior high schools.[21]

All- or nearly all-African American schools housed fifty-four percent of the African American elementary and junior high school students more than ten years after the *Mims v. Duval County School Board* case mandated the clustering of some schools in order to complete the desegregation process. The African American high schools still educated fifty-seven percent of the African American high school students. Almost all of the eighteen African American schools were located in the core city; none was in or near white areas. There was no way to integrate the African American students into white schools, or to get white students into the African American schools, without transporting some students to these schools and some away from them. Therefore, from the beginning, busing was going to have to be a part of any legitimate integration plan in Jacksonville.[22]

Everyone knew that the eighteen core-city African American schools were the remnants of the segregated system of the past. The *Charlotte-Mecklenburg* case demanded that these schools and their students be integrated, through busing, into outlying white areas. School Superintendent Dr. Cecil B. Hardesty and NAACP lawyers met in Atlanta with members of the court of appeals to work out a mutual agreement that would settle the remaining issues. The group laid the foundation for an agreement. However, when the parties returned to Jacksonville to finalize the details, the settlement fell apart and the two sides, who could not agree on a student assignment plan, returned to court. Before reviewing the case, all sides agreed that it was important that the courts study the school system to understand the complexities of the Duval situation.[23]

At the hearing, the school board presented its desegregation plan to the court. The plan was actually three plans combined into one. The school board looked at the different levels of education and came up with a different formula for each level. The elementary school plan called for the clustering and pairing of schools to produce integration. Both sides agreed that the school board plan desegregated every school in the system. Each elementary school would have an African American student body of between twenty-four and thirty-four percent.[24]

The school board's plan called for two groups of clusters. They were identified as Group A and Group B. Both the school system and the NAACP wanted fair integration with the least amount of transportation possible. The clustering plans were written with this in mind. Group A consisted of eight clusters, each including from three to six schools, and providing schooling for grades one to six. Group B consisted of twelve clusters with three to seven schools each. It differed from Group A in that it involved grades one to five only and called for the creation of sixth grade centers. All sixth graders would be educated in these schools which were located in predominantly African American neighborhoods. White students would be bused to African American areas during that year of school.[25]

The NAACP had no problem with Group A clusterings, especially since they mirrored the clusterings from Judge William McRae's August 6, 1970, order. The school board's plan had actually gone further than Judge McRae's plan. The school board's plan integrated more schools than any previous plan and made the ratio of African Americans to whites more equitable. By increasing the number of schools clustered, the board was able to integrate even more students and improve the ratio of students. For example, under Judge McRae's plan, North Shore and Long Beach Elementary Schools were clustered, creating a school with 646 whites and 799 African Americans. However, under the board's plan, Beulah Beal, Lola Culver, and Louis Sheffield were also clustered with North Shore, creating a school that was approximately seventy percent white and thirty percent African American.[26]

The NAACP's objections to the school board's plan centered on the Group B clusters. NAACP lawyers argued that it was unfair to ask African American students to ride on buses for grades one through five, while white children rode the bus only for grade six. They referred to the burden as "unconscionable if not unconstitutional." The NAACP lawyers argued that the busing burden should be shared equally between African American and white children, and if they were closing African American schools, they ought to close white schools as well. However, school board officials argued that this would be a harsh decision, because the African American schools were in such poor condition many of them were not worth saving. Before the integration process started, there had been little concern about what condition the schools that African American children attended were in. Also, there was the practical problem of getting the ratios necessary, with only about thirty percent of the system's students being African American and seventy percent being white. The school system's most serious problem was that there were not enough African American students at white schools. They argued that closing some of the African American schools and shipping the students to predominantly white schools was the best way to solve this problem.[27]

The school board's proposal called for closing schools in lower-income African American areas and busing those students to predominantly white schools in an attempt to get a seventy percent to thirty percent white to African American ratio at each school. According to school board officials, the schools designated for closing all had major environmental or structural problems that made saving them unreasonable. The schools were deemed either too dangerous or too unhealthy for white children, even though they had been all right for African American children during segregation. The NAACP agreed that some of the schools needed to be closed; however, NAACP lawyers argued, for the sake of the community, some of the schools should be refurbished and kept open. The schools that both sides agreed needed to be closed were Isaiah Blocker, Fairfield, and A.L. Lewis Elementary Schools. There were four other schools, East Jacksonville Elementary, Forest Park, Mt. Herman, and John E. Ford, that the NAACP argued could be kept open if they were repaired.[28]

The school board's attorneys argued that their decision to close the four schools was based on solid evidence and recommendations from the Miami Desegregation Center. The four schools had been recommended for closing by the center's 1967 plan for integrating the schools. The courts agreed with the school board's plan and rejected the notion of keeping the four African American schools open. After careful review, the courts agreed with the school board's reasoning and approved the closings. The reasons for closing the schools were: crime in the area; industry and environmental concerns; problems with the physical plants; and other issues. Judge McRae ruled in favor of the school system and ordered the plan implemented.[29]

The school board argued that John E. Ford and Mt. Herman, which bordered the I-95 Expressway and were located in the highest crime area of the city, where eighty percent of the hard narcotics were trafficked, were no longer viable educational facilities. Their lawyers said that it was impossible to create a quality educational environment at these two schools because of the chronic crime threat. The problems included truants, unusually high drop-out rates, the constant threat of invasion from vandals, and troublemakers on the school grounds. School officials had sometimes been forced to lock the teachers and students in the classrooms; but even this had not stopped assaults on teachers and students. These conditions made it difficult to recruit white teachers to the area; thus it was impossible to comply with the seventy-to-thirty ratio. East Jacksonville Elementary was located in an area which needed a major facelift before the building could be fit for educational purposes. The Miami Desegregation Center had recommended that the school, "should be abandoned as soon as possible" because it was, "clearly unsuitable for educational purposes and should be phased out." The school needed to be expanded and the neighborhood did not offer that possibility. Forest Park Elementary was a fairly modern school, situated on a 1.72-acre land site capable of housing 1,080 students.[30]

Nevertheless, the Desegregation Center said of the school, "One school is particularly displeasing in terms of location. Forest Park is a large . . . relatively new building." The problem was that the school was located between a city incinerator on the east, a polluted creek on the north, and a meat and poultry packing plant on the west. The result was that the school was regularly bombarded with the odors from the incinerator, the meat packing plant, and the sewage clogging the polluted creek. NAACP lawyers countered that the incinerator had closed and was no longer a neighborhood nuisance. However, school board attorneys argued that the creek and the meat and poultry packing plant still polluted the school's air, creating an unsafe learning environment. They were especially concerned because noxious odors continued to permeate the school cafeteria. The court agreed with the school system, arguing that the closing did not represent an undue burden, but instead, "is simply a reasonable part of a workable plan of desegregation." The argument seems clear: the schools were all right to use for African American children, but they were below standard for integrated schools with white students.[31]

The second issue the NAACP lawyers raised was the idea of the unfair burden busing placed on African American children. They argued that to bus African American kids for grades one through five represented an undue burden, because white children were only bused for grade six. The court relied on earlier opinions rendered in the *Allen v. Asheville City Board of Education* case and *Norwalk Core v. Norwalk Board of Education*. In these two decisions, courts found that it was not an unfair burden for African American children to be bused more than white children. The courts argued that, "It is a question with the Board, with the facilities available having acted in the utmost good faith, in a non-arbitrary and deliberate manner in order both to insure racial balance and to provide high quality education." The courts ruled that they would trust the school board to the extent that they did what was in the best interest of the children.[32]

The courts also ruled that the school board's plan for sixth grade centers was calculated to produce quality education and provide a healthy transition from primary to secondary schools. In essence, the court accepted the school board's plan and ordered its implementation with few exceptions. The twenty-one-mile distance between John E. Ford and the sixth grade center was originally not considered an undue burden. However, at the time the courts made that ruling, studies showing the travel time required were not in. Court-ordered tests found that students would travel an hour and a half each day if they were bused from the Beaches to downtown core sixth grade centers. Therefore, the courts rejected the clustering of Beaches schools with core-city African American schools.[33]

The courts also argued that a unitary system could be created, without busing African American students from the core city, by changing attendance zones. The Beaches' segregation was based upon their placing African American students in separate elementary and secondary schools. By integrating Fletcher Senior-Junior High School, they had integrated their junior and senior high schools. The court argued that to integrate the six elementary schools only required clustering the elementary schools. That would give each school an average fifteen percent African American student population. The Joseph Finegan Elementary School would remain untouched because of its unique position and relationship with Mayport Naval Station.[34]

Next the courts looked at the junior high schools. Jacksonville had twenty-two junior high schools and one junior-senior high school. Six of the schools were fully integrated. The school board's plan used clustering and grade centers to integrate the fifteen formerly one-race schools, creating fourteen integrated unitary schools with twenty-one to thirty-four percent African American students in each school. The school board plan closed the formerly all-black Darnell Cookman. School board attorneys argued that because of the high crime rate and neighborhood blight, the school was not conducive to quality education. Even though an urban renewal plan was promised, because the courts mandated immediate integration and the board could not wait for a promised neighborhood renovation, the school board lawyers argued the school should be closed. The school board promised to look at reopening the school if the neighborhood improved. The courts accepted the school board's rationale and ordered the school closed.[35]

There were two schools left out of the school board's plan that created a problem. Sandalwood was a newly built school, scheduled to open in September. Its projected enrollment was 1,316 whites and only six African Americans. The other school untouched by the plan was Northwestern Junior High School. It was built in 1957 and had a projected enrollment of 1,590 African

Americans. That meant that Jacksonville would have two virtually one-race schools. The board lawyers argued that the *Charlotte-Mecklenburg* decision allowed one-race schools to exist in areas where there were new schools and the neighborhood patterns had not been established. School board lawyers argued that to integrate students into Sandalwood would require busing African American students from inner-city schools.[36]

Northwestern was located in the center of the African American community and was some distance from any white school or residential area. Historically its students came from all-black elementary schools and it fed the all-black Raines High School. Under the school board's plan, its future students would come from integrated grammar schools and would attend integrated high schools. The court ruled that the school board's plan was a good faith attempt to provide a nondiscriminatory education. The court argued Northwestern's "all-black character is not the product of gerrymandering zone lines. The failure to pair or cluster Northwestern does not reflect a desire on the part of the Board to keep it segregated." There was fear that any attempt to change Northwestern's racial makeup would only destroy the racial balance at other schools.[37]

The other part of the plan dealt with Jacksonville's senior high schools. Duval County had thirteen senior high schools during the 1970-1971 school year. Raines and Stanton High Schools were defined by the system as all-African American high schools. The other eleven high schools ranged from one to forty percent African American enrollment. The board's plan called for converting Stanton High School into a vocational school with an integrated student body. School board officials argued that Stanton was the best-suited school for a vocational program, because its equipment and personnel were ideal for such a program. One-third of its student body was already involved in a vocational program.[38]

The plan called for bringing African American and white students from all over the county to Stanton. The remaining two-thirds of Stanton's students would be transferred to the eight predominantly white schools in the county. The courts accepted and approved the proposal submitted by the school board. Using the proposed school board plan, with the exception of Raines and Ribault High Schools, all of Jacksonville's high schools would be integrated, with an African American enrollment of between seven and forty percent. Even though this formula did not match the seventy-two percent white and twenty-eight percent African American formula suggested by the courts, in the county's opinion, achieving unitary status superseded the need to adhere to a strict mathematical formula.[39]

The school board's proposals for dealing with Raines and Ribault did not fit constitutional requirements. Raines and Ribault High Schools were built almost across the street from each other. The two schools served the students from the northwest section of the county. Originally, Raines educated black children while Ribault educated white students. The racial composition of the community which was served by the two schools was approximately fifty-eight percent African American and forty-two percent white. The school board's plan called for using six additional school buses to integrate the two schools. The school board rejected the use of cross-town busing to integrate Raines.[40]

To summarize the school board's plan from a student perspective is quite easy. African American children would be bused to an elementary school in a white neighborhood for their first five years of school. Then black children would attend a sixth and seventh grade center in an African American neighborhood. For junior high school, African American students would be bused to a formerly all-white school for eighth and ninth grades. Their high school years would be spent at a formerly all-white or all-African American high school. This new school was integrated and better equipped, producing a more conducive educational environment.[41]

For white children, understanding the school board's plan was even easier. White children would spend the first five years of their education in formerly all-white neighborhood schools. On most occasions these would have been the same schools they would have attended under segregation. They would then be bused to sixth and seventh grade centers located in African American neighborhoods. Next, most white children would return to a formerly all-white neighborhood school for eighth and ninth grades. Finally, white children would attend one of the newly integrated high schools, probably the one closest to their neighborhood. Once again this would probably be the school the child would have attended if the schools had not been desegregated. Students living in Baldwin and the Beaches would attend fully integrated neighborhood schools from elementary through high school.[42]

There were some issues which had to be resolved to fully implement the school board's plan. First, the school board needed to contract an additional 250 school buses to transport the students under the desegregation plan. The board had contracts to utilize 149 school buses from local bus owners. The school board used independent contractors, all local residents, to transport children to and from school. Local contractors purchased either new or used buses on their own, using their school board agreement as collateral on the loans.[43]

The problem that faced the school district was that there was no way to get that many new school buses before the school year began. The school system had access to one hundred used buses that could be delivered in September for the beginning of the school year, but that still left them more than 150 buses short. The courts ordered the school district to implement the plan as far as possible, and purchase the other buses once all of the appeals had expired. The courts did not want the school board to order more buses until the board knew if the plan was going to be adopted. If the plan were rejected, the school board might have to purchase more buses. Also, there was concern that, if the board were forced to order the additional 150 buses at $10,000 per bus, that might inflict an unbearable burden on the school board, individual contractors, and taxpayers.[44]

The first part of the integration process occurred in Duval County with the integration of the faculty and staff. From January 25 until January 30, 1970, following Judge McRae's earlier ruling, schools in Duval County were closed, as the school district undertook the process of transferring teachers and staff to reach the court-imposed seventy/thirty percent ratio at each school. The school board's plan called for the system to use a reverse seniority plan when determining transfers. Principals were allowed to protect twenty percent of their teaching staff and key administrators. Second-year teachers were the first to be transferred. Minority teachers and those protected by the principals were not involved. Kindergarten teachers and those in federally funded special education programs were also not affected by the transfers.[45]

The plans also called for no transfer of principals. Senior high school deans, who were in charge of discipline, were not transferred. Those in charge of discipline at junior high schools were also protected, no matter what their titles were. All other administrators at junior and senior high schools, including assistant principals, curriculum assistants, and counselors, were eligible for transfer to achieve the correct ratio. The principals' protected lists and rationales were reviewed by the assistant superintendent for operations, Dr. Harold Campbell. He had to approve each principal's list. Teachers expressing a genuine objection to the transfer could appeal and have their cases reviewed by a committee composed of representatives from the district, school, and classroom levels. The teachers had to submit a written appeal to the committee.[46]

The 1970-1971 school year represented a major shift in the school integration process for Duval County. For the first time since the case began, the school district had introduced a workable plan for integrating the schools. The black and white teachers would be shared by the various schools according to an established ratio and the students would be integrated. However, the burden for integration was clearly being placed on African American children.

Though the plan was not perfect, it represented a good first step toward equal education in Jacksonville. However, everyone suspected that there would be much more work ahead.

Notes

1 Charles Ogletree, *All Deliberate Speed: Reflections on the First Half Century of Brown v. Board of Education* (New York: WW Norton, 2004), 132.

2 Howard Ball, *A Defiant Life: Thurgood Marshall and the Persistence of Racism in America* (New York: Crown Publishers, 1998), 197.

3 Ball, *A Defiant Life,* 193, 197; Juan Williams, *Thurgood Marshall: American Revolutionary* (New York: Three Rivers Press, 1998), 335-344.

4 "1968 Like a Knife Blade, The Year Severed Past From Future," *Time,* January 11, 1988.

5 Steven Lawson, *Running for Freedom: Civil Rights and Black Politics in America Since 1941,* 3rd ed. (Chichester: Wiley-Blackwell, 2009), 140.

6 Stephen E. Ambrose, *Nixon: The Triumph of a Politician 1962-1972,* vol. 2 (New York: Simon and Schuster, 1989), 187.

7 Richard Reeves, *President Nixon: Alone in the White House* (New York: Simon and Schuster, 2001), 116-117; Richard Kluger, *Simple Justice: The History of Brown v. Board of Education and Black America's Struggle for Equality* (New York: Alfred A. Knopf, 2004), 761.

8 Ambrose, *Nixon: The Triumph of a Politician,* 316; Ogletree, *All Deliberate Speed,* 132.

9 Kluger, *Simple Justice,* 761-762.

10 Ibid., 608; "The Congress: A Fight to the Finish," *Time,* December 20, 1971.

11 Kluger, *Simple Justice,* 608-609, 761-762.

12 Ambrose, *Nixon: The Triumph of a Politician,* 433; Kluger, *Simple Justice,* 762; Mims v. Duval County School Board, No. 4598-Civ-J, June 1971, 8.

13 *Mims v. DCSB,* 9.

14 Ibid.

15 Kluger, *Simple Justice,* 608-609, 762-763; Swann v. Charlotte-Mecklenburg Board of Education, 431 F.2d 138, Argued: October 12, 1970, Decided: April 20, 1971.

16 Ibid.

17 *Mims v. DCSB,* 11-12.

18 Ibid., 10.

19 Ibid.

20 Jacksonville Branch NAACP v. Duval County School Board, Appeal No. 99-12049-EE 19, 36.

21 *Mims v. DCSB,* 13.

22 Ibid., 11.

23 Ibid., 11-12.

24 Ibid., 13.

25 Ibid.

26 Ibid.

27 Ibid., 16.

28 Ibid., 15.

29 Ibid. 19.

30 Ibid., 15-16.

31 Ibid.

32 Ibid., 19.

33 Ibid. 20.

34 Ibid. 10.

35 Ibid., 11.

36 Ibid.

37 Ibid., 11-12.

38 Ibid., 22.

39 Ibid., 23.

40 Ibid., 24.

41 Ibid.

42 Ibid., 25.

43 Ibid.

44 Ibid., 13.

45 *Florida Times-Union,* January 7, 1970.

46 Ibid.

Chapter Seven

Integrated But Not Unitary

As 1990 approached, the Duval County Public School desegregation struggle was entering its thirtieth year. The problem of achieving equal education and unifying the public school system had proven more difficult and had lasted longer than anyone could have expected. Though both sides wanted the lawsuit ended, the NAACP was unwilling to end the process until they ensured that African American children were equally served by the public school system. As the business community celebrated Jacksonville's economic development, racial issues and school desegregation continued to plague local officials and embarrass civic and business leaders desperate to attract investors. Despite the pressure from local officials, NAACP lawyers agreed that they had a responsibility to see that an integrated unitary public school system was established in Duval County before they halted their legal actions. The organization's lawyers argued that it was important to continue to pressure the courts to enforce their rulings.

There was excitement throughout Jacksonville on September 6, 1988, when Judge John H. Moore declared the Duval County Public School System integrated and unitary. In making this ruling, Judge Moore sought to end the court's oversight of Jacksonville's public schools after nearly thirty years of litigation. In his ruling, Moore concluded that no evidence of discrimination in extra-curricular or transportation policies existed within the public school system. He also ruled that the school board had taken affirmative actions to ensure minority student achievement. The remaining discrimination was the last vestige of the dual system and was not the result of any overt school action. Judge Moore's decision effectively ended forced busing in Jacksonville, a very unpopular integration tool used by the courts since the early 1970s. NAACP lawyers were shocked by the judge's decision, because they knew that Jacksonville did not have a unitary system. While many local white residents cheered Moore's ruling, school officials counseled caution because they knew that there were still areas of concern. The decision to relieve the school system of court supervision both surprised and encouraged many people who were hoping to attract new residents and businesses to the city. School Superintendent Herb Sang expressed cautious praise for the decision before promising no drastic changes would occur. He asked for time to study the implications of Judge Moore's decision before the school district made additional changes.[1]

Sang was relieved by Moore's decision and hoped to move on to other areas where he could improve the school system. He had been praised for the improvements the Duval County School System had made over his term. He did not have a good relationship with the NAACP but was popular in segments of the African American community, because he had improved the scores at several predominantly African American schools in the city. Sang believed that cross-town busing posed an undue burden on African American children and parents. He instead believed in neighborhood schools as the most effective way to educate children. Busing made it difficult for parents to be engaged in their children's education and it also limited the involvement that children could have in after-school activities. Sang made an agreement with local ministers to have no school meetings on Wednesday nights, because the ministers wanted the parents in Bible study. In return, the ministers would provide encouragement and transportation to African American parents to get them to their children's schools for open houses and teacher meetings.[2]

Another group that was buoyed by Judge Moore's decision were white parents. Many of them were glad to see the long litigation come to an end. They also welcomed the end of cross-town busing which took their children to African American neighborhoods for schooling. However, many in the black community jeered the judge's decision and encouraged the NAACP to appeal Moore's ruling. NAACP attorneys wasted little time appealing Moore's decision, citing obvious areas where the school board had failed to carry out court-mandated reforms. Amazingly, Judge Moore had overlooked the fact that the district had several schools that were identifiably one-race and teacher transfer orders to balance faculty ratios had been ignored. With the appeal pending, the school integration issue continued to dominate headlines in Duval County during the late 1980s and early 1990s, as the NAACP was vilified for again taking the school system back to court for another round of legal wrangling. Whether because of fatigue or community pressure, both the school board and the NAACP showed a determination to work together to solve the problems. This cooperative spirit led to a series of negotiations that produced an agreement which, for at least a short time, lowered the volume in the rancorous discussions over Jacksonville's public schools.[3]

Neither the school board nor the NAACP was comfortable with Judge Moore's ruling. Both sides agreed that, though improvements had been made, there were still several areas where more could be done. In appealing Judge Moore's ruling, the NAACP lawyers cited numerous areas where they believed that the school board had failed to meet its obligations regarding desegregation. The school board had never fully complied with the 1971 *Mims v. Duval County School Board* injunctive that teachers be assigned on a seventy percent white and thirty percent African American basis at each school, one of the more easily accomplishable goals. They also pointed out that the school board had never met the *Mims* injunctive requirements concerning student assignments. There were still numerous schools that were nearly all-black or all-white. These were obvious, glaring, measurable areas where the school board had failed to carry out court-mandated changes. How Judge Moore could have ignored these violations was unclear and his judgment stunned the black community. Wendell Holmes, one of two African Americans on the school board, expressed dismay over the judge's order, referring to it as "premature."[4]

On September 15, 1989, the Eleventh Circuit Court reversed Judge Moore's decision and remanded the case back to the lower court. The court of appeals cited several areas of concern for the school system. First, there were schools that had administrative staff personnel consisting of one race matching the majority of the student body, a clear violation of the *Mims* injunctive. This finding proved that the school board had never complied with the *Mims* requirement that teachers be assigned on a seventy percent to thirty percent white to African American ratio at each school. This could have been done because it only required transferring teachers to meet a specific goal. The ruling found, "approximately thirty schools have varied consistently by more than 10% from the target ratio since 1972." Superintendent Sang argued that, because principals had the final say on staff transfers, and teachers' preferences were always considered, it was difficult to get the desired ratio. Teachers preferred to work near, or in, their neighborhoods, so transferring them was difficult. The school board had never met the *Mims* requirements in regard to student assignments, either. The court stated, "Segregation in the district as a whole has increased since 1972. In that year eight schools had majority black populations; in 1985, twenty-seven schools fell into that category." As a result the school system was once again placed under the 1971 court order. This left the school board and the NAACP with two choices. They could either continue to fight in the courts or they could attempt a negotiated settlement.[5]

As the two sides contemplated their next step, the school board ousted Superintendent Herb Sang. He had guided the school system since February 1, 1976, and was nationally recognized for his reforms. However, with the school system still mired in the integration process, several school board members felt it was time for a change. On March 31, 1989, Sang resigned as school superintendent, ending a productive thirteen-year reign. He was temporarily replaced by Dr. Charles Cline, who served in an interim position for two months.

On April 24, 1989, Dr. Larry Zenke, a former aide to Cecil Hardesty, returned to Jacksonville as superintendent of the Duval County Public School System. Zenke had served in the school system before, from March 1970 through August 1973, when he was director of elementary education in Duval County at the relatively young age of thirty. Zenke, as director of elementary education, was responsible for the direction of the one hundred elementary schools in the district. When he had previously left Jacksonville, he was sure that it would not be long before the city's schools were integrated and unified. Zenke took the position of school superintendent thinking that the school system had been desegregated, and that he would be allowed to continue the impressive work he had begun in Orlando. There he had improved student and district performance while serving as deputy superintendent of instruction from 1973 until 1976. Zenke, a native of Galesville, Wisconsin, had spent five years teaching and two years as a principal in Chicago before moving to Florida to do graduate work in education at the University of Florida. He moved to Gainesville in 1968 to work on his doctoral degree. Zenke worked in a federally funded program designed to train urban school administrators. As part of his training, he was required to spend three months as an administrative intern to the superintendent of the Miami-Dade County Public School District.[6]

The three months Zenke spent working as an administrator in Dade County were invaluable for molding his ideas about education. This was the fourth largest school system in the nation. He learned the complexities involved in running a large multicultural school district. He was also introduced to the intricate racial mindset of white Southerners. As a Northerner, he was not familiar with the elaborate racial etiquette of the South. His Miami experience taught him a great deal about racial attitudes and the difficulties of working across racial lines.[7]

One of the first things Zenke did when he took the job in 1970 was to investigate the school system to see how it operated. He immediately observed that it operated on a dual basis with black and white schools. He also recognized that the African Americans schools were in an abominable state and that the white community had little interest in improving conditions in these schools. In August 1970 he was part of the team that implemented the court-ordered plan for integrating the one hundred public elementary schools in the district. Zenke's wife, Jo Ann, got a teaching job working in the district. She volunteered to work in a predominantly African American school to demonstrate to others that her husband was not asking teachers to do anything that he wouldn't ask his own family to do. For two more years, from 1971 until 1973, Zenke worked to integrate the remaining elementary schools that needed to be integrated. He went as far as to have his oldest daughter, Lisa, bused to a formerly all-black inner-city school to show parents they had nothing to fear from busing. Once again he wanted to prove the point that he was not asking the community to do anything that he was unwilling to do himself. When he left Jacksonville in 1973, he assumed that the district would be relieved of court supervision soon because of the progress made during his time in the system.[8]

When Zenke came back to Jacksonville as superintendent in April, 1989, he believed that he could concentrate on creating a first-class educational system in Jacksonville. Zenke had intimate knowledge of Jacksonville's school system from his previous work in the city. He thought he knew what was needed to make improvements to the district. No one was more disappointed and surprised than Zenke when the appeals court, on September 15, 1989, reversed Judge Moore's ruling. He had taken the superintendent's job not long after Judge Moore's ruling. Therefore, as he returned to Jacksonville, he thought that the federal courts would not be interfering with his plans. The appeals court's decision forced him to shift his priorities from improving the school system to getting the district out from under the court's jurisdiction. Zenke found six areas where the school district had yet to comply with federal mandates.[9]

In 1990 both the school board and the NAACP came to the conclusion that the endless round of litigation had to end. With Zenke running the school system, NAACP officials believed that they had a better chance of negotiating a solution. Zenke and NAACP president Willye Dennis suggested that the two sides get together and discuss the issues to see if they could come to a mutually beneficial compromise. It was obvious that they would not get far if the lawyers continued to argue between themselves in endless rounds of court proceedings. Each side searched for a neutral third party who could mediate between the two warring sides and help them come up with a fair and equitable agreement acceptable to both the constituents and the courts. Recognizing that each side had its own agenda, there was hope that, through compromise, an acceptable agreement could be reached.[10]

Dennis had intimate knowledge about Jacksonville's racial climate and was very familiar with the school board's tactics. She mistrusted the board and any proposal they might advocate. Dennis was a Jacksonville native who understood the complex racial environment in which she worked. She had experienced a number of tragedies in her life, which strengthened and prepared her for the struggle with the school board. She was a tenacious and resilient fighter who could not be intimidated by school officials and she was indifferent to public opinion. Both of her parents had died when she was just fifteen. After their deaths, she lived with a sister before moving to Atlanta, where she attended Clark College. While at Clark in the early 1950s, she came face to face with America's racial policies when she attempted to have lunch at a downtown restaurant in Atlanta with several friends from foreign countries. Though she was the only American citizen, she was the only person the restaurant owner refused to serve. This incident both angered and insulted her. She questioned the value of her American citizenship when she could not be served in an American restaurant. When she returned to campus, she joined the NAACP, vowing to fight racism and ensure that all Americans were treated equally.[11]

After graduating from Clark, Dennis returned to Jacksonville where she attempted to get a job as a librarian. At that time, Jacksonville had no African American librarians. In fact, blacks could not even get an application for a civil service job. When Dennis went to the civil service office to get an application, she was met with the familiar greeting, "We don't hire niggers!" Dennis replied, "That's too bad for niggers, but I want an application." Dennis challenged the rule, demanding that she be allowed to apply for a librarian job. She raised such a disturbance that Mayor Haydon Burns, whose office was down the hall, came to her defense, forcing the Civil Service Board to give her an application. Though it took two more years, she eventually got to take the civil service exam and became the first African American hired through the

Civil Service Board. She worked for the Jacksonville Public Library System for twenty-seven years before retiring as chief of the children's division. For Dennis, the school issue was similar to what she had experienced earlier with the Civil Service Board. She knew that eventually, with enough time and commotion, the school board would relent, because the law and right were on her side.[12]

Dennis understood the importance of the negotiations and the sensitive nature of the issues to be debated. As NAACP president, she was aware of the passionate emotions stirred by racial and educational issues. She had been the target of death threats throughout the school integration battle, so she understood the sensitive nature of school integration. On December 18, 1989, Walter Leroy Moody took the threats a step further when he mailed a bomb to the NAACP headquarters in Jacksonville. Miraculously, a string of coincidences saved Dennis from the bomber. Even though Dennis handled the package, morning meetings forced her to delay opening her mail until later in the afternoon. On the way back to the office, her car stalled and she chose to go home for the day. That evening she heard news reports about bombs being mailed to people in packages similar to the one she had handled earlier that day. She called the police, who investigated and found a very powerful pipe bomb in the package she had received. Had she opened the package that morning, most likely she would have been killed by the blast! Dennis knew that many people had grown tired of the NAACP's challenges and had threatened violence against her and the other members of the organization. Most of the threats had been ignored, but after the bomb scare, Dennis knew the pressure had been ratcheted up.[13]

Walter Leroy Moody was eventually arrested, tried, and convicted of the bombings. At the time, Moody was a fifty-five-year-old Rex, Georgia, man who hated the court system. After a short stint in the military and prison, he began experimenting with bombs. In 1972, he was arrested when a bomb he made to kill a car dealer who had repossessed his car exploded prematurely and seriously injured his wife. In 1988 his case was appealed to the Eleventh Circuit Court, where Judge Robert Vance served as a justice.

Judge Vance, who was African American, was one of the three judges who denied Moody's appeal. On December 16, 1989, Judge Vance was killed by a bomb sent to his home by Moody. Moody then sent several bombs to other people to make law enforcement officials think the bombings had a racial overtone. More than one hundred Federal Bureau of Investigation agents investigated the case along with Alcohol, Tobacco, and Firearms officers and state and local officials. An officer who was familiar with this 1972 investigation was able to link Moody to the bombings. Moody was eventually tried and convicted on all charges stemming from the bombing and his attempts to tamper with witnesses in his original trial. In February 1997, he was sentenced to die in Alabama's electric chair.[14]

As the NAACP and school board began negotiations, the racial atmosphere around the city, state, and nation was tense. The parameters of the negotiations were clear. Both sides wanted to continue desegregating the school system and student body, but each side realized that they were somewhat constrained by their constituents. There was a need to add more money to the $60,000,000 set aside for new schools and repairing of older schools. They wanted to ensure that they would have parental involvement in creating magnet school programs. They wanted to establish a process for desegregating the teachers and administrators to establish the seventy to thirty ratio at each school. There was general agreement that the magnet school program could be used as a tool for attracting white students to African American schools. Therefore, it could be a powerful tool in integrating hard-to-integrate predominantly black central city schools.[15]

As these negotiations began, both sides knew that they faced obstacles. For example, while the superintendent could negotiate on behalf of the school system, he could not force the elected school board to abide by his commitments, because the superintendent was an employee of the school board. Also, there was no guarantee that the community would accept an NAACP-negotiated deal. There was literally millions of dollars in development money at stake as the NAACP and the school board entered into negotiations. Several prominent local developers were ready to invest in housing and community projects, but they could not move until they were assured that the courts would allow the school board to build new schools in the developing areas. The problem was that most of the developing neighborhoods were located in predominantly white areas outside the urban core where most African Americans lived. Therefore, though both sides wanted a negotiated settlement, these challenges had to be overcome.

Along with these obstacles, there were several areas of disagreement between the school board and the NAACP. One area that was generally mentioned was the difference in opinion concerning how best to integrate the students. The NAACP supported a controlled-choice program with immediate mandating of parental choices. They had come to believe that parents could not be trusted to do the right thing and therefore should be compelled to participate in integrative programs. They also wanted assurances that the school board would abide by its previous agreements. The NAACP no longer trusted the board to implement what they had agreed upon, because on several occasions the elected school officials had ignored commitments and unilaterally carried out their own wishes. The school board preferred long-term programs that attracted students to schools by using incentives such as magnet programs. They wanted to develop desegregation strategies that had a definitive end date. They also wanted to avoid any strategy that compelled parents to send their children to areas outside of their own neighborhoods. There were still few white students attending predominantly African American schools and few incentives for them to do so. The school board also wanted the flexibility to make changes to their agreements without getting approval from the NAACP or the courts. As elected officials, they were very concerned with public opinion and also with ensuring that they did not overreach parental prerogatives.[16]

In reality, both sides had to be cognizant of what the community they represented wanted. The African American community wanted majority African American teachers in majority black schools. They also wanted equal-quality education for their children. They knew that their children had historically been short-changed in their educational experience by the Duval County Public School System. If there were special programs and opportunities available to white children, black parents wanted those same things made available to their children. White parents, for the most part, wanted the elimination of busing to achieve racial balance and an end to the endless court filings. There were many white parents who had come to embrace the notion of neighborhood schools. They wanted their children to attend the local schools in their own neighborhoods from elementary through high school, believing that was the best way to foster school and neighborhood pride.

The business community was also interested in a solution to the school controversy for a number of reasons. They wanted an educational system that produced a quality workforce and attracted more business investment to the city. Business owners also wanted to know that if they invested in developing areas, there would be new schools in those areas. Finally, they wanted an end to the rancorous racial conversations about education and a return to efforts to improve the public schools to bolster the city's national image. While the school problems were being discussed, simultaneous negotiations were taking place with the National Football League in an effort to bring a professional football team to Jacksonville.[17]

Between January and July of 1990, Willye Dennis and Larry Zenke entered into historic negotiations on school desegregation. These negotiations represented the first time the two sides had sat down together to try to work out an agreement. The NAACP asked for and got assistance from its national office to help the local officials frame their demands. Zenke convinced the school board to hire a desegregation consultant to advise it on effective integration strategies. They also solicited community involvement, enlisting parents and community leaders in helping them develop and implement their magnet programs. The two sides established three goals for the meeting. First, they wanted to improve educational opportunities for all students. Second, they wanted to reduce the mandatory busing program that had been used to achieve racial integration. Finally, they wanted to meet the court requirements for desegregating the public schools.[18]

One of the most popular solutions for school officials was the so-called controlled choice proposal. Controlled choice called for no student's being guaranteed a particular school. All parents were given the chance to select admission to their preferred desegregated schools outside of their residential neighborhoods. Controlled choice was used to govern all student assignments. One essential feature of the Duval County School Board plan was the elimination of all individual school attendance boundaries. The plan called for the adoption and enforcing of desegregation that would guarantee minority- and majority-race students genuine proportional access to all schools and programs of choice. It allowed parents and students to make multiple school choices, but it did not guarantee them their first choice. The school board's plan offered an effective parent information and outreach process. Implementation of this plan called for the grandfathering in of students at their present schools as long as the district-wide integration level was at fifty percent. The schools had to be within five to ten percent of the county's racial mix.[19]

The school board and NAACP discussions resulted in a series of compromises designed to produce a unitary system providing equal education to all students. The agreement they reached was called a Corrected Stipulation Agreement by the courts. It was grounded in three areas of concurrence. First, both parties agreed that the system of mass busing had failed as a means of student desegregation. Second, it was obvious that the litigation had to end and an agreement based upon the accord was needed. Third, it was mutually agreed that any future school board desegregative efforts would revolve primarily around elementary schools and only secondarily around middle and high schools.[20]

By 1990 no one doubted that the Duval County Public School System was integrated. The school board had taken a number of affirmative actions to ensure that the schools operated in an integrated manner. The difficulty with ending the litigation was how to measure a unitary system. Both parties agreed that, "the school system will not achieve unitary status until it maintains at least three years of racial equality in six categories: student assignment, faculty, staff, transportation, extracurricular activities, and facilities."[21]

The agreement called for the school board to operate all its programs in a nondiscriminatory manner. There were specific mandates agreed to by the board to measure their achievement. The second part of the agreement dealt with the student assignment plan. Both parties agreed to replace the mandatory student assignment plan with a voluntary one. This agreement was important because both the white and African American communities were tired of cross-town busing. The voluntary school choice plan utilized magnet schools to recruit students across attendance zones to African American and white schools.[22]

The negotiated settlement accomplished the following things. It ensured parental involvement in determining and creating magnet schools, and it attempted to replace forced busing with voluntary student transfers to schools with enhanced academic programs. The Corrected Stipulation reorganized the Duval County Public School System. The entire district was divided into seven administrative zones. The school system set an enrollment of at least twenty percent African American and forty-five percent white at all schools in zones 1 through 5. In zones 6 and 7, the district was to operate each school within ten percent of the zone-wide racial composition at its grade organizational level.[23]

Beginning with the 1991-1992 school year, the school district got rid of the sixth and seventh grade centers that had been an important component of the 1971 desegregation plan. The agreement called for a complete reorganization of the school system, shifting from a K-5, 6-7, 8-9, 10-12 grade system to a K-5, 6-8, 9-12 grade system. This created the popular middle school program with a 9-12 grade high school. Beginning with the 1991-1992 school year, Raines, Sandalwood, Mandarin, Englewood, Wolfson, and Paxon High schools all added ninth-graders to their student bodies. In addition, Andrew Jackson High School was converted into a middle school during the 1991-1992 school year. Raines received a magnet program in science and mathematics and Mandarin got a magnet program in African American history and culture. To attract students to high schools that were especially difficult to integrate, such as Raines, Ribault, Wolfson, and Ed White, the plan utilized popular magnet programs that appealed to white parents. Most of the students at Stanton were reassigned to Raines High School.[24]

For the middle schools, the proposal called for Paxson Junior High to remain a middle school. The seventh grade center at Oceanway was dissolved into an enlarged Oceanway Elementary. The students who would have attended that school were moved to Ribault Middle School during the 1990-1991 school year and to Highlands Middle School the following year. Matthew Gilbert High School was renovated and turned into a middle school. The students who would have attended the school were sent to either Southside or Dupont Junior High Schools during the 1990-1991 school year. Landon Junior High School was converted into a middle school during the 1991-1992 school year, and given a magnet program. The ninth graders who would have attended Landon were sent either to Englewood, Wolfson, or Sandalwood High Schools. Southside's ninth grade was moved to Englewood while Dupont's ninth grade was moved to Wolfson High School.[25]

The other part of the agreement dealt with the elementary grades. All of the current educable mentally handicapped (EMH) and educable mentally retarded (EMR) students were re-evaluated. There was a concerted effort to find African American students and teachers to participate in the gifted programs. The conclusion to the report called for the school board and the NAACP to work together to stay out of the courts. They built in a level of flexibility and mandated actions, with specific deadlines combined with periodic adjustments that were designed to move the process forward through continuing negotiations and agreements. They agreed that local control was preferable to court-ordered busing. The NAACP also preferred mandated decisions rather than the voluntary measures that the community preferred. Finally, they agreed to seek involvement from students, parents, staff, and the entire community in developing desegregation solutions that achieved their stated goals.[26]

The school board and the NAACP also agreed to open seven new schools during the 1990-1991 school term in rapidly growing white areas. To compensate for this move, the school board was responsible for securing $60 million in new funding for needed facility upgrades to inner city and northwest quadrant schools, which had long been neglected. This new money would allow for dramatic improvements in the quality and quantity of instruction and technology for inner-city schools. The agreement also provided for elementary, middle, and high school magnet programs to be placed in those schools, which the NAACP and school board hoped would attract white students. It committed the district to timely completion of all needed bonded projects and eliminated so-called standalone schools. These were schools that were integrated by virtue of neighborhood integration. A seven-member team with representatives from the NAACP and school board was created to oversee improvements in facilities and instructions.[27]

The agreement established a seventy to thirty percent ratio of whites to African Americans for teachers and administrators at all schools, a long-sought-after goal of the *Mims* case. It also ended forced busing for 14,000 students. Willye Dennis and other members of the NAACP were pleased with the negotiated settlement. The *Florida Times-Union* quoted Dennis as saying, "We feel this plan is educationally driven." Reverend Henry Green, president of the AME Ministerial Alliance, an organization composed of some sixty ministers, praised the proposal: "I think the concept of the plan offers some hope to the African American community." Fred Matthews of the NAACP's Education Committee praised the way the proposal was written because it required the school system to actually do things instead of just expecting the NAACP to trust them. He pointed out that the school board only had permission to open four of the seven schools. They had to make a $30 million deposit into the fund for the African American schools in order to open the other three schools. The court approved the school board plan on July 13, 1990, retaining jurisdiction to enforce it.[28]

By June 1991, NAACP lawyers were already challenging the school board's implementation of the agreement. The NAACP asked the court to initiate a controlled-choice plan in addition to the magnet program as a way of assigning elementary students. The court ordered an evidentiary hearing to discuss the issues the NAACP lawyers brought up. Judge Frank Johnson focused on five specific issues raised by NAACP lawyers: (1) The alleged dissemination by the school board of a so-called neighborhood school letter. (2) The issue of staff assignments by race. (3) The board's student transportation policy. (4) An issue concerning the facilities committee. (5) The district court's refusal to modify the plan and use a controlled-choice plan for elementary students. The court had problems with the neighborhood letter assigning students to neighborhood schools and it also had a problem with the duration and nature of the committee's duties regarding its study of educational programs.[29]

On May 11, 1993, the school board unilaterally announced its intentions to construct nine new schools in rapidly developing suburban areas to alleviate overcrowding. The NAACP immediately rejected the plan and threatened to sue. Willye Dennis argued that there were several schools in African American neighborhoods that had vacant seats. She demanded that the school board address those seats before looking to build new schools. Superintendent Zenke admitted that there were 860 spaces available in schools in the predominantly black northwest quadrant, but he argued that neighborhood schools were preferable to the parents. The school board joined Zenke in rejecting the NAACP's argument and announced its plan to go ahead with its proposal.[30]

When the two sides could not agree on how to solve those issues, Judge Moore sent the case back to court. However, he advised both sides to submit to arbitration with Judge Harvey E. Schlesinger, Judge Moore's brother. The two parties failed to reach an agreement, and on October 1, 1996, the school board filed a suit asking the courts to declare a unitary school system and release the district from the court's jurisdiction. School board officials argued that they had done all they could to achieve unitary status.[31]

The NAACP argued that between 1991 and 1995, the school board had repeatedly violated the spirit of the agreement and had not taken affirmative actions to reduce the level of segregation within the school system. They were also angry that the school board continued to build new schools in predominantly white out-lying areas when there were inner-city schools which had numer-ous empty seats. In May 1995 the school board applied for federal funds to finance its magnet program with the promise that it would achieve acceptable desegregation ranges at twelve schools by 1997. If the board failed to reach those ranges, they would agree to intro-duce a controlled-choice plan. The NAACP opposed this applica-tion, arguing that it was premature.[32]

In August, Judge Moore appointed Judge Harvey Schlesinger as a mediator between the two sides to solve their disputes. The NAACP lawyers argued that the school board had been working against them in their efforts to desegregate the remaining segre-gated schools. They provided several examples of what they believed were bad faith efforts made on the part of the school sys-tem. The mediation efforts of Judge Schlesinger failed to produce a compromise. The court studied the school board's request before calling for a hearing on it. By 1996 the courts had allowed school districts to have partial unitary status. In the 1968 *Green v. County School Board of New Kent County* case, the courts outlined six areas that should be used to determine unitary status. Those areas were: student assignment; faculty assignment; staff assignment; facilities and resources; transportation; and extracurricular activi-ties.[33]

Jacksonville had made strides since the original case was filed in several of those areas. By the 1990s, the city's population had increased dramatically to more than one million people. With city-county consolidation, Jacksonville had a landmass of 851 square miles, making it the largest city in the nation. The school system's enrollment had fluctuated during the period from 1967 until 1996. During the 1967 to 1968 period, Jacksonville's public school enrollment stood at 119,738 students, of whom 86,564, or seventy-two percent, were white and 33,172, or twenty-eight percent, were

African American. During the 1972-1973 school year, when the school board implemented Judge Gerald Tjoflat's order, school enrollment declined significantly. By the 1983-1984 school year, enrollment had fallen to 87,604 students, of whom 56,285, or sixty-four percent, were white and 31,319, or thirty-six percent, were African American. This did not mean that the city's white population was decreasing, only that white parents were finding alternatives to public education for their children.[34]

Between 1985 and 1996, enrollment increased, even though the ratio of white to African American students leveled off at sixty percent to forty percent. After the school board and the NAACP came to an agreement that had the two sides working together, student enrollment once again began to climb. By 1991 the enrollment had reached 111,146 students, with sixty-three percent white and thirty-seven percent African American. By the 1996-1997 school year, enrollment had increased to 125,971, with 75,105 white students and 50,866 African American students. The racial mix was still at sixty percent white to forty percent African American. The number of schools had increased to 142. There were still thirty schools with a student population of seventy-five percent or more African Americans. The school district continued to have a significant level of segregation but the educational system was improving.[35]

Some of the students were in special schools, which were not included in the agreement. The school board and NAACP lawyers agreed to use the benchmark of seventy-five percent to determine if a school was identifiably African American. The parties divided the elementary schools into four categories. The first group had enrollments of between twenty and fifty-one percent black. They were defined as naturally integrated or stand-alone schools. Both parties agreed that these schools had a racially integrated student body as a natural by-product of the evolving demographics factors surrounding the schools' location.[36]

The second category of elementary schools were those with an African American enrollment of seventy-five percent or higher. These schools were referred to as preferred option or racially identifiable schools. Both the NAACP and the school board wanted to concentrate their efforts on desegregating those schools. The third category of schools were those with a fifteen percent or less enrollment of white students. These schools were described as identifiably African American schools.[37]

Defining a school system as segregated proved difficult. There were several factors that had to be considered when making this decision. First, and most obvious, was that there were more white students than African American students and one could expect some identifiably white schools because of neighborhood segregation. The most important detail for the desegregating forces was to make sure that there were no identifiably African American schools. The courts argued that desegregating identifiably white schools was irrelevant because the African American schools were the issue.[38]

The fourth category of elementary schools was defined as those that did not fit into any of the previous categories. They were schools with African American enrollment of between sixteen and nineteen percent or between fifty-six and seventy-four percent. The school district opened a new office called the Desegregation Planning Office. This office identified the twenty-eight elementary schools that were not integrated and developed educational programs to solve their problems. The programs they developed were designed to provide a high-quality education to as many area students as the school could reasonably handle in a desegregative fashion and also to attract and retain opposite-race students to fulfill the desegregation goals of the proposal.[39]

As the school issues began to dominate the local news, city officials became increasingly concerned. The educational crisis was taking away from the progress the city was making in other areas. In 1994 John Delaney was elected mayor of Jacksonville. Delaney, like Zenke, was a transported northerner who had moved from Lansing, Michigan, to Jacksonville with his family as a teenager. He attended high school in Jacksonville, graduating from the predominantly white Terry Parker High School in 1974. After high school, he attended the University of Florida where he earned a BA in History in 1977 and a law degree in 1981. After graduating from law school, he served in several city positions. He was the general counsel and then chief of staff during Mayor Ed Austin's administration. Delaney was a new-generation Republican who championed government as a tool for improving people's lives. Not long after his election, he initiated a bold new proposal called The Better Jacksonville Plan, which called for the city to spend an astounding $2.2 billion on a series of municipal projects designed to make the city more livable. The plan proposed preservation projects, along with land grants to parks. According to City Charter Revision 761:

There is hereby established "The Better Jacksonville Plan," for the purposes of managing growth, improving and constructing roads, protecting natural lands and waterways and targeting economic development and providing public facilities. Among other quality of life improvements, The Better Jacksonville Plan, if approved by the citizens of Jacksonville, will improve roads to reduce traffic congestion and direct growth through a Countywide road and infrastructure improvement plan for $1,500,000,000. . . . By investing in enhanced neighborhood streets and parks, protecting natural resources and providing better public facilities for residents and encouraging growth in targeted areas, The Better Jacksonville Plan will help ensure a strong City for the future. (Ord. 2000-572-E, § 1)[40]

The Better Jacksonville Plan had its origins in a September 5, 2000, vote when residents across Jacksonville overwhelmingly voted to approve it. It was a blueprint for managing the city's future growth. The proposal called for a $2.25 billion comprehensive growth management strategy that expanded and upgraded roads; modernized and improved infrastructure; emphasized environmental preservation; and targeted economic development with new and improved public facilities throughout the city. The plan was to be funded through a half-cent sales tax and by better utilizing existing revenue sources. City officials set aside $1.5 billion for road and infrastructure improvements, directly benefiting neighborhoods in all parts of the city. Furthermore, they called for targeted economic development to create jobs in economically depressed areas. The plan included funds to encourage land preservation, rebuild neighborhood parks, and modernize sewer infrastructure in critical areas. Finally, the plan called for providing residents with quality public facilities such as modern neighborhood libraries; a sports and entertainment arena and baseball park; and a new county courthouse. According to the program's website, "The Better Jacksonville Plan marries all of these key elements into a design that will encourage and support responsible and managed growth while creating a better quality of life for all of Jacksonville's residents."[41]

With all of the improvements and progress made in Jacksonville there was a growing movement to end the school desegregation case. Several prominent leaders began pressuring school officials to make the necessary adjustments to complete the court-mandated changes. However, the NAACP lawyers and the school board lawyers seemed to be at an impasse as they haggled over the details of the agreed-upon plan. As the two sides continued to argue back and forth, the courts once again stepped in and demanded the two sides sit together to mediate their disputes.

On January 12, 1996, newly appointed judge William Terrell Hodges ordered representatives from the NAACP and the school board to get together to see if they could settle the dispute between them before embarking on yet another long court battle. Judge Hodges asked U.S. District Judge Harvey E. Schlesinger to mediate between the two factions. The NAACP was represented by Anthony Rodgers, Jacksonville branch president; attorney Michael Sussman; Wylene Dozier, first vice president; Robert Flowers, second vice president; Michael Rutledge, third vice president; Olivia Gay, treasurer; and Paulene Ingraham-Drayton, education committee chair. The school board was represented by Larry Zenke, superintendent; Cheryl Donelan, school board chairwoman; board members Gwendola Jones, Billy Parker, Linda Sparks, and Susan Wilkinson; Ernst Mueller, assistant general counsel; and Maree Sneed, board attorney.[42]

The two groups met and began a series of negotiations aimed at settling the final differences between them. It was soon obvious that the negotiations would be difficult and possibly fruitless. The Duval County School System had changed and there was disagreement over whether or not the school board's integrative efforts had kept up with the changes.

Between 1991 and 1997, student enrollment in Duval County had increased by 30,000 students. There was a severe shortage of classrooms for students who lived in the newly developed neighborhoods in outlying areas. Between 1991 and 1995 the school district and NAACP officials held constant consultations about three issues: student assignments, potential sites of new schools, and educational equality. Willye Dennis and Larry Zenke held several meetings in which they discussed several compromise sites for the new construction. They specifically discussed school sites in East Arlington. They wrote a proposal calling for the new schools to be built in so-called grey areas. However, this idea was quickly deemed unfeasible because it called for closing some predominantly black schools. Also, the areas available for school construction were not suitable because of soil condition, pollution, lot sizes, or nearby commercial development. Zenke argued that the school board had met its obligation of consulting and went ahead with purchases of school sites in overcrowded areas. The two sides could not agree on this important issue.[43]

School board lawyers argued that the NAACP should not complain about their rejection of a plan which the NAACP itself found unacceptable. Furthermore, they argued the law did not require the board to adopt the most desegregative alternative available when there were other potential problems with the available options. Superintendent Larry Zenke faced a crucial hurdle when two properties that the school district was considering buying became available. On March 7, 1995, Jim Howard, Duval County

Public Schools Director of Facilities, wrote to the assistant superintendent of facilities services:

[The seller] says that if the DCSB turns down purchasing the two parcels tonight that his clients will put them on the market. They feel that they have held property and worked with the DCSB for over two years. Because of this and the fact that they have held the line on the price, at less than one-half of the current value, at this time wishes to place these parcels back on the market for full current value.[44]

Zenke informed Bill Randall, Jacksonville Branch NAACP President, both verbally and in writing that the school district was going to purchase the property prior to the board action. Just purchasing the two East Arlington sites did not necessarily mean that the school board would build on them. Sometimes the board purchased land and held it to sell or trade for other sites. In June 1995, shortly after purchasing the land, the school board formed a desegregation committee to make recommendations on new school sites. The board invited representatives from the NAACP to serve on the committee. However, the NAACP refused to participate in this effort, squandering an opportunity to influence the site selection process. The committee's first action upon convening was to invite NAACP representatives to participate. Again, the NAACP declined.[45]

In November of 1995, the desegregation committee issued its report. Superintendent Zenke utilized this report in creating his five-year facilities plan, which was a comprehensive proposal for growing the district's facilities to meet its needs. To appease the NAACP, Zenke ordered that all of the facilities ensure equity. Zenke's plan was designed in conjunction with desegregation consultants Dr. David Bennett and Dr. Robert Peterkin, who advised the school board on desegregation issues. Bennett, who was white, was a Minnesota-based desegregation expert highly recommended by NAACP lawyers. Peterkin, an African American, had been hired by Zenke in 1995 to help with implementing the NAACP-negotiated agreement. Peterkin was the director of the Urban Superintendents' Program and a senior lecturer in educational policy and administration at the Harvard Graduate School. The plan was then given to the NAACP for their perusal. After reviewing the proposal, the NAACP lawyers rejected it. They outlined their objections in writing prior to their court-ordered mediation meetings. Because of the NAACP's objections, the school board chose not to implement the plan until after their mediation sessions with Judge Schlesinger.[46]

After six months of fruitless negotiations, the school board decided to amend the plan and then implement it. They informed the NAACP of their decision, and without further consultation, implemented Zenke's amended plan. In October 1996, the board informed the NAACP that they were beginning construction on the Abess Boulevard Elementary School on one of the sites they had purchased in East Arlington. In 1998 they also began construction on other educational facilities: Chets Creek Elementary, Baymeadows Elementary, Baymeadows Middle, and Old Middleburg Road School. All of the schools opened with black student enrollments within the Corrected Stipulation Agreement goals.[47]

The NAACP objected to the school openings. They countered the board's arguments by pointing out that there were still a number of schools that had staff and faculty that were decidedly one race. They pointed to Andrew Jackson Senior High School, Paxon Senior High School, Ribault Senior High School, Matthew Gilbert Middle School, Northwestern Middle School, and William Raines Senior High School, all of which had coaching staffs that were more than sixty percent African American. They also indicated six schools which had head coaches who were black, mirroring the majority race of the schools. NAACP officials also pointed out that Mandarin Senior High School and Ed White Senior High School had each hired a staff of head coaches that was less than twenty percent African American.[48]

The school board's representative, Peterkin, argued that it was difficult to hire coaches because the pay, especially for middle schools, was low, and the teachers had to play a dual role of teacher and coach. Therefore, the coaching staff in middle school came from the teaching faculty, reducing the number of available candidates. He went on to argue that, since the faculty pool was only thirty percent African American, that reduced the applicant pool even further. Peterkin argued that the board had gone to great lengths to create racial diversity in hiring and assigning coaches and that African American coaches were well represented district-wide.[49]

As the year came to an end, the school board members were confident that they had done all they could to establish an integrated unitary school system in Duval County. With the backing of many in the community, the board decided to apply for unitary status, and to petition the federal court to relieve it of court supervision. As the school district prepared to go to court, the issues and arguments were clear, but many held their breath. The basic issue was whether the spirit or letter of the law was more important. The NAACP wanted the school board to follow the letter of the agreement while the school board wanted to adhere to the spirit of the agreement.

Education correspondent Laura Diamond outlined the different perspectives of the school board and the NAACP in a *Florida Times-Union* article on November 11, 1999. Diamond stated, "In determining if a school system deserves unitary status, courts are obligated to look at specific areas. Disagreements exist between the NAACP and the Duval County school system as to whether schools have adequately corrected past discrimination in these areas." The areas are student assignment, facilities, faculty/staffing, and extracurricular activities. The NAACP and school board disagreed on all of these areas. For example, on the sticky issue of student assignment, the NAACP believed that the school board had been unwilling to use aggressive measures to push white parents to send their children to African American schools. Therefore, the magnet or neighborhood school option was a cop-out which allowed white parents to send their children to predominantly white schools.[50]

The school board officials argued that the Corrected Stipulation did not require compulsory assignments. Their voluntary plan met the requirement. Their lawyers also argued that even though the magnet programs considered race when assigning students, more than two-thirds of them had achieved racial balance, which exceeded what the agreement required. The school board believed that they had fulfilled the spirit of the agreement.[51]

On the issue of facilities, once again the NAACP and school board saw things differently. The NAACP argued that the school board had opened several racially identifiable white schools without consulting the NAACP. They also had built five other schools without conferring with the NAACP, a clear violation of the agreement. The school board argued that there had been extensive consultation and communication with the NAACP for years before they proceeded with construction. They specifically pointed to the numerous discussions between former Superintendent Larry Zenke and former NAACP president Willye Dennis.[52]

On the issue of faculty staffing, the NAACP was adamant that the school system had not sustained the required racial balance of faculty for three years when it applied for unitary status in October 1996. Their lawyers pointed out that during the 1994-95 school year, twenty percent of the schools did not meet the racial requirement. Before the system could be declared unitary, the 1990 agreement stipulated it must maintain the racial balance for three years. The school board argued the 1990 agreement stipulated that the schools meet the racial balance for three years before being declared unitary. They did not see the three-year timetable as a precursor to unitary status.[53]

On the issue of extra-curricular activities, the NAACP argued that the school system had to produce a detailed plan ensuring that extra-curricular activities were operated in a non-discriminatory and desegregative way. NAACP lawyers argued that the school board failed to provide such a plan. They noted the greater selection of clubs at predominantly white schools. They also noted that schools with extra-curricular activities had little participation from black students. School board lawyers argued that extra-curricular activities were voluntary, and principals had done all they could to ensure equal access. Middle school and high school principals "frequently encourage black students to participate." Also, the 1990 agreement did not specify a quota for a racial balance in extracurricular activities.[54]

The two sides outlined their arguments in briefs presented to the courts as they prepared to do battle once again. Judge William Terrell Hodges was assigned to hear the case. After listening to the two sides' arguments, Hodges declared the Duval County Public School System unitary and desegregated on May 26, 1999. In his ruling, Hodges went through the 1990 Corrected Stipulation and assessed the efforts of the school board and the critique of the NAACP lawyers. Judge Hodges ended his long decision with the words, "According to the reasons stated in this Order, the Duval County School Board's Motion for Unitary Status is Granted. The Duval County School District is hereby declared unitary in all respects."[55] This decision freed the school district to borrow money to update technology and improve facilities at the schools in the district. The decision showed a triumph of a developing strategy of utilizing magnet programs as an alternative to busing.

The judge's decision did not shock most followers of school desegregation cases. The *Florida Times-Union* staff writer Bruce Bryant-Friedland wrote:

The decision by a federal judge to pull the plug on Duval County's longstanding desegregation case yesterday fits a national pattern. One by one, lawsuits aimed at ensuring that black children sit side-by-side with white children are coming to a close in big-city school districts across the country. And now that the unrest in those cities, sparked by such measures as involuntary bussing, fade into the recesses of newspaper archives, the schools are said to remain as they were: black and white.[56]

Thus, the courts were beginning to move in a new direction. The NAACP was fighting a rising tide of conservatism. Many in the white community were successful at rejecting the traditional weapons used to integrate schools. Bryant-Friedland seemed to summarize the new developing spirit when he wrote, "Black leaders need to focus on making sure that their children's schools are as good as, or superior to, their white counterparts." He understood that the legal and social landscape was once again shifting.[57] The NAACP filed an order challenging the judge's decision. On September 15, 1999, their lawyers filed briefs asking that the judge's decision be reversed. Everyone knew that the court's decision would either end or prolong the city's long struggle for school integration.

Notes

1 *Florida Times-Union,* September 15, 1985.

2 Interview with Herb Sang by phone, January 25, 2011.

3 *Florida Times-Union,* September 15, 1985.

4 Interview with Willye Dennis, NAACP president, FTU, September 15, 1985.

5 Jacksonville Branch NAACP v. Duval County School Board, No. 85-316-Civ-J-16, (11th Cir. Sept. 15, 1989).

6 Interview with Larry Zenke, March 16, 2011.

7 Ibid.

8 Ibid.

9 Ibid.

10 Ibid.

11 *Florida Times-Union,* January 13, 1996.

12 Ibid.

13 James Thurman, *Practical Bomb Scene Investigation: Practical Aspects of Criminal and Forensic Investigation* (Boca Raton: CRC Taylor and Francis Press, 2006), 377-379.

14 Athan G. Theoharis, *The FBI: A Comprehensive Reference Guide* (Phoenix: ORYX Press, 2000), 98-99.

15 Desegregation Points. This is a talking point sheet given out by the NAACP. There are no page numbers, no author, and no publication information.

16 Ibid.

17 Ibid.

18 "Desegregation: Building for the Future," *Florida Times-Union,* January 13, 1996.

19 Judy Poppell, "The Desegregation of a Historically Black High School in Jacksonville, Florida." (PhD diss., University of North Florida, 1988), 210.

20 Jacksonville Branch NAACP v. Duval County School Board, No. 85-316-Civ-J-10C, (11th Cir. May 27,1999), 4.

21 *NAACP v. Duval County School Board, opinion,* 5.

22 "Desegregation: Building for the Future."

23 Jacksonville Branch NAACP v. Duval County School Board Corrected Stipulation and Agreement, No. 85-316-Civ- J-16, (11th Cir. 1990), 2.

24 "Desegregation: Building for the Future."

25 Ibid.

26 *Jacksonville Branch NAACP v. Duval County School Board, No. 85-316-Civ-J-10C,* 96, 111.

27 "Desegregation: Building for the Future."

28 *Florida Times-Union,* January 13, 1996.

29 *Jacksonville Branch NAACP v. Duval County School Board, No. 85-316-Civ-J-10C,* 3.

30 Jacksonville Branch NAACP v. Duval County School Board, Appellant's Brief in Chief, September 15, 1999, Docket No. 99-12049-EE, 32, 39.

31 Ibid., 10; *Jacksonville Branch NAACP v. Duval County School Board, No. 85-316-Civ-J-10C,* 7.

32 Ibid., 2.

33 Ibid., 118.

34 Ibid., 10.

35 Ibid.

36 Ibid., 11.

37 Ibid., 12.

38 Ibid., 23; *Jacksonville Branch NAACP v. Duval County School Board Corrected Stipulaton and Agreement*, 5.

39 Ibid., 4.

40 Chapter 761 – The Better Jacksonville Plan. http://www.coj.net/ Departments/Better-Jacksonville-Plan/BJP-Ordinance.aspx

41 Better Jacksonville Plan. http://www.bringyouhome.com/ betterjacksonville.html

42 *Florida Times-Union*, January 13, 1996; *Jacksonville Branch NAACP v. Duval County School Board Corrected Stipulation and Agreement*, 4.

43 *Jacksonville Branch NAACP v. Duval County School Board, No. 85-316-Civ-J-10C*, 70-73.

44 Ibid., 46.

45 Ibid., 45-46.

46 Ibid., 47.

47 Ibid.

48 Ibid., 72, 95.

49 Ibid., 95-96.

50 "Desegregation Arguments at a Glance," *Florida Times-Union*, November 11, 1999.

51 Ibid.

52 Ibid.

53 Ibid.

54 Ibid.

55 *Jacksonville Branch NAACP v. Duval County School Board, No. 85-316-Civ-J-10C*, 72, 140.

56 *Florida Times-Union*, May 28, 1999.

57 Ibid.

Chapter Eight

The Battle is Over: What Have We Learned?

Following the May 27, 1999, decision by Federal Judge William Terrell Hodges declaring the Duval County Public School System integrated and unitary, the NAACP faced a crucial but daunting decision. It could either move on, concentrating on other areas where discrimination was an issue, or continue the fight for equal education by attempting to push for additional changes to the Duval County Public School System.

Since its early filings in the late 1940s, the NAACP's national organization had been pushing for racially integrated public school systems that catered to all students, faculty, and staff fairly and equally. Though the organization had faced tremendous opposition and criticism, through its efforts all of the legally sanctioned policies supporting discrimination in the public sphere had been dismantled. Blacks and whites were socially integrated on levels never imagined by their grandparents. The quality of African American schools and facilities had been dramatically improved since the late 1950s and early 1960s, when the integration process began.

Because of NAACP pressure, school districts had spent billions, first on avoiding integration, and later on implementing integration plans designed to undo years of discriminatory policies. The integration plans were designed to force reluctant, predominantly Southern, school districts to do what they did not want to do, which was to integrate their African American children into historically segregated white schools. White school officials were compelled to integrate their African American children into the same schools that their own children attended. They also had to develop policies and guidelines that ensured African American faculty and staff an equal chance at advancement opportunities in the system. Through NAACP efforts, school districts were forced to equalize teachers' pay and open up more administrative opportunities for minority teachers. The integration fostered by NAACP pressure had forced white Southerners to admit that many of the racial biases they held were not based in fact, but instead on racial prejudice. However, as many other concerned African Americans had painfully learned, NAACP influence could not eliminate the de facto segregation that resulted from individual choices made by free citizens.

The NAACP had worked tirelessly to rid the nation of discriminatory laws. However, for many in the African American community, segregation and discrimination remained facts of life. African Americans believed that school integration was the magic bullet that would open the hearts and minds of reluctant whites. Many hoped that, through daily contact and better legislation, some of the built-up prejudices could be alleviated. Dr. Martin Luther King Jr. noted, "The job must be done through education and religion. Well, there's half-truth involved here. Certainly, if the problem is to be solved then in the final sense, hearts must be changed. Religion and education must play a great role in changing the heart. But we must go on to say that while it may be true that morality cannot be legislated, behavior can be regulated. It may be true that the law cannot change the heart but it can restrain the heartless. It may be true that the law cannot make a man love me but it can keep him from lynching me and I think that is pretty important, also."[1] School integration had gone a long way toward changing the behavior of white Southerners and many of the worst aspects of black life in the South had been alleviated.

As the South was succumbing to federal pressure, school districts were demonstrating their commitment to integrated education by pushing through aggressive plans for improving their schools. Many of these districts were run by integrated school boards dedicated to providing the best education possible to all of the children they served. The federal courts were taking note of these efforts and began rewarding the school districts by relieving them of court supervision. Even though very few of the school districts had reached perfection, many of them had made remarkable progress and were proclaiming that they had done all they could, in light of the political climate, to ensure equal educational opportunities for all of their students.

All over the nation, school districts were being declared unitary and integrated even though they had not completely eliminated racially identifiable schools, because the segregation was not caused by overt school policy, but instead by personal choices. As the country became more integrated and African Americans began to move into formerly all-white enclaves, many of the new residents developed a class-centered outlook. There were several African Americans who adopted a more conservative tone, deemphasizing racial issues and directing their attention to class issues. American attitudes about racial injustice were changing and there were fewer people interested in continuing to wage multi-generational struggles to integrate schools. Additionally, numerous stakeholders in Jacksonville were pressuring the NAACP to let the court's decision stand so that the city and school district could move on to other issues. In particular there was pressure to improve the academic performance of the students.

Such was the case as the NAACP assembled its board in June 1999 to discuss its next move. For the NAACP, the decision of whether or not to continue the fight was an easy one. The organization had never shied away from unpopular actions if the members believed the battle they were waging was a righteous one. The NAACP board voted unanimously, 28 to 0, to challenge Judge Hodges' ruling and appeal the decision. The NAACP's board voted to continue fighting until the school system treated each student, regardless of race, equally. Jacksonville Branch NAACP President Isaiah Rumlin said, "My desire, wishes and prayers are that we as a city have some degree of leadership that can come together, sit down and resolve this so children have equal education at all levels. . . .We do not feel the school system is unitary at this point."[2] The NAACP's board disagreed with Judge Hodges' assessment that the school board had done all it could to implement the well-publicized agreement the two sides had negotiated in 1990. Even though the school board had made remarkable progress during the 1995-1996 school year in pushing through reforms and attempting to implement major portions of the plan, there were still areas of concern for the NAACP. School board lawyers also believed that the Jacksonville courts were biased against them and they expected to have a much more favorable ruling if they appealed to the Eleventh Circuit Court of Appeals in Atlanta. There the three-judge panel had proven more receptive to their arguments in the past.[3]

For the NAACP's board the major concern was still the clearly identifiable achievement gap between African American and white children. Many on the board believed that the school board had failed to adequately address this important issue. School board officials readily agreed that Jacksonville had an achievement gap; however, they argued that it was not the fault of the school board and, therefore, not an issue that could be addressed in the lawsuit. Clearly, African American children were not performing as well as white children in schools. However, this "achievement gap" was a national phenomenon and not a local problem the Duval County Public School System could solve. School Board Chairwoman Linda Sparks noted, "Across the nation, school districts have been declared unitary, and there are probably achievement gaps in all of them. . . . It's hard to become unitary when your school district is distracted by so many things that don't have to do with education." For Sparks and others in the school system, they had done all the school district could do to ensure equal education.[4]

Judy Poppell, the school system's director of academic programs and a key player in helping the schools comply with the desegregation agreement, agreed that an achievement gap existed, but that "the school system clearly has not given up on addressing the inequalities."[5] She also felt that the NAACP should allow the case to die and begin working with the school system to fix remaining problems outside of the court system. Poppell pointed to programs like America's Choice and the Urban Systemic Initiative, which focus on helping low-achieving students, as proof that the school system was trying to deal with the achievement gap. For many the court cases were an unwelcome distraction, which took focus away from other issues needing attention. Many school board officials made the same argument that if the school board were removed from court order, they could focus more on other issues.[6]

At that time John Fryer was the school system's superintendent. He was overjoyed that the courts had stepped in and stopped the lawsuit. He believed that Superintendent Zenke had already set up enough programs and policies to ensure that the school district served each child equally. He wanted to continue to ensure equality but felt that there were other areas that the school system needed to work on without court supervision. He also believed that the charge that there was an achievement gap was unfair. "Every school district which attempts to integrate sees the same thing. Affluent parents remove their children from school systems that go through integration. People commonly call it 'White Flight' but what it should more accurately be called is 'wealth flight.'"[7] Fryer said that there was no realistic way to guard against people with money moving to new areas, or taking their children out of public schools and putting them into private schools, to avoid contact with children they deemed undesirable. School districts should not be blamed for parental actions they could not control. Fryer said being declared unitary and integrated did not stop the equalization process but, instead, helped speed it up by freeing the district to attack solvable problems.[8]

However, after nearly forty years of broken promises, the NAACP was not prepared to trust the school district to do the right thing without significant outside pressure. Education for black children had obviously improved since the bad days of segregation, but black children in Jacksonville were still not getting the same education that white children were receiving. Until they did, the NAACP was obligated to continue its fight. The African American members of the school board were also not ready to declare the school district unitary. African American school board member Gwen Gibson, who was also a practicing attorney, said, "Healing? There is no healing. The fact that there is a pronouncement that the district is unitary doesn't mean that the sun shines brighter. Many of the problems we started out with are still with us."[9] Gibson said teachers in inner-city schools were still dealing with a lack of supplies and books, and there were inequities in promotion and staffing. "I get calls from all over the district. Adults and children are still suffering and there is no process–no written procedure–for handling complaints."[10] Gibson understood why the NAACP wanted to challenge Judge Hodges' decision. She had spent many years advocating for improvements to African American education in Jacksonville. She understood that Jacksonville was a historically difficult place to make racial progress.

Gwendolyn Gibson was a native of Tallahassee, Florida, who had moved to Jacksonville with her family in 1972. Gibson was amazed at how open white residents of Tallahassee were to integrating their schools when she was growing up. However, she immediately noticed that Jacksonville residents put up far more resistance than the residents of Tallahassee. Gibson was a graduate of Florida A&M University and the University of Florida Law School. Her husband worked for the Duval County Public School System, serving as a teacher at Matthew W. Gilbert Middle School. She was immediately shocked by how difficult it was to reach agreement on what, to her, were simple and easy educational reforms in Jacksonville. Not long after arriving in Jacksonville, she worked on the board of Legal Aid where she became actively engaged in a number of community activities. The one issue that constantly resurfaced was education. Gibson became actively engaged in educational issues because of her husband's work and concern about her children's education. In 1990 Gibson was a member of the NAACP, as the Duval County Public School System was trying to work through their negotiated settlement with the organization. She was amazed at how much opposition there was to what, to her, seemed like a logical and fair proposal. She was so upset by the experience that, in 1990, she ran for the school board to ensure that African American schools and children were served equally by the agreement.[11]

In Gibson's opinion, the NAACP was using the wrong strategy with its emphasis on magnet schools to get white children to attend black schools. Instead of wasting time trying to get white students into black schools, she believed that the organization should fight for more funding for African American schools and programs. She believed that there was an overemphasis on integration and not enough emphasis on equality. The achievement gap between black and white students was, to her, a clear sign that black and white children were not being served equally in Duval County. Also, she argued that the physical plants and teaching methods used at predominantly black and white schools were totally different. Even though there had been improvements, the schools were not equal and certainly not unitary. She could not understand how Judge Hodges could miss this. Gibson left the school board and the city in the early 2000s when her husband retired from the system and they both moved to Daytona. She was once again refreshed by the attitude that the local residents had toward education in Volusia County. Even though she continued to keep tabs on the Jacksonville situation, she was sure that things would not appreciably improve.[12]

NAACP lawyers agreed with Gibson's assessment and appealed Judge Hodges' decision to the Eleventh Circuit Court of Appeals. The three-judge panel heard the case and carefully considered all of the arguments. Both the NAACP and the school board presented a plethora of experts who testified for and against the various positions. The NAACP argued that the school board was not acting in good faith and that it was still not doing everything it could to ensure an equal education for all children. The NAACP lawyers pointed to several areas where the school system was failing. African American schools were not staffed, operated, or administered the same as white schools. This had, in turn, led to black children not receiving the same quality of education as white children. Their lawyers also argued that instead of carrying out the spirit of the negotiated agreement, the board had consistently violated it and circumvented its spirit.

The school board's lawyers used a number of impressive statistics to make the argument that they had gone above and beyond the call of duty to ensure equality among all students. They contended that the inequities which remained were not the result of overt school board action but were instead the vestiges of America's segregationist past. There were still racial issues dividing blacks and whites but these were not problems that the school board could solve. Even the statistics, which seemed to show segregation increasing and African American children experiencing more negative outcomes, were a reflection of increased numbers of black students, not of increased segregation and discrimination.[13]

The courts accepted the school board lawyers' arguments and, on November 19, 2001, after nearly forty-one years of litigation before five district court judges, two different circuit courts of appeal, and a three-judge panel representing the Eleventh Circuit of the United States Court of Appeals, unanimously ruled that the Duval County Public School System had done all it could to integrate the county's public schools. After many premature pronouncements, the more than forty-year ordeal finally ended, not with a bang but a whimper. Though the courts ended the case, questions remained about what had been accomplished. The Duval County Public School System was declared unified and integrated, even though everyone knew that the system still had racially identifiable schools, and there were still charges that whites and upper and middle class children continued to receive a better education than lower class students in predominantly African American neighborhoods. The court's decision forces us to ask the question, "Integration for what?" Why did the NAACP and the many African American families carry on this decades-long struggle? Was it to integrate the schools, or was it to provide a high-quality education for all the children in Duval County? Also, were the costs associated with the lawsuits worth it? Did Jacksonville gain or lose from the long-drawn-out struggle to integrate its schools? Did the protracted school integration battle help or hurt race relations in the city? Finally, what price did those who waged the struggle pay?

The many judges who sat through the oral arguments and read the written responses from the various parties in the school integration cases had to deal with the shifting priorities of those who championed these cases. They also had to adjust to the changing demands of the community as the battle shifted from a racial to a class struggle. The racially segregated Jacksonville of the 1960s was replaced by an integrated, consolidated city where blacks occupied several positions of power. When the NAACP originally filed the case in 1960, there were no African Americans on the school board or the city council. By 2001 blacks were sitting on both of these august councils. During the forty years of litigation, the city, state, and nation had dramatically changed and the leaders of the public school system no longer openly supported segregation and discrimination. Florida's population had more than tripled during this period, rising from 4,951,560 to 15,982,378. By the 2010 census, Florida's population had increased to 18,801,310.[14] By 2001 Florida was one of America's largest and most diverse states. Hispanics had found a comfortable niche in society, transforming the traditional racial dynamics from black and white to black, white, and brown. Between 1960 and 2010 Jacksonville's population had mushroomed from 522,169 to 864,263.[15] The demographics of those enrolled in the Duval County Public School System fluctuated during this period as it, like the nation, had become increasingly browner. As the integration process heated up and busing became a tactic, white students fled the system in droves. In the early 1960s, more than seventy percent of the students enrolled in the schools were white. By 2000 that number had declined to under sixty percent. The number of identifiably black schools had actually increased over the years as more whites moved out of the public schools and into private schools, leaving more African American and Hispanic students in the public schools. Between 1989 and 1999, the number of identifiably black schools had increased from eighteen to thirty, as more whites, especially those assigned to schools in black neighborhoods, moved into private schools.[16]

The United States had changed and school systems changed along with the country. In 2008 Barack Hussein Obama was elected as America's first African American president. Taking advantage of a colossal economic collapse, Obama put together a grassroots campaign that energized progressive whites and American youth to win a national election. Many argued that we were seeing the end of race as a political issue. However, within weeks of Obama's taking office, many could see that even though we had made strides, race continued to be a dominant issue separating blacks and whites. Historian Peniel Josephs says, "If civil rights marches, urban riots, and black militancy sparked a national dialogue on race during the 1960s that at times threatened to go down a slippery slope of racial hysteria, Obama's election has likewise triggered national contemplation over the meaning of race and democracy in the twenty-first century."[17] Blacks and whites cooperated over class lines on many controversial issues.

As the divide between the rich and poor increased, the disparities in education also grew. Dropout rates increased and the perceived quality of a public education was reduced. As the nation moved in a decidedly conservative direction, educational issues were scrutinized as state governments looked for ways to reduce taxes and cut state budgets. Educational budgets were often the target of politicians looking for ways to make a name for themselves. They cut or reduced educational spending to show they were willing to make tough financial decisions. As conservative commentators introduced alternatives to the newly integrated public schools, there was a corresponding denigration of the public school system. State legislatures, more interested in cutting state budgets than ensuring educational excellence, reduced spending and cut taxes, gutting educational budgets along with funding for other social programs. When the quality of education declined, those same legislators accused teachers and administrators of poor performance and advocated educational alternatives to public education.

In addition, the African American community was ravaged by the destruction of the traditional family structure. As two-parent families disappeared and more children were reared in single-family homes, a number of new pathologies developed which harmed their communities. Between 1962 and 2000, what Senator Daniel Patrick Moynihan had considered a possibility in the 1960s had become a reality. According to Child Trend Databank, by 2000 nearly seventy percent of children born to black parents were born in a single-parent home.[18] By 2003, of the 52.6 million students in grades K-12 in the U.S., 12.8 percent of whites, 39 percent of Hispanics, and 69 percent of African Americans lived in homes where there was no male figure.[19] Many African American communities were plagued by drug use, violence, and illicit sexual behavior, which devastated these communities and undermined many of the social and economic gains made during the previous civil rights era. These behaviors also weakened the educational foundations of the African American community, leading to declining graduation rates and high levels of incarceration. In her well-received book, *The New Jim Crow*, Michelle Alexander argues that reduced educational spending is directly tied to the increase in spending on prisons; part of a continuing caste system designed to keeps minorities on the bottom.[20]

A number of African American scholars and experts have opined about these problems but few have found viable solutions. As the nation saw a decline in traditional ideas about faith, family, and society, there was a corresponding decline in support for the institutions that undergirded these ideas. The number of African Americans attending church declined significantly along with the number of people who got married. As the nation debated ethical and moral issues, school issues took on new importance, since many of these debates were played out in school curriculum battles. What was lost were the children who, in ever increasing numbers, began to leave school without graduating.

Of the many problems which have plagued education in contemporary society, none has been more debated than the dropout rate. In America, literally millions of school-age children drop out of school before graduation. This decision can have devastating consequences for the students themselves and for the communities they reside in. There has been a compelling link between dropout rates and incarceration rates. These two problems have gone hand-in-hand in Jacksonville.

On any given day, nearly 23 percent of all young black men ages 16 to 24 who have dropped out of high school are in jail, prison, or a juvenile justice institution in America, according to a disturbing new national report

released today on the dire economic and social consequences of not graduating from high school.

Dropouts become incarcerated at a shocking rate: 23 of
every 100 young black male dropouts were in jail on any
given day in 2006-07 compared to only 6 to 7 of every 100
Asian, Hispanic or white dropouts. While young black
men are disproportionately affected, the report found
that this crisis cuts across racial and ethnic lines. Male
dropouts of all races were 47 times more likely to be
incarcerated than their peers of a similar age who had
graduated from a four-year college or university.[21]

Jacksonville has been dealing with the dropout problem for several years. It feeds into the notion of the city's being the murder
capital of Florida. This is yet another example of how school and
social issues are intricately linked. Michelle Alexander noted in
The New Jim Crow, "The young men who go to prison rather than
college face a lifetime of closed doors, discrimination, and ostra-
cism."[22]

As local residents dealt with integration issues, a number of
other concerns that were associated with school integration also
had to be considered. Many people were touting the progress the
nation had made on racial concerns, yet the relatively easy process
of integrating the schools had proven remarkably difficult. It led
many to ask the question, "Just how far have we come on racial
issues?" When there are clear disparities between the experiences
of African Americans and whites, most African Americans have
been pre-programmed to immediately look for racial explanations.
This response is not based on some paranoid racial delusions, but
is instead the result of years of racial discrimination supported by
seemingly innocuous laws designed to help society but, in actuality, maintaining the inequities in the system.

Therefore, when African Americans ended up right back where
they started, they were immediately suspicious that they were once
again the victims of some racial scheming. Blacks in Jacksonville
had waged a long, determined battle to ensure that their children

received a quality education which was just as good as that of any other person in society. Sadly, even after this struggle, in many cases African American children still found themselves lagging behind whites in many important areas. John Fryer, the former superintendent of schools, said the underlying problem was not race but, rather, fear. People were afraid of each other and this had kept the two races apart. Integration helped break down the fear on both sides. Some African Americans who were very suspicious of whites and did not trust them were changed by their experiences in integrated schools. On the other side, there were whites whose fear of blacks allowed them to do irrrational things to blacks. Though conditions had not become perfect, progress had been made. This progress was sometimes overlooked as people concentrated on other negative events.[23]

For example, though the number of racially identifiable schools in Jacksonville had actually increased, it was clear that the schools were no longer legally segregated. The federal courts argued that the presence of one-race schools did not necessarily mean that the school district was not unitary. There were several instances in which a school district was declared unitary even though there were numerous essentially one-race schools. For example, in the 1983 *Ross v. Houston* case, the courts ruled the school district unitary and integrated even though fifty-five of the 226 schools were ninety percent or more African American. Houston's school district was thirty-eight percent African American, twenty percent white, and forty-two percent Hispanic. That school district saw an increase of thirty-three racially identifiable schools during the period of federal court supervision. The courts stated, "Constructing a unitary school system does not require a racial balance in all of the schools. What is required is that every reasonable effort be made to eradicate segregation and its insidious residue." The federal courts recognized that racial housing patterns and individual decisions could not be legislated or changed by court action. If the school system had make reasonable efforts to end its dual operations the courts gave them credit.[24]

Several district courts have looked at the school districts' good faith efforts to implement court-ordered student assignments and also how the school district has been operated historically. Though many school districts have never fully integrated, they have nonetheless received court approval because they no longer operate on a racially discriminative basis. A number of courts gave school districts unitary status even though there were several schools that had student populations that did not fall into the specified racial composition demanded by the courts. In these cases the court looked at other factors in making its decision. Also, the courts took into consideration the progress that each community had made toward racial healing. In 1995 Jacksonville residents had elected Nat Glover as one of the South's first African American sheriffs in the modern era. Also, Earl Johnson, the lawyer who filed the first school desegregation suit, was elected to the newly created consolidated city council from an at-large seat. This showed that white attitudes towards blacks were changing. These factors also influenced the court's decision.

Conservatives applauded the courts' decisions to turn school issues back over to local authorities. Many conservatives were leery of multigenerational lawsuits demanding integration of public school systems, with what many of them referred to as nondescript goals. They made the argument that these suits represented the worst solution to fixing the racial gap in public schools. Conservative analyst Abigail Thernstrom noted, "We've got a horrible racial gap in academic skills and we've got to close that gap, but busing wasn't doing it."[25] A number of conservative critics argued that the notion that we could socially engineer an equalized society was naïve. They instead suggested that we concentrate on naturally evolving strategies that did not have predetermined outcomes. Stan Hawkins, an Atlanta-based attorney who represented the public schools in De Kalb County, Georgia, in their effort to close the suit against their system, said, "Federal courts are not designed, nor do they have the role, to solve educational problems in this country." Like many conservatives Hawkins believed that any top-down solution to a local problem was illegitimate. He favored a reduced role by federal authorities in local issues.[26]

However, those who supported the lawsuits saw the developing trends and argued that, without force or threat, school districts would revert to their old ways and we would see the resegregation of the public school systems. There was little evidence that school districts would do the right thing without court pressure. In fact, the evidence showed that they were willing to attempt a number of illegal and unethical schemes to avoid integration. Gary Orfield, the Harvard education professor who writes about educational issues, made the argument that school districts were rapidly resegregating and, if the courts released their heavy hand, there would be nothing to stop the movement. Orfield and his fellow researchers raised the clarion call that the nation needed to be on guard against the potential of returning to the segregated society of the past. Even the NAACP seemed to be resigned to the fact that the traditional solutions to integration were failing to achieve the desired results. John Evans of the De Kalb County NAACP was quoted as saying, "You cannot attract white folks to black communities."[27]

When interviewed years later about the school desegregation suit, Willye Dennis was very unapologetic about the long struggle the NAACP waged for equal education. She continued to believe that the school board had not done enough to ensure equal education for Jacksonville's black children. She was particularly concerned about the situation at Raines and Ribault, two predominantly African American schools which had failed to meet established state standards. Dennis said, "I don't blame those kids. I blame the School Board and the Courts which have both failed to do their job. Those kids are just as talented as any kids in this city. The difference is that the people in power have refused to give them all the tools they give the other kids."[28] Dennis believed that, though Jacksonville had made progress on racial issues, many of the same challenges she faced years ago growing up in the city were still prevalent in the contemporary society she inhabited.[29]

Dennis's feelings were somewhat mirrored by the feelings of Wendell Holmes. Holmes had been a part of the school desegregation process from the beginning. He also believed that African American children continued to be shortchanged by the school system. Though tremendous progress had been made, none of it had come easily. The school system had fought the NAACP and those who supported integrative policies all the way. In the end those who had waged this struggle were asked to trust that those who had spent decades blocking school integration efforts had done everything they could to make up for past sins.[30]

In the case of the Duval County Public Schools the courts concluded that, "It simply is not possible to identify the 'race' of a school by the racial composition of its administration or faculty, the quality of its building, or the level of program services and resources that the District provides." In the areas where the school board had the power to make changes, they made the necessary changes. They transferred teachers and administrators to get the proper racial balances and spent $60 million to improve and upgrade selected inner-city schools. The school district had been very proactive in developing race-neutral practices in operating all of its programs and operations. John Fryer, the former superintendent, says that being declared integrated did not end the school system's effort to ensure quality education; rather, it enhanced it.[31]

There are few people who can argue that public school integration did not open the society to African Americans, offering them more opportunities than in any previous era. Through school integration, African American children were given a chance to compete with white students and demolish some of the intellectual inferiority theories that were prevalent. The first children who integrated public schools performed well and helped break down some of the early fears whites may have had. Equally important was that many of these children took advantage of their opportunities and continued to use their education to move into important leadership positions.

School integration gave Jacksonville's white community a chance to interact with African Americans in different social settings. Having the advantage of hindsight, we now know that the dire predictions of Jacksonville developing into a resegregated society or school system did not materialize. In reality, with the end of the desegregation case, the school board went on to concentrate on a massive building program, which produced modern well-equipped schools throughout the county. Nevertheless, there are still lingering racial issues which continue to plague the system and city. No one would argue with the idea that we have far too many racially identifiable schools in Jacksonville. The question which remains is: How much of that problem can be attributed to the operational practices of the school board?

Former Jacksonville Public School Superintendent Larry Zenke said that people owed a debt to the NAACP and others who fought for school integration. The level of general integration that we see today is a direct consequence of the integration of the public schools and the lowering of racial tensions. School integration helped change the society and improve conditions for both African Americans and whites. It opened new opportunities for working together that had not been seen before. Despite the fact that African Americans continue to believe that they are not equally served by the school system, they recognize that the conditions in African American schools are much better than they were when the lawsuits began.[32]

Wendell Holmes served on the Duval County School Board for twenty-two years. He was intimately familiar with the school board's work. Holmes believed that the school board could have done more. The whole gamut of services provided to students was unequal. The schools serving white students were always better than the schools serving African American students. "We started this struggle to address areas where our children were receiving less quality education than other students." By identifying these areas and forcing the school board to deal with them, they successfully destroyed the dual system. Holmes was motivated to join the school board because of his concern about the education his children were receiving. As part of the NAACP, Holmes worked with the organization on educational issues. He was a member of the Citizens Committee for Better Education in Duval County.[33]

Larry Zenke, the former Duval County Public School System superintendent, understood why Judge Hodges made the decision he did. There were six so-called *Green* factors which had been established by the courts to determine if a school system was unitary and integrated. The school board had done all they could do to ensure a fair education for all children in Duval County, given the political and social restraints they faced. According to the standards established by the courts, the school district was unitary and integrated. However, he also understood why African American leaders were still upset. There were several aspects of the way the school system operated that disadvantaged African American children. There were still disparities in allocations of funds and opportunities, depending on where students lived.[34]

Former Jacksonville mayor and current University of North Florida president, John Delaney, was also relieved that the courts removed themselves from the school battle. Delaney, a veteran of the public school system, was born in Lansing, Michigan, but moved to Cincinnati, Ohio. In 1972 his family moved from Cincinnati to Jacksonville, settling in the Arlington area. He was somewhat surprised by the racism he saw in the city. Delaney graduated from Terry Parker High School, went on to the University of Florida, and then to the University's Law School. He served as a state attorney for several years, eventually rising to chief assistant under State Attorney Ed Austin.

When Austin was elected mayor of Jacksonville in 1991, he tapped Delaney as the city's general counsel. Delaney rose to chief of staff and, in 1995, was elected mayor. Delaney, a Republican, served two terms as mayor, from 1995 until 2003. During his tenure, he oversaw the massive Better Jacksonville Plan, which relied on a sales tax to fund a $2.5 billion dollar municipal improvement program. The school superintendents were really in a bind because they had to work with the dysfunctional school board, where all it took was four votes to stop anything.

School integration had definitely improved the city and helped the people work together more effectively. The problem with race in the U.S. is that there are some people who see racism in everything, while others don't see racism in anything. As long as these two groups have their way, we cannot make much progress. We solve problems when the two sides get together and negotiate a fair agreement. The Jacksonville of 1972 and the Jacksonville of 2012 are two radically different places, and much of the credit should go to school integration. Even though the schools had a period of regression during the past few years, the good news is that they are coming back.[35]

When summarizing the significance of Jacksonville's long struggle to integrate the public schools, Larry Zenke summed up why the fight was worth it. Zenke said that when he arrived in Jacksonville in 1970 there were two Jacksonvilles: one black and the other white. They were separate and vastly unequal. Within three years the one hundred elementary schools were integrated and attempts were being made to equalize the system. When he returned to the city in 1989, he lived in an apartment for a few months while the builders completed construction on his home. He noticed that each afternoon an interracial group of young men played basketball at the playground of his apartment. The young men were not segregated by race but instead had whites and blacks playing together on both teams. Through school integration, students had developed relationships with people of different races, and these relationships sometime extended to their parents.

By 2012 Jacksonville had an African American mayor and he was sitting in a restaurant near two interracial couples. None of that would have been possible had we not integrated the public schools, opening up opportunities for white and black children to interact together in classroom settings. This interaction led to socializing, which eventually led to dating, and that inevitably led to interracial marriage, which today is commonplace. This breaking down of barriers went both ways as African Americans became more comfortable with whites and whites became more comfortable with blacks. School integration had fostered the naturally occurring neighborhood integration.[36]

School integration has not been a panacea for America's racial problems. However, what is clear is that school integration has been a very important factor in improving race relations nationwide. If you just use Jacksonville, Florida, as a model, you can clearly see the potential that equal education has for equalizing society. School integration helped move the nation from a place where African Americans were legal pariahs to a position where the president is now an African American. Similarly, through school integration and the interracial cooperation it has fostered, Jacksonville has gone from a place where African Americans could not even stand and snack at a downtown restaurant to a city where an African American is now the mayor. After forty years of lawsuits, arguments, and political fights, Jacksonville finally got their integrated and unitary school system. It is a system which clearly has problems but, as John Delaney stated, is coming back. The city is much stronger as an integrated city than it ever was under the old segregated system. Historians will continue to argue about why it took so long and whether or not the system will ever be completely integrated or just desegregated. School integration has been a great equalizer, offering opportunities which never would have been available without it.

Notes

1 Dr. Martin Luther King Jr., Western Michigan University, December 18, 1963.

2 *Florida Times-Union,* June 15, 1999.

3 Ibid.

4 Ibid.

5 Ibid.

6 Ibid.

7 Interview with John Fryer, May 16, 2012.

8 Ibid.

9 *Florida Times-Union,* May 30, 1999.

10 Ibid.

11 Interview with Gwendolyn Gibson, by phone, May 11, 2012.

12 Ibid.

13 Jacksonville Branch NAACP v. Duval County School Board, No. 85-316-Civ-J-10C, (11th Cir. May 27,1999), 116.

14 Florida Population Growth, http://censusscope.org/us/s12/chart_popl.html

15 http://www.census.gov/2010census/data/index.php

16 *Jacksonville Branch NAACP v. Duval County School Board, No. 85-316-Civ-J-10C,* 8.

17 Joseph Peniel, *Dark Days, Bright Nights: From Black Power to Barack Obama* (New York: Basic Civitas Books, 2010), 228-229.

18 http://www.childtrendsdatabank.org/pdf/75_PDF.pdf

19 U.S. Department of Education National Center for Education Statistics, National Household Education Surveys Program (Washington, DC: NHES US Department of Education, 2003), 19.

20 Michelle Alexander, *The New Jim Crow: Mass Incarceration in the Age of Colorblindness* (New York: The New Press, 2010), 184-5.

21 http://www.clms.neu.edu/publication/documents/The_Consequences_of_Dropping_Out_of_High_School.pdf, October 2009.

22 Alexander, *The New Jim Crow,* 185.

23 Interview with John Fryer, May 16, 2012.

24 *Jacksonville Branch NAACP v. Duval County School Board, No. 85-316-Civ-J-10C,* 60.

25 *Florida Times-Union,* May 29, 1999.

26 Ibid.

27 Ibid.

28 Interview with Willye Dennis, July 24, 1999.

29 Ibid.

30 Interview with Wendell Holmes, March 18, 2011.

31 *Jacksonville Branch NAACP v. Duval County School Board, No. 85-316-Civ-J-10C,* 61; Interview with John Fryer, May 16, 2012.

32 Interview with Larry Zenke, May 10, 2012.
33 Interview with Wendell Holmes, May 15, 2012.
34 Interview with Larry Zenke, May 15, 2012.
35 Interview with John Delaney, May 31, 2012.
36 Interview with Larry Zenke, May 15, 2012.

Conclusion

On May 17, 1962, as Americans participated in commemoration activities for the one hundredth anniversary of the American Civil War, Dr. Martin Luther King Jr. delivered an impassioned plea to President John F. Kennedy asking for a "Second Emancipation Proclamation." Hoping to take advantage of the celebratory spirit aroused by the Civil War anniversary, King wrote a presidential proclamation which he hoped would give the president the necessary incentive to move the country forward on racial reconciliation and civil rights. This new Emancipation Proclamation would be in the form of an executive order outlawing segregation. If President Kennedy accepted the challenge, his move would put him in the same category as Abraham Lincoln, another president of great moral courage, who took a politically unpopular racial position because it was right. King delivered this manifesto as the nation was once again in a life-and-death struggle over the meaning of democracy and freedom. Civil rights, and particularly African American civil rights, were once again tearing at the social fabric of the American society.

Historian David Blight, writing in the *New York Times* on May 16, 2012, said King infused his executive-order campaign with the gravitas of the centennial of the Civil War and Emancipation. "What we need to do," he told Clarence B. Jones, his trusted legal adviser, "is to get Kennedy to issue a second Emancipation Proclamation on the anniversary of the first one." On June 6, 1961, at a news conference in New York, King explicitly invoked the memory of the Civil War: "Just as Abraham Lincoln had the vision to see almost one hundred years ago that this nation could not exist half-free, the present administration must have the insight to see that today the nation cannot exist half-segregated and half-free."[1] Though many will argue that we have slain the segregation monster, the equally daunting monster of inequity still remains.

Like Lincoln in the 1860s, we as Americans must come to the realization that the nation can no longer accept the current inequities in public education. The situation as it exists today in education is a recipe for disaster. With the nation slowly growing grayer, the need for improvements in education will grow louder as teachers will be faced with increasingly diverse classrooms. Also, the appallingly high dropout rates foretell a dreadful future where we will not have enough trained workers for our more and more technologically advanced society. The nation is divided not only on racial lines but, today, as our communities are being destroyed and rebuilt, the lines of demarcation are increasingly being drawn along class lines. The protests of the ninety-nine percenters echo in the ears of those who are growing more concerned about the economic divide. More than 150 years after the ratification of the Thirteenth Amendment, it may be time for another amendment mandating equal education for all children.

Though such a move would immediately be castigated as a political ploy, nevertheless, it would be a clarion call showing that we recognize the problem. The United States is falling behind other nations in education, and even though our best students continue to excel, those who are in the middle and below are increasingly being left behind. A Second Emancipation Proclamation would finally close the circle and end the one-hundred-fifty-year odyssey from slavery to freedom for all of America's people. Education is not a racial issue; it is a civil rights issue because education is still the great equalizer, while unequal education is the great divider. Too many people have fallen for the convincing lie that education is a luxury and not a necessity. We need good schools just as much as we need a good military and a good government. In fact, in many ways we need good education more because, with a well-educated populace, we will solve the other two problems.

Twelve years ago, when I began this book, I had no idea how difficult it would be to tell this story. Originally, I thought I had an easy tale of white prejudice and black heroism against nearly impossible odds. The story was an old familiar one about brave African American parents fighting an evil segregated public school system on behalf of their much-maligned children. Initially, I hoped to produce a manuscript about the gallantry of the NAACP leadership fighting for integrated schools in Jacksonville. However, the youthful optimism that I expressed twelve years ago has been replaced by the cold hard truth that this is a very complicated story. Once we moved into the 1980s, the narrative changed, as many in the African American community found themselves more interested in improving schools in their neighborhoods than integrating into predominantly white schools. The change in attitude was an acknowledgement that racial prejudice in the city had not subsided. Something I have learned while researching this book is that Southerners' racial attitudes are seemingly impervious to societal change. Despite the cataclysmic changes that have occurred over the past forty years, race continues to be the major issue dividing black and white Southerners.

Despite the elections of President Barack Obama and Mayor Alvin Brown, black and white Southerners continue to see things through a racial prism. As former Jacksonville mayor John Delaney said, "Whites don't ever see any racism, while African Americans see racism in everything."[2] That is the most intractable problem when writing on subjects that have a racial component. Blacks and whites see these issues from totally different perspectives; therefore, it is very difficult to have an open and honest dialogue between the two groups because they seem to be speaking two radically different languages. Having attended the local schools in Jacksonville, I am intimately familiar with much of the story I write about. I was a part of the early integration efforts of the 1970s and left the school system in June 1983. Several of my family members also served as teachers and administrators in the system, so I knew about school issues from a number of different perspectives.

I personally knew the story of integration and racism in Jacksonville because I was a part of it. I attended school with the children of several of the key figures I am writing about. However, my experiences were relevant to this book only for a portion of the story because, when I left, the school story was still being written. The educational narrative shifted abruptly as I moved into the contemporary era and found that, as with most stories, the actual narrative is more complicated than originally thought. Today, with school-aged children of my own, I understand that school integration involves much more than a racial struggle: it encompasses moral, economic, and class issues which resist any simple explanation. It involves parental choices, entitlements, and questions of power and prejudice. It is a much deeper story than black and white, that includes "haves and have-nots," as well as questions of right and wrong and of school equity. It requires us to gauge the motives of parents who make decisions about their children's education that are personal and difficult, but are often viewed as racist, classist, and wrong by those on the outside looking in.

I grew up in the Arlington area of Jacksonville. This was a safe, conservative, white middle-class neighborhood, which had good schools and a comfortable environment. My family was one of the few African American families in the area. The community was not completely open to integration but, like most areas, followed the law and did what it could to ease the transition to a new integrated reality. Today, the Arlington area is a mixed-raced community with schools that are struggling to come back from years of declining test scores and community change. The safety of the neighborhood has declined and the community now has a much higher crime rate than it had in the past. As African Americans moved in, whites who could afford to leave did so, making the area more integrated but less financially stable. White students fled the schools, leaving them to the newly arriving African Americans who were not as financially successful as the whites who left. The new children who attended the schools were not such good students as those who had left.

This process repeated itself numerous times in various neighborhoods in Jacksonville. As the city's neighborhoods became more integrated, the schools saw a corresponding reduction in the number of white students. As the schools became browner, scores declined and the schools had increasing disciplinary problems. The white flight from schools added even more pressure to the quality of the school system as many of the best students withdrew from the public school system and entered predominantly white private schools. The reasons for these withdrawals vary, but anecdotally we can assume at least some involved racial issues.

Changing laws could not alter the perceptions of many white parents that an influx of people who were different in background and race would equate to a lower quality education. Public school integration and equality continue to be the last barriers to complete racial equality. They are the foundation of all other social measures in society. If we can get this right, we can solve all the other related racial and economic problems. Jacksonville is a great model for understanding how these issues relate to the nation. It is a large conservative area which has shown glimpses of progressive action. It is a city that is still writing its story on race, much as the United States is still writing its story.

Though there is little chance that President Obama or any other president will have the courage to navigate the troubled racial waters of American history, it is comforting to think that things are improving. As we continue to make painful decisions about economic priorities, educational issues will come under increasing scrutiny. For the sake of our children, I hope that politicians will do what is smart and not what is expedient.

Notes

1 *New York Times*, May 16, 2012.
2 Interview with John Delaney, by phone, May 31, 2012.

Bibliography

Books

Ambrose, Stephen E. *Nixon: The Triumph of a Politician 1962-1972*, vol 2. New York: Simon and Schuster, 1989.

Anderson, James. "Ex-Slaves and the Rise of Universal Education in the New South, 1860-1888." In *Education and the Rise of the New South,* edited by Robert Goodenow and Arthur White, 2-16. Boston: G.K. Hall and Co., 1981.

Ball, Howard. *A Defiant Life: Thurgood Marshall and the Persistence of Racism in America.* New York: Crown Publishers Inc., 1998.

Bartley, Abel. *Keeping the Faith: Race Politics and Social Development in Jacksonville, Florida 1940-1970.* Westport: Greenwood Press, 2000.

Bennet, Lerone. *Before the Mayflower: A History of Black America.* Chicago: Johnson Publishing, 2003.

Bigelow, Lee. *Public Schools of Duval County.* Prepared for the State Library Project, Works Progress Administration, Jacksonville Florida, 1939.

Cochran, Thomas. "History of Public Education in Florida." Master's thesis, University of Pennsylvania, 1921. Lancaster: The New Era Printing Company.

Davis, T. Frederick. *History of Jacksonville, Florida and Vicinity 1513 to 1924.* Jacksonville Florida Historical Society, 1925.

DuBois, W. E. B. *Black Reconstruction in America 1860-1880.* New York: Touchstone Books, 1935.

Dyckman, Martin A. *Floridian of His Century: The Courage of Governor Leroy Collins.* Gainesville: University of Florida Press, 2006.

Finkelman, Paul. *Dred Scott v. Sandford: A Brief History with Documents.* New York: Bedford/St. Martin's Press, 1997.

Foner, Eric. *From Slavery to Freedom: A History of African Americans*, 7th ed. New York: McGraw-Hill, 1994.

——.*Reconstruction: America's Unfinished Revolution, 1863-1877*. New York: Harper & Row Publishers, 1988.

——.*The Story of American Freedom*. New York: WW Norton & Company, 1998.

Franklin, John Hope and Alfred A. Moss. *From Slavery to Freedom: A History of African Americans*, 8th ed. New York: Alfred K. Knopf, 2000.

Gibbs, Jonathon. *Report of the Superintendent of Public Instruction of the State of Florida, For Year Ending September 30, 1873*. Tallahassee: Hamilton Jay State Printer, 1874.

Gold, Pleasant. *History of Duval County Including Early History of East Florida*. St. Augustine: The Record Company, 1929.

Green, Ben. *Before His Time: The Untold Story of Harry T. Moore, America's First Civil Rights Martyr*. Gainesville: University of Florida Press, 2005.

Howard, John. *The Shifting Wind: The Supreme Court and Civil Rights From Reconstruction to Brown*. Albany: State University of New York, 1999.

Jones, Maxine D. and Kevin McCarthy. *African Americans in Florida*. Sarasota: Pineapple Press, 1993.

Jordan, Winthrop. *White Over Black: American Attitudes Toward the Negro, 1550-1812*. Chapel Hill: University of North Carolina Press, 1968.

Kluger, Richard. *Simple Justice: The History of Brown v Board of Education and Black America's Struggle for Equality*. New York: Alfred A. Knopf, 2004.

Kyvig, David. *Explicit and Authentic Acts: Amending the US Constitution 1776-1995*. Lawrence: University of Kansas Press, 1996.

Lawson, Steven. *Running for Freedom: Civil Rights and Black Politics in America Since 1941*. Philadelphia: Temple University Press, 1991.

——.*Running for Freedom: Civil Rights and Black Politics in America Since 1941*, 3ʳᵈ ed. Chichester: Wiley-Blackwell, 2009.

Logan, Rayford. *The Betrayal of the Negro: From Rutherford B. Hayes to Woodrow Wilson*. New York: Collier Books, 1968.

Martin, Richard. *The City Makers*. Jacksonville: Convention Press, 1972.

——.*Consolidation Jacksonville/Duval County: The Dynamics of Urban Political Reform*. Jacksonville: Crawford Publishing Company, 1968.

McNeil, Genna Rae. *Groundwork: Charles Hamilton Houston and the Struggle for Civil Rights*. Philadelphia: University of Pennsylvania Press, 1983.

McPherson, James. *The Negroes' Civil War: How American Blacks Felt and Acted During the War for the Union*. New York: Ballantine Books, 1991.

——.*Ordeal By Fire: The Civil War and Reconstruction*, 2ⁿᵈ ed. New York: McGraw-Hill Press, 1992.

Nieman, Donald. *African Americans and Education in the South*. New York: Garland, 1994.

——.*Promises to Keep: African Americans and the Constitutional Order 1776 to the Present*. New York: Oxford University Press, 1991.

Ogletree, Charles. *With All Deliberate Speed: Reflections on the First Half Century of Brown v Board of Education*. New York: WW Norton & Co., 2004.

Reeves, Richard. *President Nixon: Alone in the White House*. New York: Simon & Schuster, 2001.

Richardson, Joe. *The Negro in the Reconstruction of Florida, 1865-1877*. Tallahassee: Florida State University Press, 1965.

Duval County Public Schools A Survey Report: Division of Surveys and Field Services. George Peabody College for Teachers, Nashville, Tennessee, 1965.

Schwartz, Gerald, ed. *A Woman Doctor's Civil War: Esther Hill Hawks' Diary*. Columbia: University of South Carolina Press, 1989.

Scott, J. Irving. *The Education of Black People in Florida.* Philadelphia: Dorrance Press, 1974.

Sitkoff, Harvard. *The Struggle for Black Equality: 1954-1980.* New York: Hill & Wang, 1981.

Thompson, Leslie. *A Manual or Digest of the Statute Law of the State of Florida, Of a General or Public Character, in Force at the End of the Second Session of the General Assembly, Approved December 10, 1845.* Boston: Charles C. Little and James Brown, 1847.

Trelease, Allen. *Reconstruction: The Great Experiment.* New York: Harper & Rowe Publishers, 1971.

Thurman, James. *Practical Bomb Scene Investigation: Practical Aspects of Criminal and Forensic Investigation.* Boca Raton: CRC Press-Taylor & Francis Group LLC, 2006.

Theoharis, Athan G. *The FBI: A Comprehensive Reference Guide.* Phoenix: ORYX Press, 2000.

Tushnet, Mark. *The NAACP Legal Strategy Against Segregated Education, 1925-1950.* Chapel Hill: UNC Press, 1987.

Walch, Barbara. *New Black Voices: The Growth and Contributions of Sallye Mathis and Mary Singleton in Florida Government.* Jacksonville: Barbara Walch, 1990.

White, Arthur. *Florida's Crisis in Public Education: Changing Patterns of Leadership.* Gainesville: University of Florida Press, 1975.

Williams, Juan. *Thurgood Marshall: An American Revolutionary.* New York: Random House Press, 2000.

Williamson, Joel. *After Slavery: The Negro in South Carolina During Reconstruction, 1861-1877.* New York: WW Norton & Company, 1965.

Winsboro, Irvin D. S. *Old South, New South, or Down South?: Florida and the Modern Civil Rights Movement.* Morgantown: University of West Virginia Press, 2009.

Woodward, C. Vann. *The Strange Career of Jim Crow,* rev. 3rd ed. New York: Oxford University Press, 1974.

Documents

Florida, *Superintendent Reports,* 189031-35.

Jacksonville Looks At Its Negro Community: A Survey of Conditions Affecting the Negro Population in Jacksonville and Duval County, Florida, Conducted by a Survey Committee of the Council of Social Agencies. Jacksonville: Council of Social Agencies, 1946.

Jacksonville Looks At Its Negro Community: Brief Report of the Bi-Racial Follow-Up Committee. Jacksonville Bi-Racial Fellowship, March 1948.

The National Negro Bluebook North Florida Edition. Jacksonville: Florida Blue Book Publishing Company, 1926.

Program for the Benefit of the Piano Fund Stanton High School and Brief History December 3 & 4, 1917.

Report of the Surveys of the Schools Duval County, Florida, including City of Jacksonville. The Institute of Educational Research Division of Field Studies, Teacher's College, Columbia University, 1927.

A Report to the Duval County Board of Public Instruction: Florida School Desegregation Consulting Center University of Miami. Coral Gables: University of Miami, 1968.

School Board History. Document received from the School Board containing information gleaned from County Archives of Florida, No. 16 Duval County, 123, book no. F352, H673, I#16.

State of Florida. Constitution 1885. State of Florida Archives.

Newspapers

Atlanta World, 1942.

Baltimore Afro-American, 1941.

Daily Florida Union, 1877

Florida Times-Union, 1959, 1960, 1964, 1965, 1967, 1969, 1970, 1985, 1993, 1996, 1999, 2000, 2001, 2004, 2005, 2007.

Florida Star, 1960.
Jacksonville Advocate, 1980.
Jacksonville Journal, 1964.
New York Times, 1958, 1959, 1960, 1964.
Pittsburgh Courier, 1942, 1964.
Southwestern Christian Advocate, 1874, 1877.
St. Petersburg Times, 2004.
The Star Zion, 1889.

Articles

Puryear, R. W. "Desegregation of Public Education in Florida-One Year Afterward." *Journal of Negro Education*, vol. 24, no. 3, (Summer 1955), 221.

Cooper, Algia. "Brown v BOE and Virgil Darnell Hawkins 28 Years and Six Petitions to Justice." *Journal of Negro History*, vol. 64, no. 1, (Winter, 1979), 1-6.

"Racial Fury Over Sit-in," *Life*, September 12, 1960, 37.

"Promise of Trouble," *Time*, September 12, 1960, 27.

"Earl Johnson: Florida's Unsung Hero," *Florida Historical Quarterly*, vol. XLVI, no. 3-4, July-October 1995, 71-74.

"1968 Like a Knife Blade, The Year Severed Past From Future," *Time*, January 11, 1988, 16-27.

Skirt! January 17, 2011.

"A Cure for City Blight–The Jacksonville Story." *US News and World Report*, January 3, 1972, 25.

Crooks, James B. "Jacksonville Before Consolidation." *Florida Historical Quarterly*, vol. LXXVII, no. 2, (Fall 1998), 156.

Richardson, Joe. "Christian Abolitionism: The American Missionary Association and the Florida Negro," *Journal of Negro History*, vol. 40, issue 1, (Winter 1971), 35, 37, 41.

"The Congress: A Fight to the Finish," *Time*, December 20, 1971, 8-12.

"October 15, 2003: Congresswoman Brown Announces Passage of Eddie Mae Steward Postal Bill," http://www.house.gov/corrinebrown/press108/pr031015.htm, June 7, 2007; *Florida Times-Union,* May 28,1999.

Interviews

Hurst, Rodney. Phone interviews, August 26 and August 28, 1995.

Brant, Ish. Personal interview, September 24, 2001.

Foster, Gordon. Personal interview, February 16, 2010.

Sang, Herb. Phone interview, January 25, 2011.

Dennis, Willye. Personal interview, January 2, 2000.

Poppell, Judy. Personal interviews, September 27, 2001, October 16, 2001, and December 20, 2001.

Holmes, Wendell. Personal interviews, November 8, 2012 and May 16, 2012.

White, Dr. Alvin. Personal interview, March 22, 2006.

Parker, Billy. Personal interview, September 20, 2001.

Johnson, Janet. Personal interview, September 7, 2000.

Pearson, Mary. Personal interviews, December 29, 1994, August 11, 1995, and February 17, 1996.

Zenke, Larry. Personal interview, March 30, 2001.

Sussman, Michael. Personal interview, June 27, 2007.

Reynolds, Vicky. Personal interview, April 4, 2001.

Jordan, Stan. Personal interview, April 4, 2001.

Delaney, John. Personal interviews April 25, 2001 and May 31, 2012.

Thompson, John. Personal interview, October 30, 2001.

Manuel, Ken. Personal interview, March 29, 2007.

Tanzler, Hans. Personal interview, March 23, 2002.

White, Walter. Personal interview, December 28, 1992.

Frier, John. Personal interview, May 16, 2012.

Webb, Grace Payne. Personal interview, March 25, 2015.

Unpublished Manuscripts

Judith Poppell. "The Desegregation of a Historically Black High School in Jacksonville, Florida." PhD diss., University of North Florida, 1998.

Damon Miller. "Jacksonville Consolidation: The Process of Metropolitan Reform." Senior thesis, Princeton, 1968.

Barbara Jackson. Unpublished paper, University of Florida Library, 1981.

Court Cases

Board of Public Instruction of Duval County, Florida v. Braxton, 402 F. 2d 900, (5 Cir. 1968).

Braxton v. Board of Public Instruction of Duval County, Florida, 442 F. 2d 1339, (5 Cir. 1964).

Hardesty, Dr. C.D. and Yardley D. Buckman. Present Status of Braxton et al v. B.P.I., No. 4598-Civ-J, (M.D. Fla., 1969). (This is an analysis of the case.)

Jacksonville Branch NAACP v. Duval County School Board, No. 85-316-Civ-J-10C, (11 Cir. 1999).

Jacksonville Branch NAACP v. Duval County School Board, No. 85-316-Civ-J-16, (11 Cir. 1989).

Jacksonville Branch NAACP v. Duval County School Board, Appeal No. 99-12049-EE, (11 Cir. 1999).

Mims v. Duval County School Board, No. 4598-Civ-J-T, (11 Cir. 1971).

United States and Linda Stout et. al v. Jefferson County Board of Education, No. 372 F. 2d 836, (5 Cir.1966).

Websites

http://www.southeastequity.org/

The Better Jacksonville Plan www.coj.net/Departments/Better-Jacksonville-Plan/BJP-Ordinance.aspx.

Jacksonville, Florida Public Library Digital Collections Document: Biographical information about Rufus Elvin Payne, cdm16025.contentdm.oclc.org

Index

K

King, Martin Luther 107, 171, 177, 228, 249

L

Lincoln, Abraham 12, 249
Lloyd, Gran 94

M

Marshall, Thurgood 65–69, 92, 175
McDaniel, Vernon 64
McRae, William 106–107, 114, 128, 181, 185, 187, 192
Mims v. Duval County School Board 184, 199, 211
Moody, Walter Leroy 204–205
Moore, Harry T. 64
Moore, John 197–199, 202, 212–213

N

NAACP 1, 57, 59–62, 64–67, 87, 89–92, 96, 98–100, 106, 113, 115–116, 118–119, 123– 124, 130, 157, 169–170, 172, 176, 181, 183–187, 197–200, 202–208, 210–214, 217–222, 224, 227–235, 241–243, 250
Nathan Bedford Forrest High School 87–89
Nixon, Richard 175, 177–180

P

Parker, Billy 87–88, 218
Payne, Rufus E. 46
Peabody Report 126–127, 168
Pearson, Pat 104–105

Pearson, Rutledge 90, 169, 171–172
Poppell, Judy 230

R

Raines High School 190–191, 209, 220, 241
Russell, Albert J. 26, 28

S

Sang, Herb 198, 200
school boycott 115, 157, 171
Scott, Irving 93–94
Shaw, Leander 91
Simpson, Bryan 96–97, 100– 101, 103, 116
Stanton High School 29–33, 46, 92, 107, 190, 210
Steward, Eddie Mae 113, 115
Swann v. Charlotte-Mecklenberg 182

T

Tanzler, Hans 115

U

University of Miami Desegregation Center 103, 111, 114, 116–120, 122–123, 125–126, 128, 130, 181, 187

Z

Zenke, Larry 200–202, 207, 212, 215, 217–219, 222, 231, 243–245